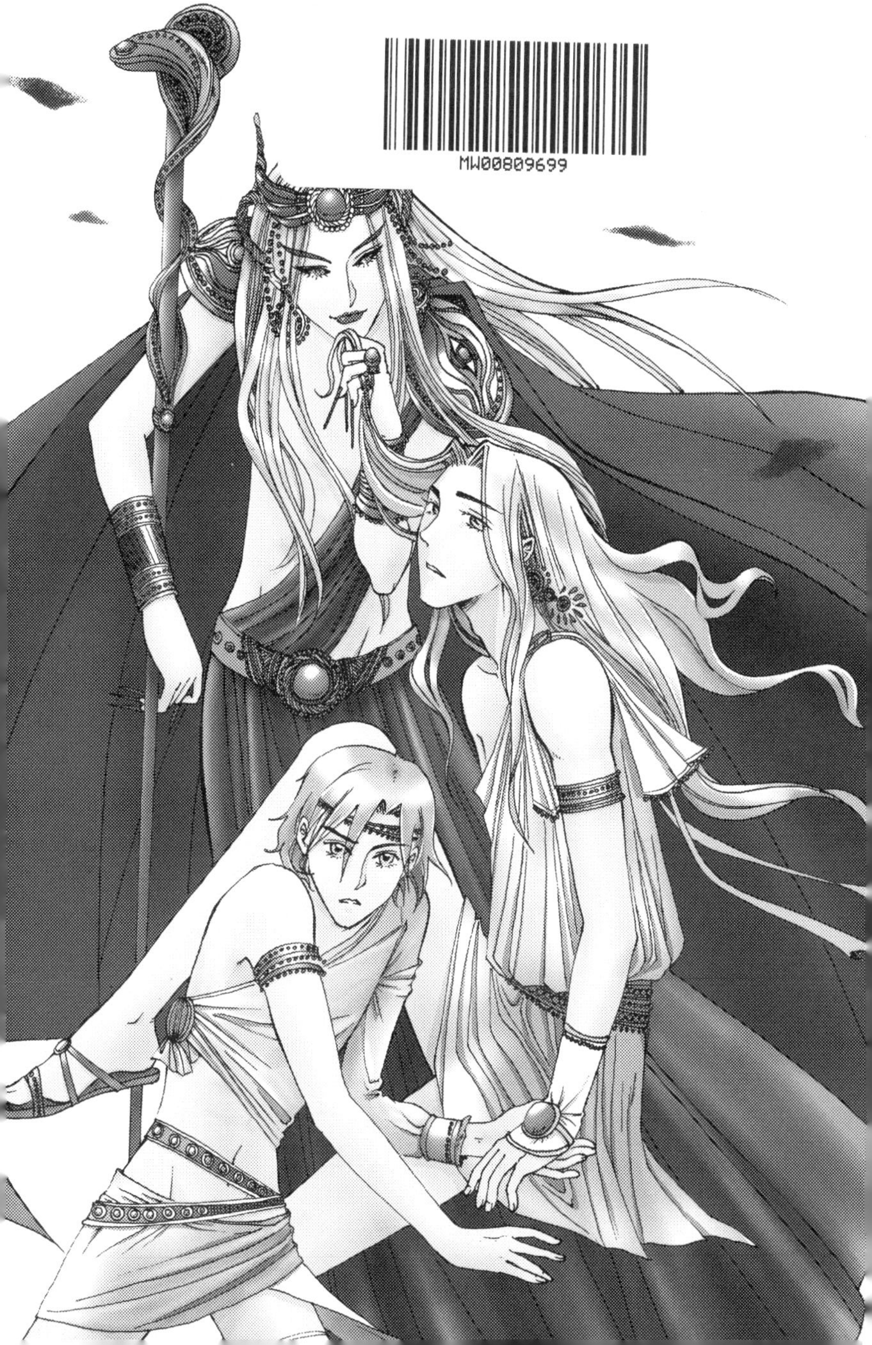

Spirit Marked

Story by Colter Hillman
Art by Yishan Li

Clockwork Heart

Story by Lawrence Rider
Art by Studio Kosaru

Yamila Abraham, Managing Editor
Laila Reimoz, Assistant Editor

All characters depicted in sexual situations are aged 18 or older.

Printed in the United States of America

ISBN: 0-9767441-6-3

ISBN 13: 978-0-9767441-6-0

Published by Yaoi Press October 2005.

www.yaoipress.com

10 9 8 7 6 5 4 3 2 1

A BOY'S LOVE GRAPHIC NOVEL

STORY BY COLTER HILLMAN
ART BY YISHAN LI
LETTERING BY LAILA REIMOZ
EDITED BY YAMILA ABAHAM

~ALSO~

CLOCKWORK HEART

STORY BY LAWRENCE RIDER
ART BY STUDIO KOSARU
LETTERING BY LAILA REIMOZ
EDITED BY YAMILA ABAHAM

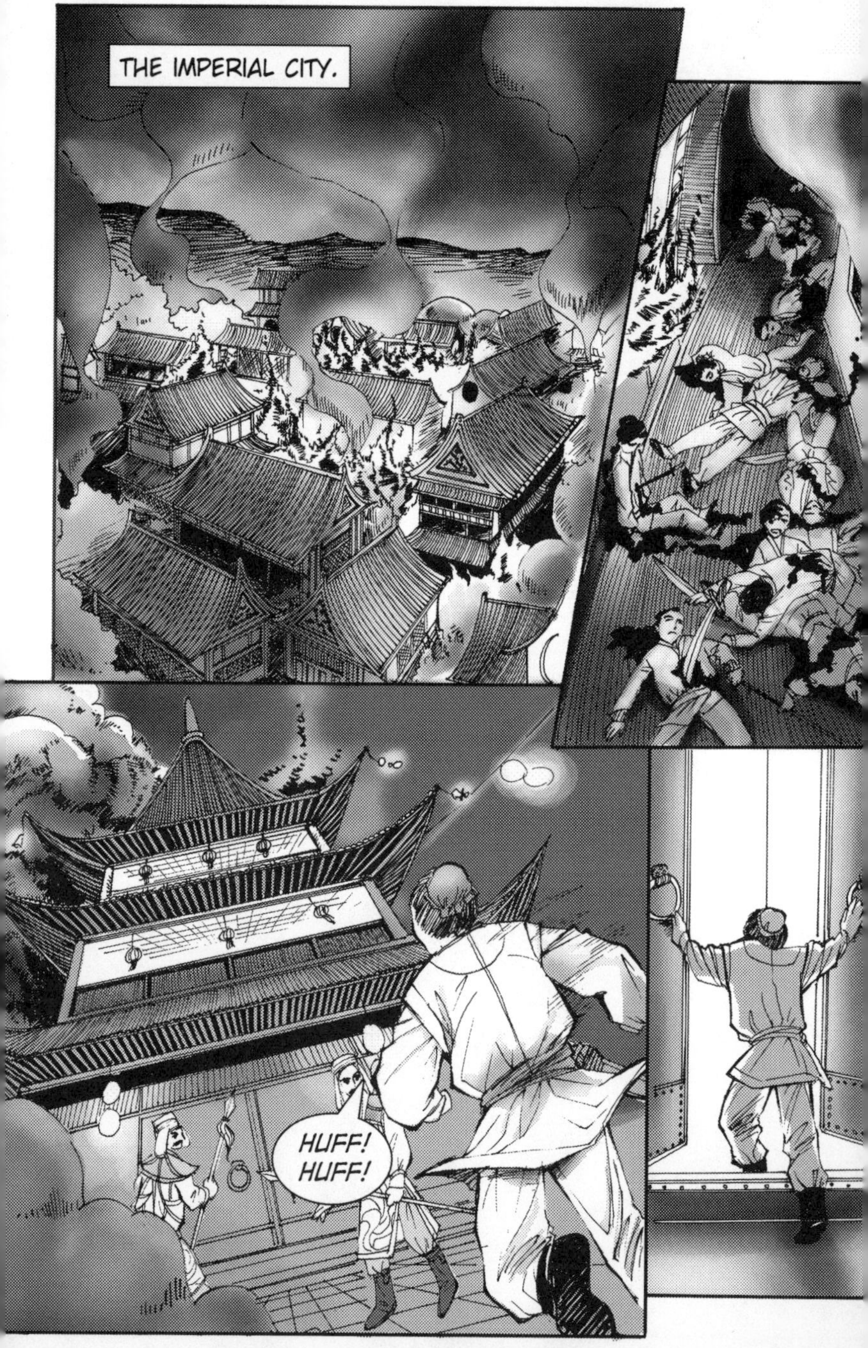
THE IMPERIAL CITY.
HUFF! HUFF!

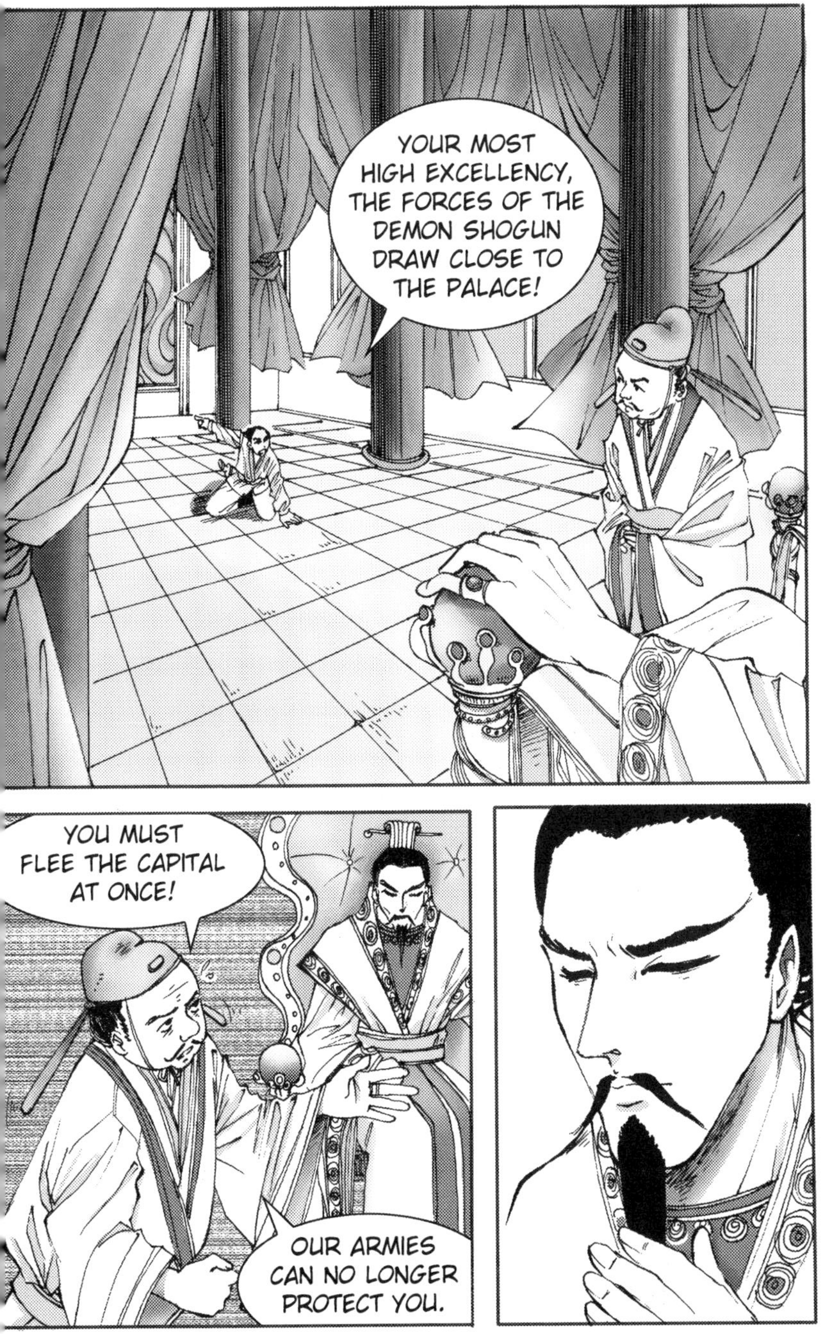
YOUR MOST HIGH EXCELLENCY, THE FORCES OF THE DEMON SHOGUN DRAW CLOSE TO THE PALACE!
YOU MUST FLEE THE CAPITAL AT ONCE!
OUR ARMIES CAN NO LONGER PROTECT YOU.

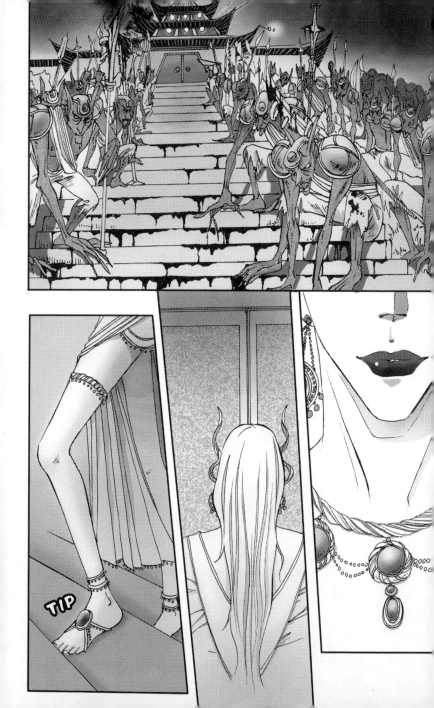

TIP

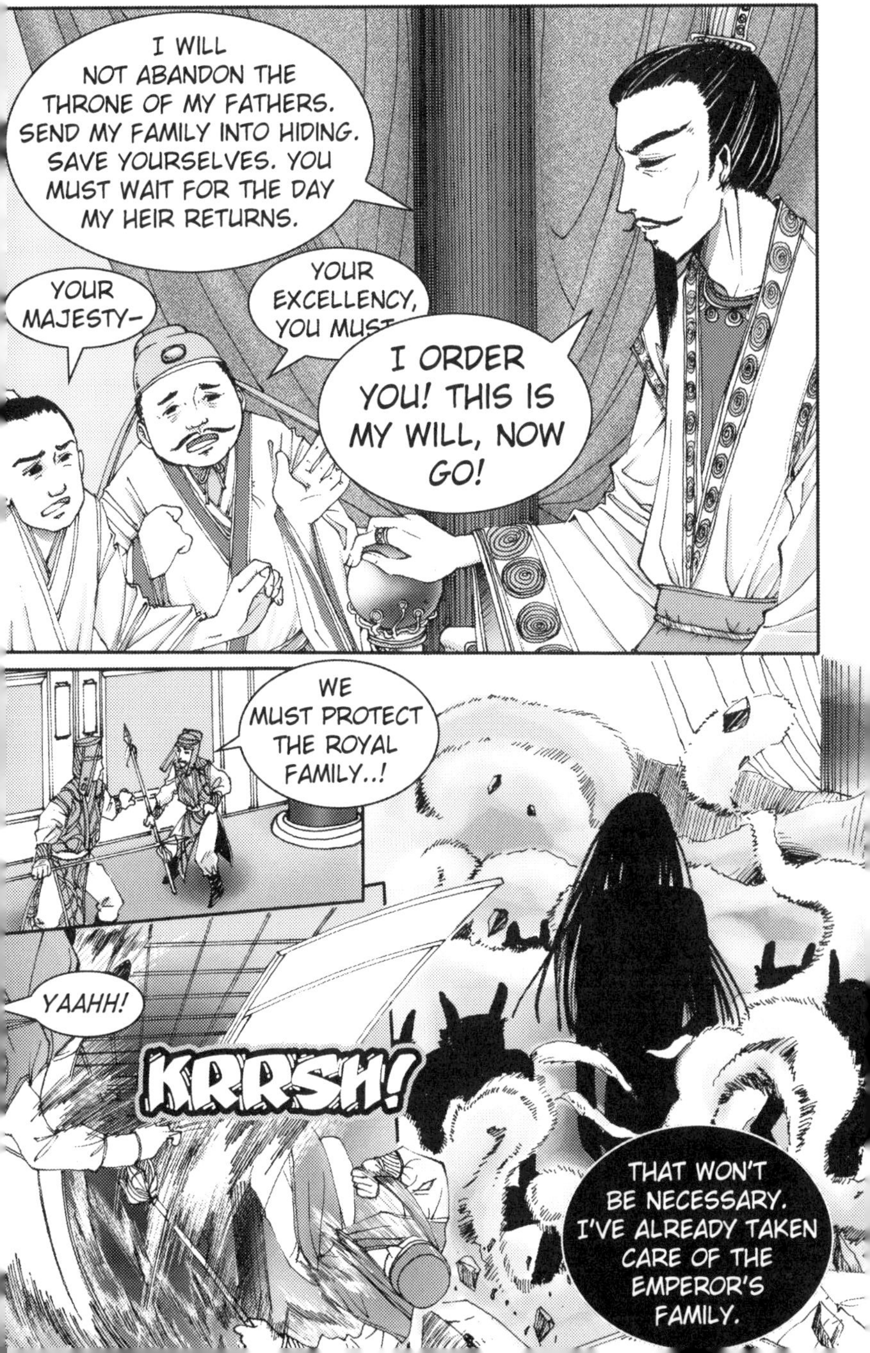
I WILL NOT ABANDON THE THRONE OF MY FATHERS. SEND MY FAMILY INTO HIDING. SAVE YOURSELVES. YOU MUST WAIT FOR THE DAY MY HEIR RETURNS.
YOUR MAJESTY-
YOUR EXCELLENCY, YOU MUST
I ORDER YOU! THIS IS MY WILL, NOW GO!
WE MUST PROTECT THE ROYAL FAMILY..!
YAAHH!
KRRSH!
THAT WON'T BE NECESSARY. I'VE ALREADY TAKEN CARE OF THE EMPEROR'S FAMILY.

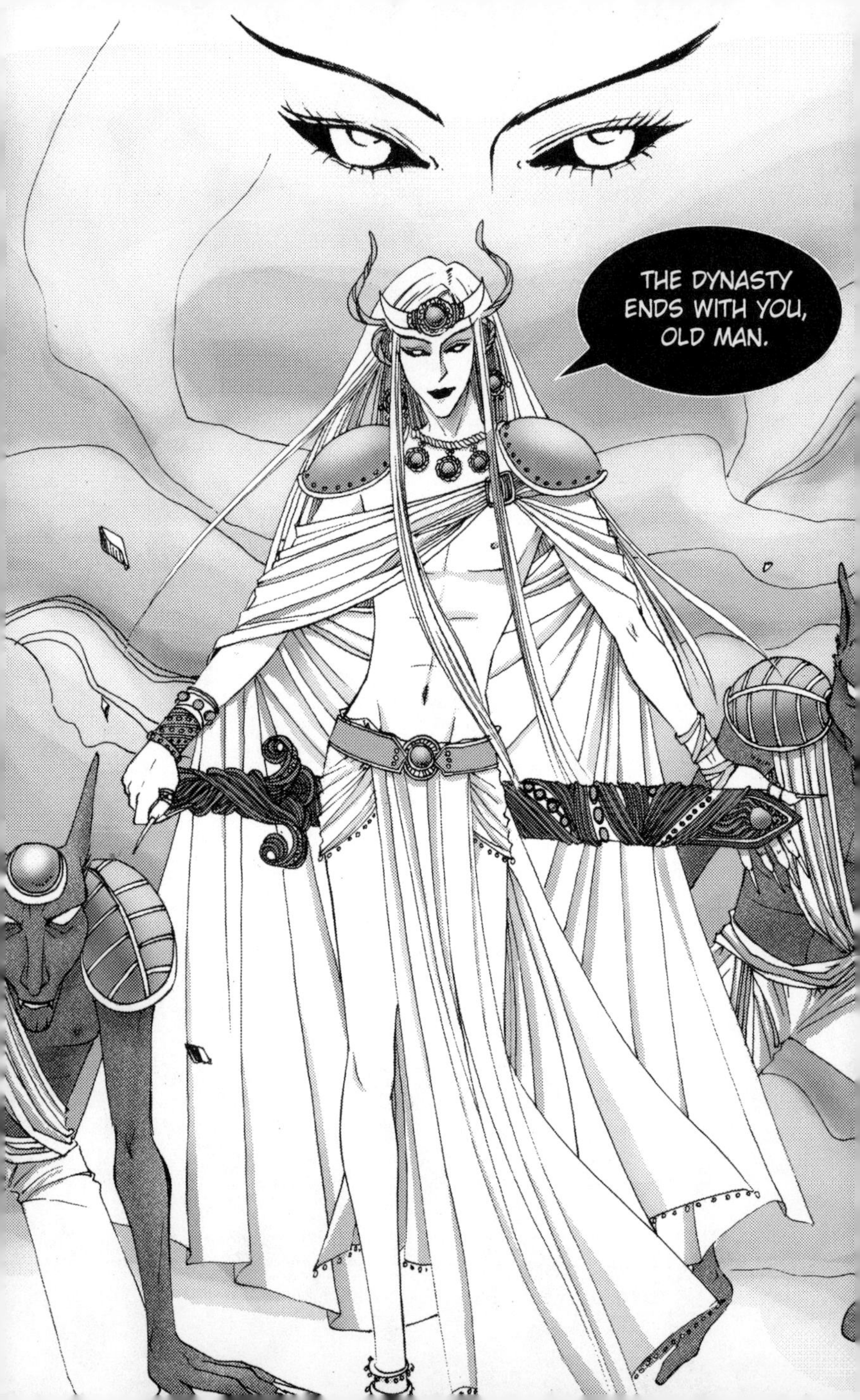
THE DYNASTY ENDS WITH YOU, OLD MAN.

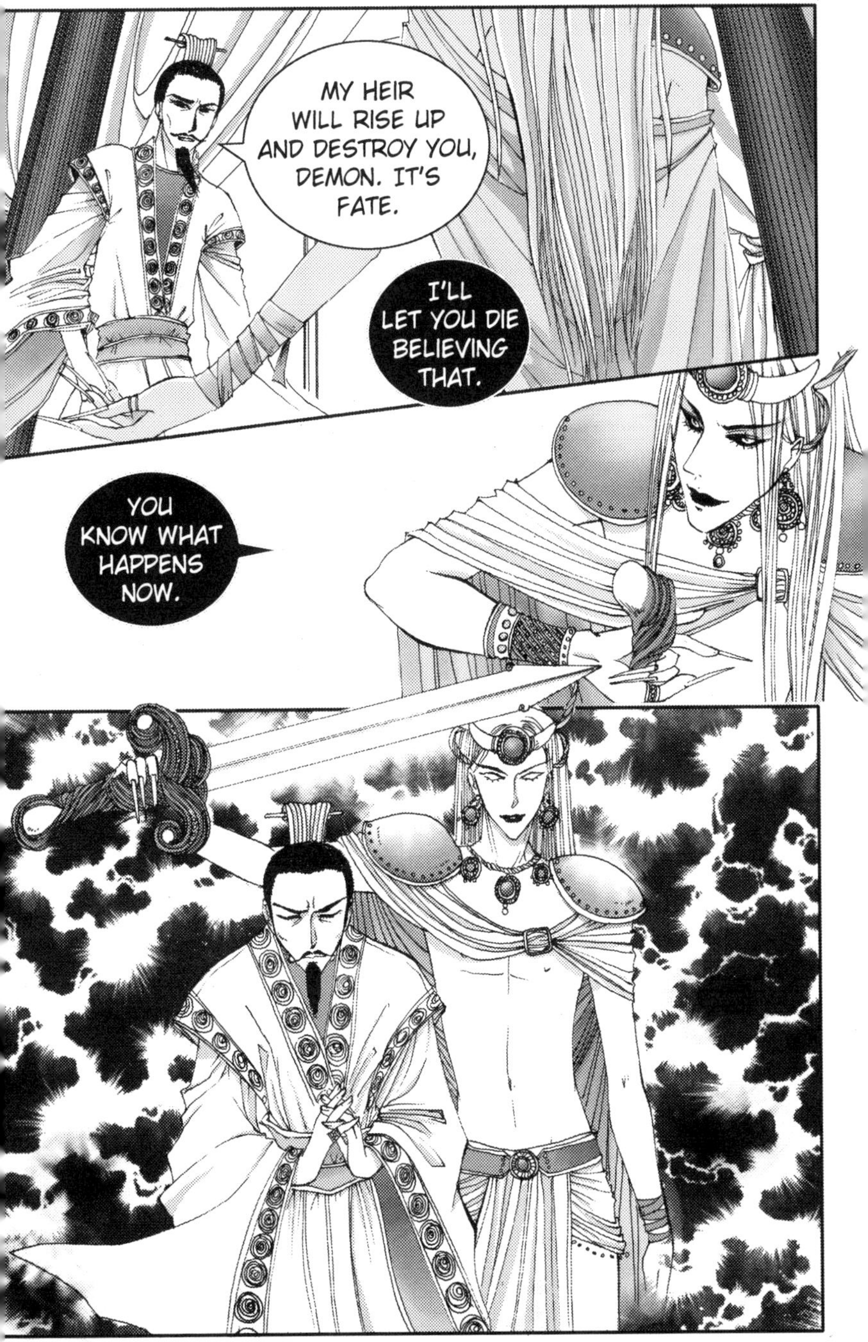
MY HEIR WILL RISE UP AND DESTROY YOU, DEMON. IT'S FATE.
I'LL LET YOU DIE BELIEVING THAT.
YOU KNOW WHAT HAPPENS NOW.

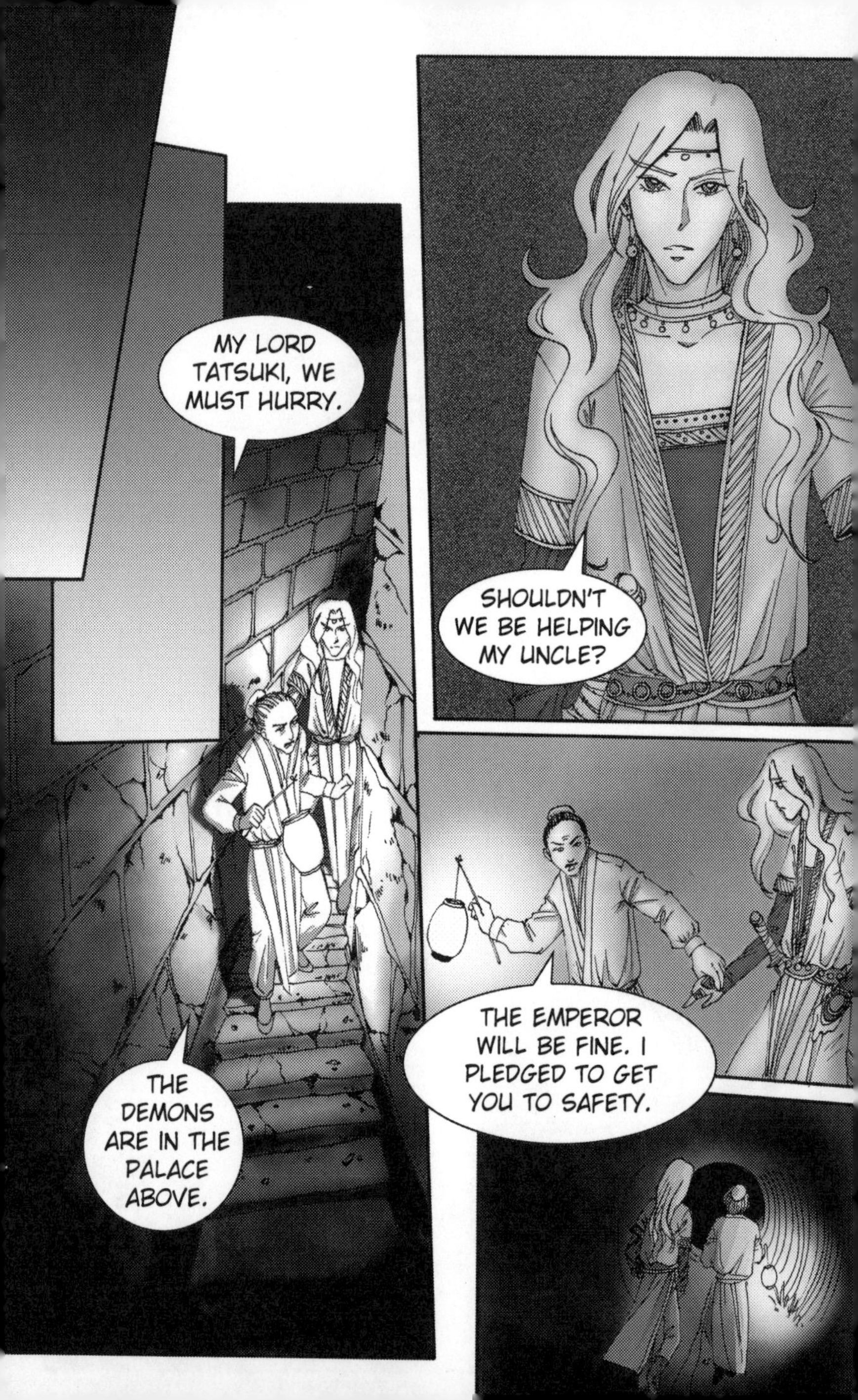
MY LORD TATSUKI, WE MUST HURRY.
THE DEMONS ARE IN THE PALACE ABOVE.
SHOULDN'T WE BE HELPING MY UNCLE?
THE EMPEROR WILL BE FINE. I PLEDGED TO GET YOU TO SAFETY.

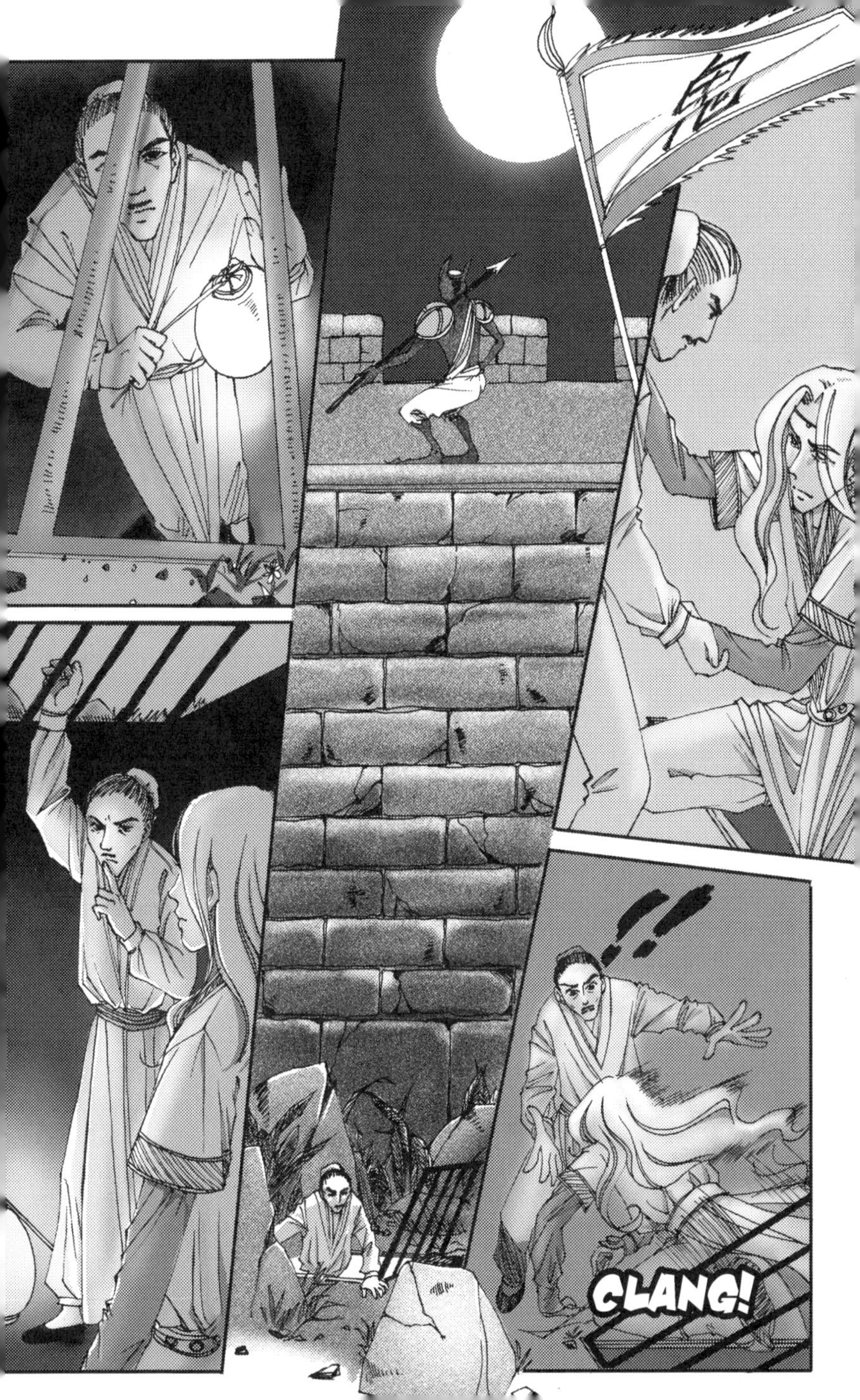
CLANG!

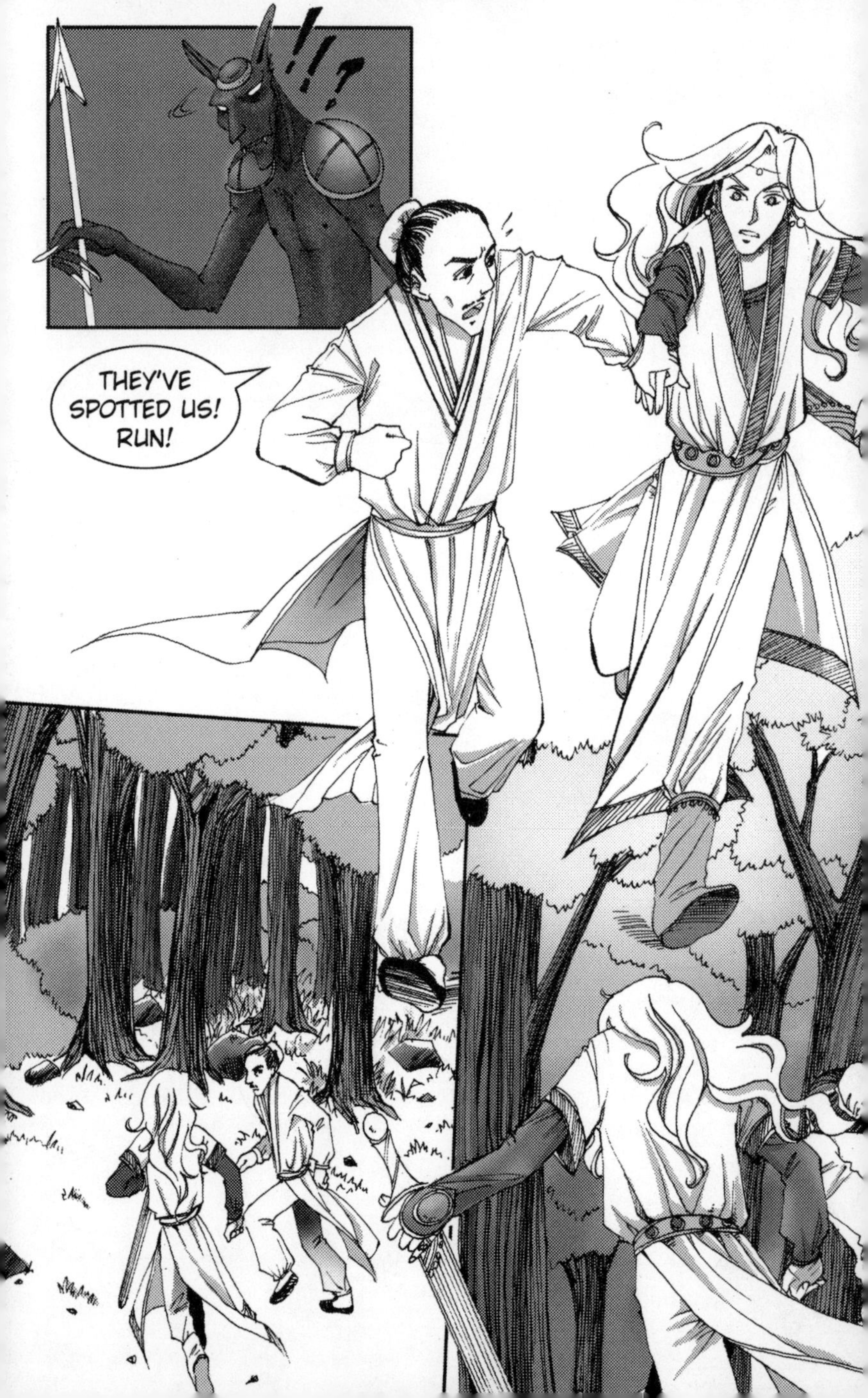
!!?
THEY'VE SPOTTED US! RUN!

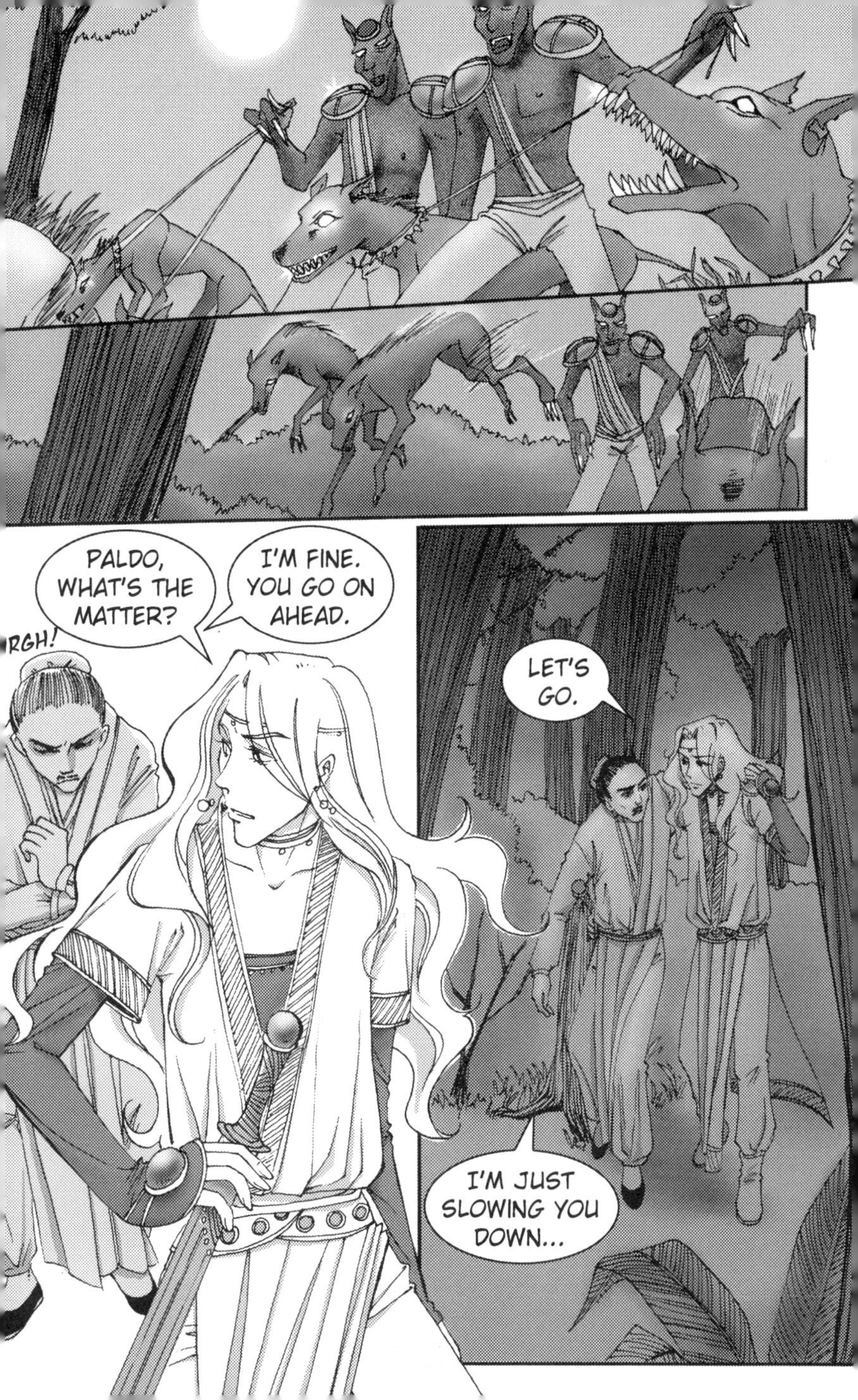
RGH!
PALDO, WHAT'S THE MATTER?
I'M FINE. YOU GO ON AHEAD.
LET'S GO.
I'M JUST SLOWING YOU DOWN...

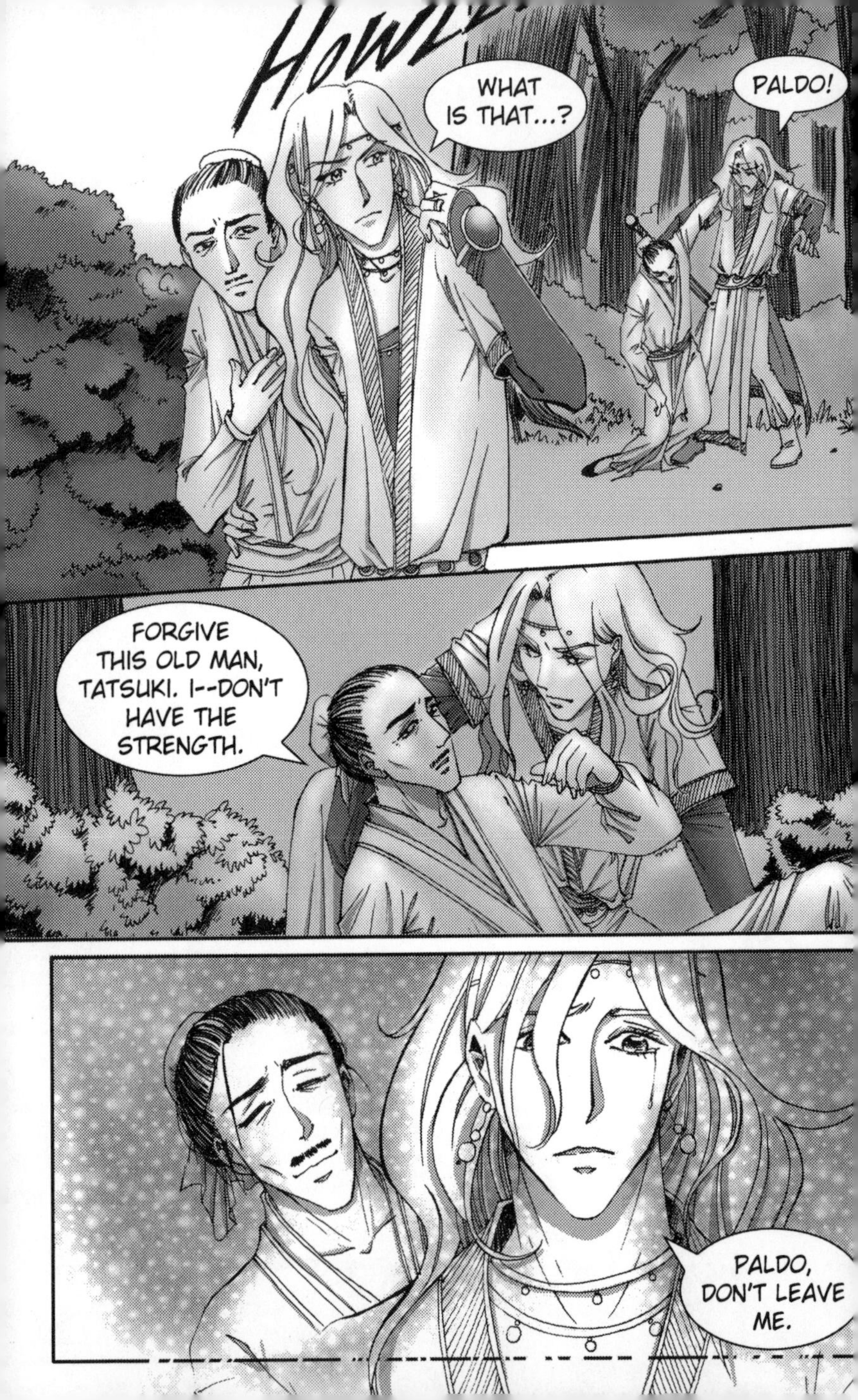
HOWL
WHAT IS THAT...?
PALDO!
FORGIVE THIS OLD MAN, TATSUKI. I--DON'T HAVE THE STRENGTH.
PALDO, DON'T LEAVE ME.

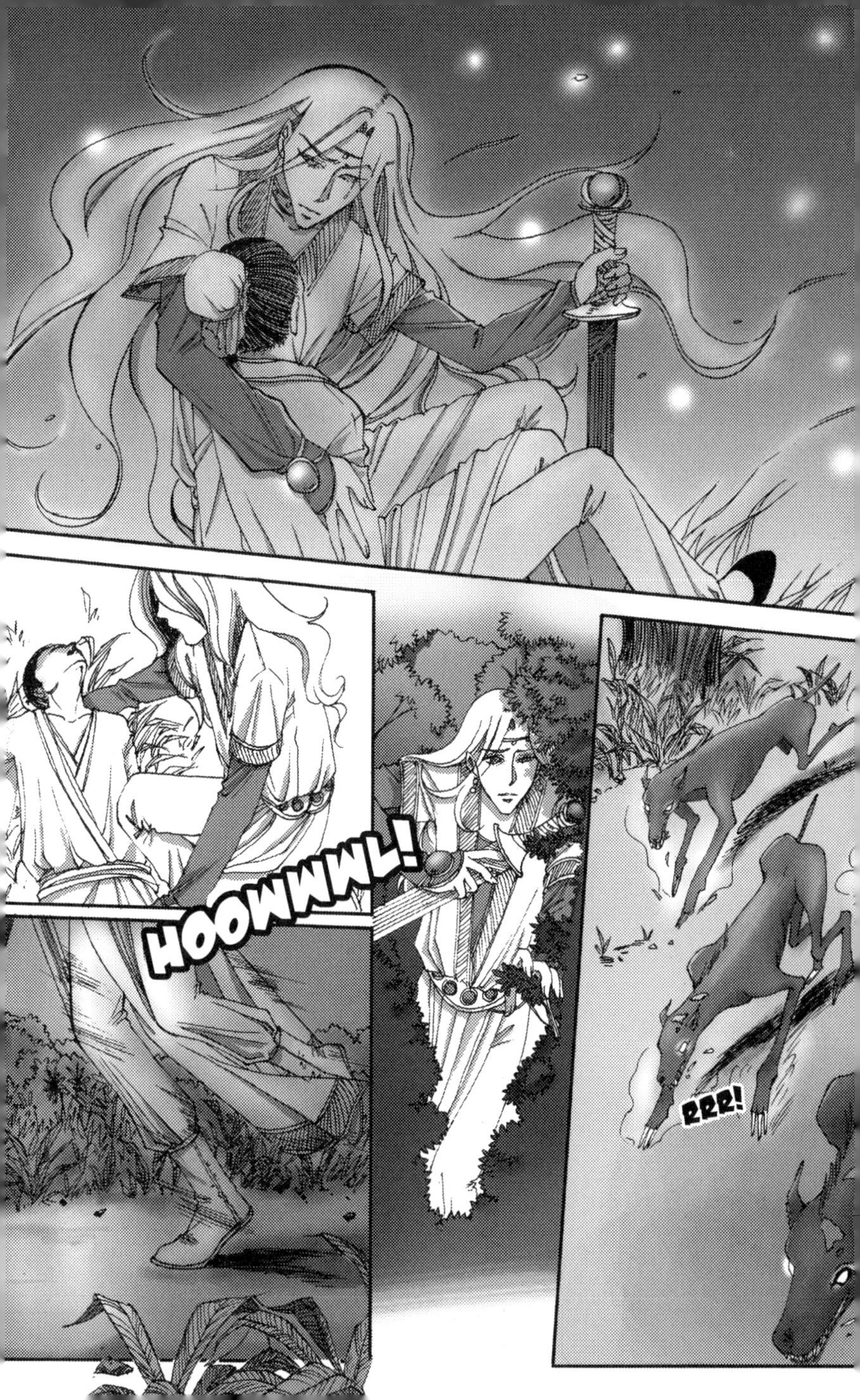
HOOWWWL!
RRR!

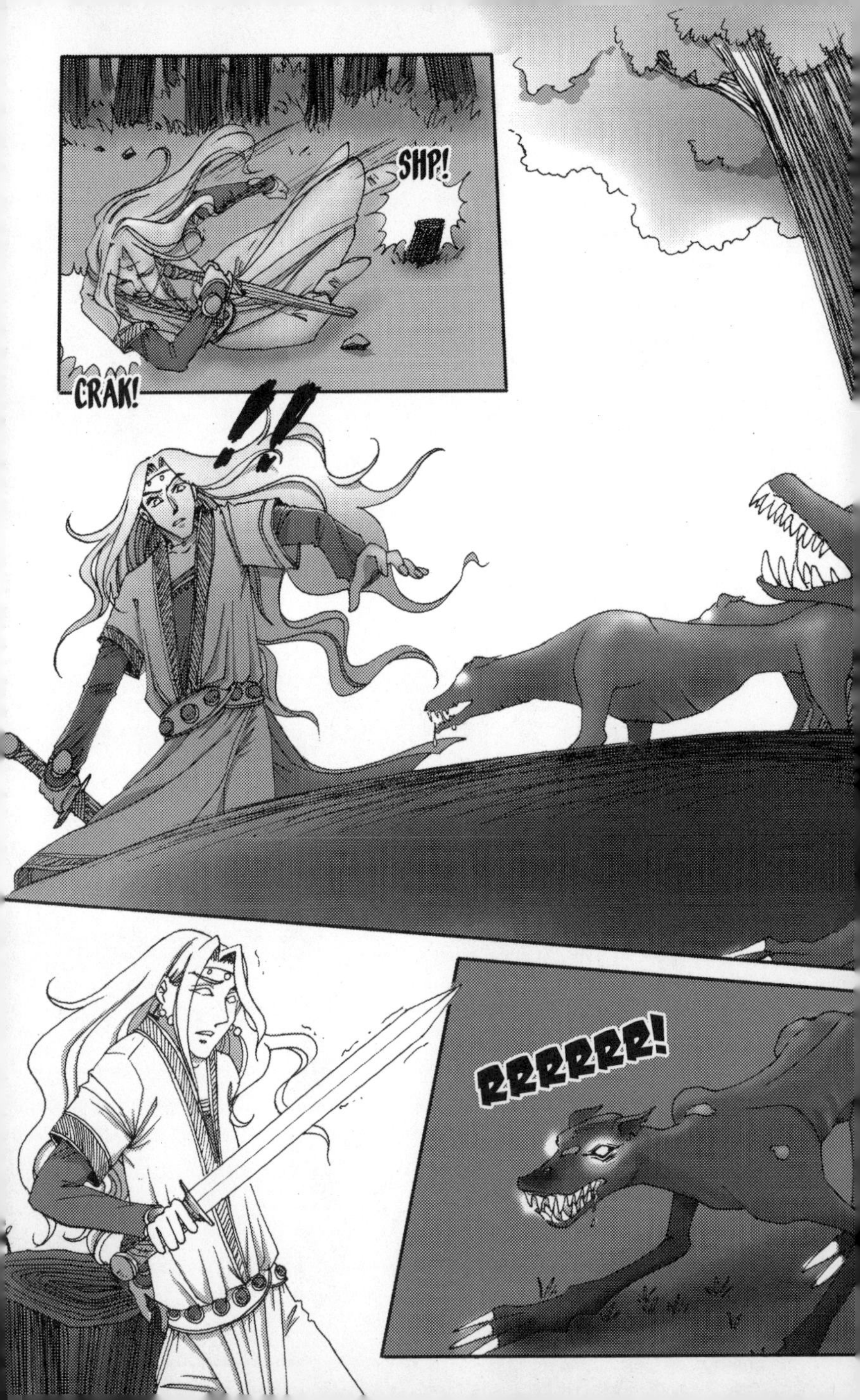
SHP!
CRAK!
!!
RRRRRR!

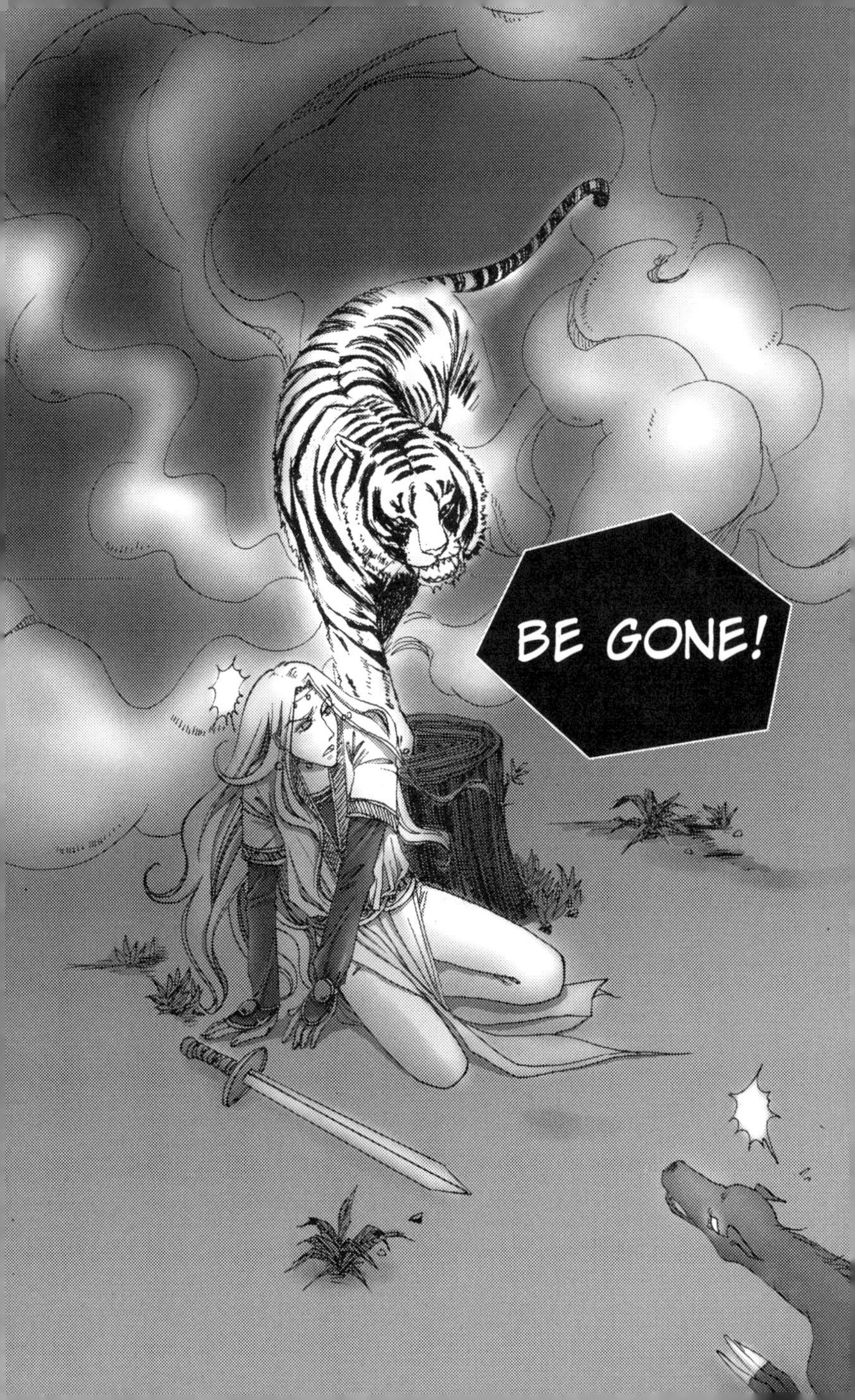
BE GONE!

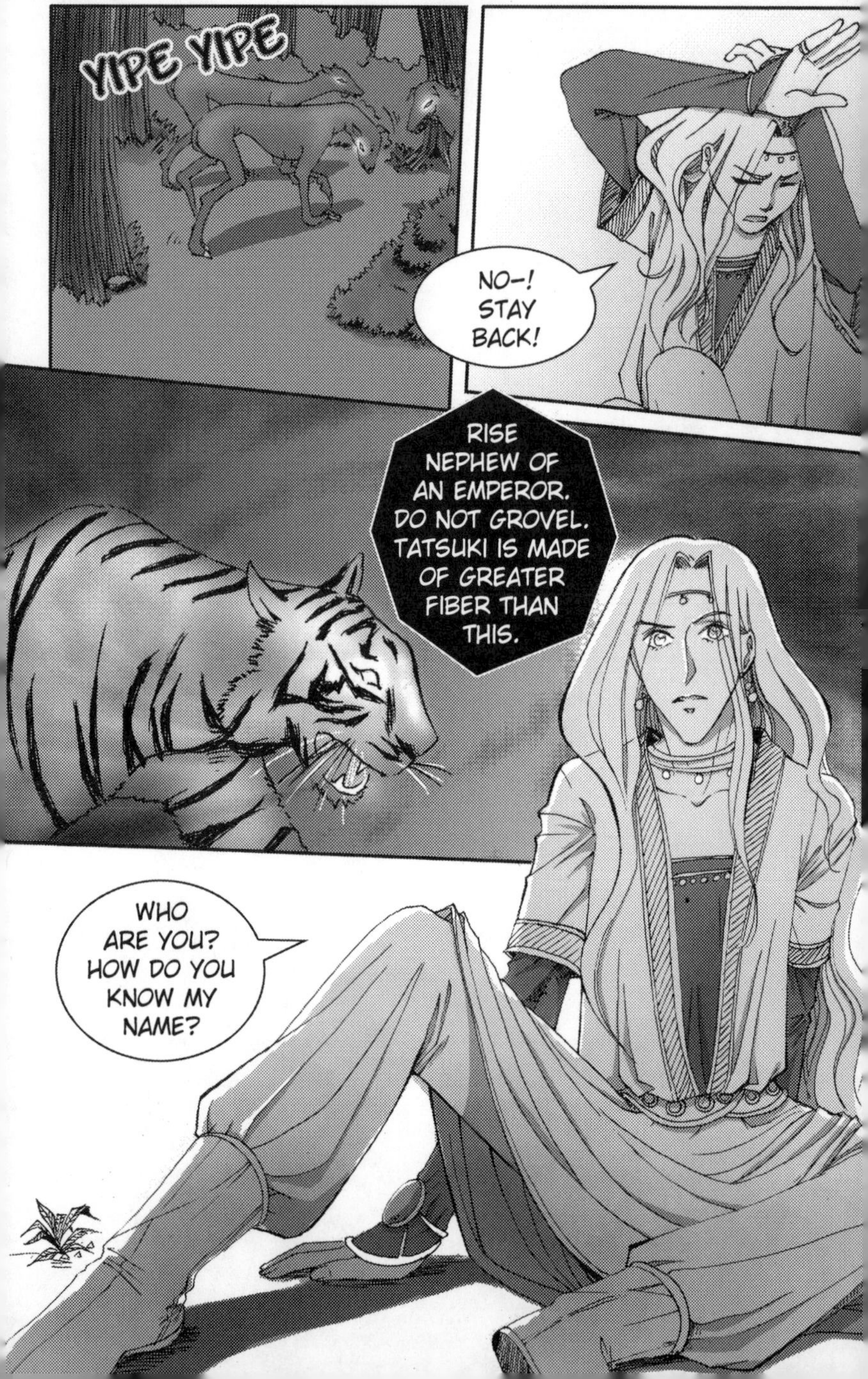
YIPE YIPE
NO–! STAY BACK!
RISE NEPHEW OF AN EMPEROR. DO NOT GROVEL. TATSUKI IS MADE OF GREATER FIBER THAN THIS.
WHO ARE YOU? HOW DO YOU KNOW MY NAME?

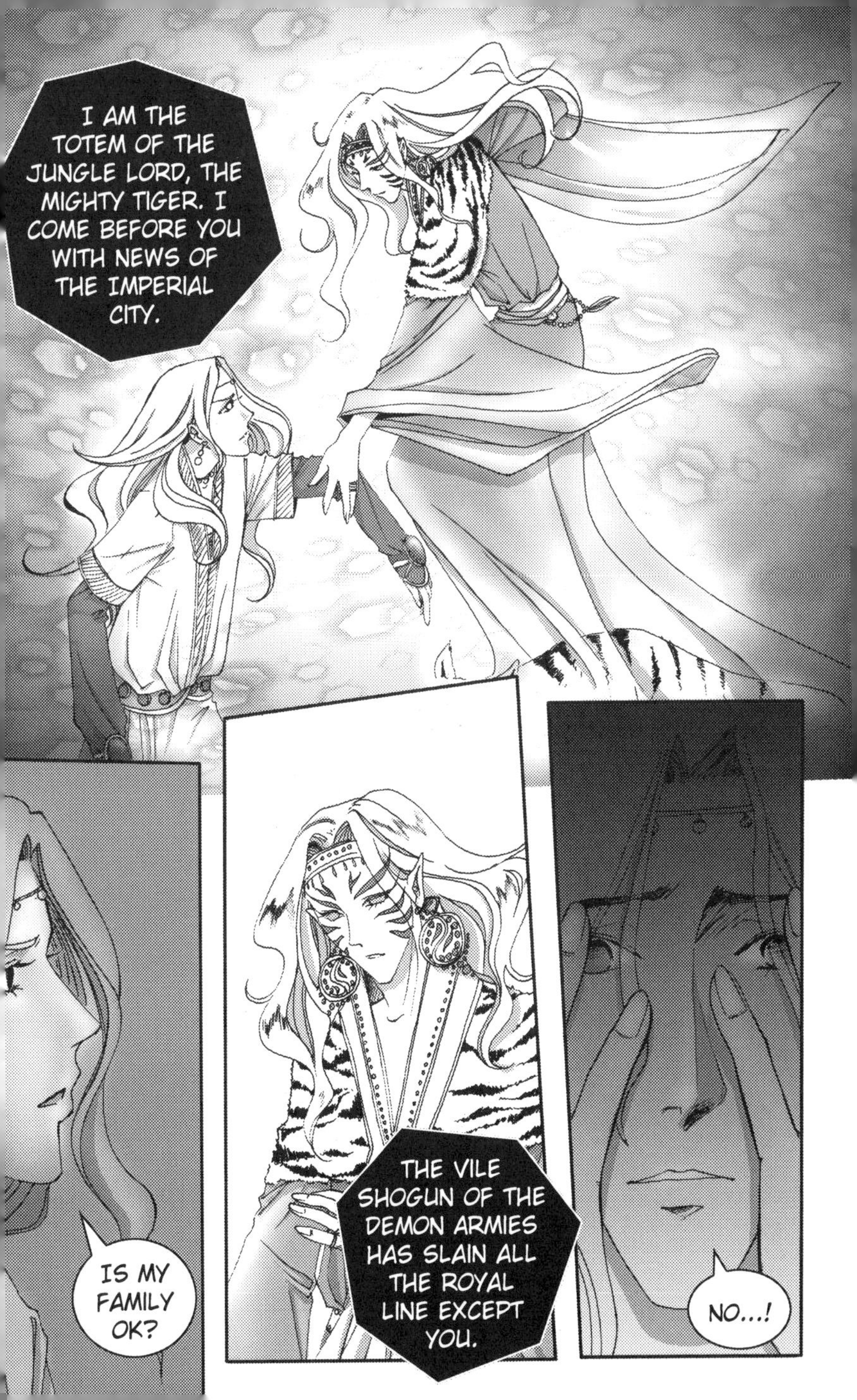
I AM THE TOTEM OF THE JUNGLE LORD, THE MIGHTY TIGER. I COME BEFORE YOU WITH NEWS OF THE IMPERIAL CITY.
IS MY FAMILY OK?
THE VILE SHOGUN OF THE DEMON ARMIES HAS SLAIN ALL THE ROYAL LINE EXCEPT YOU.
NO...!

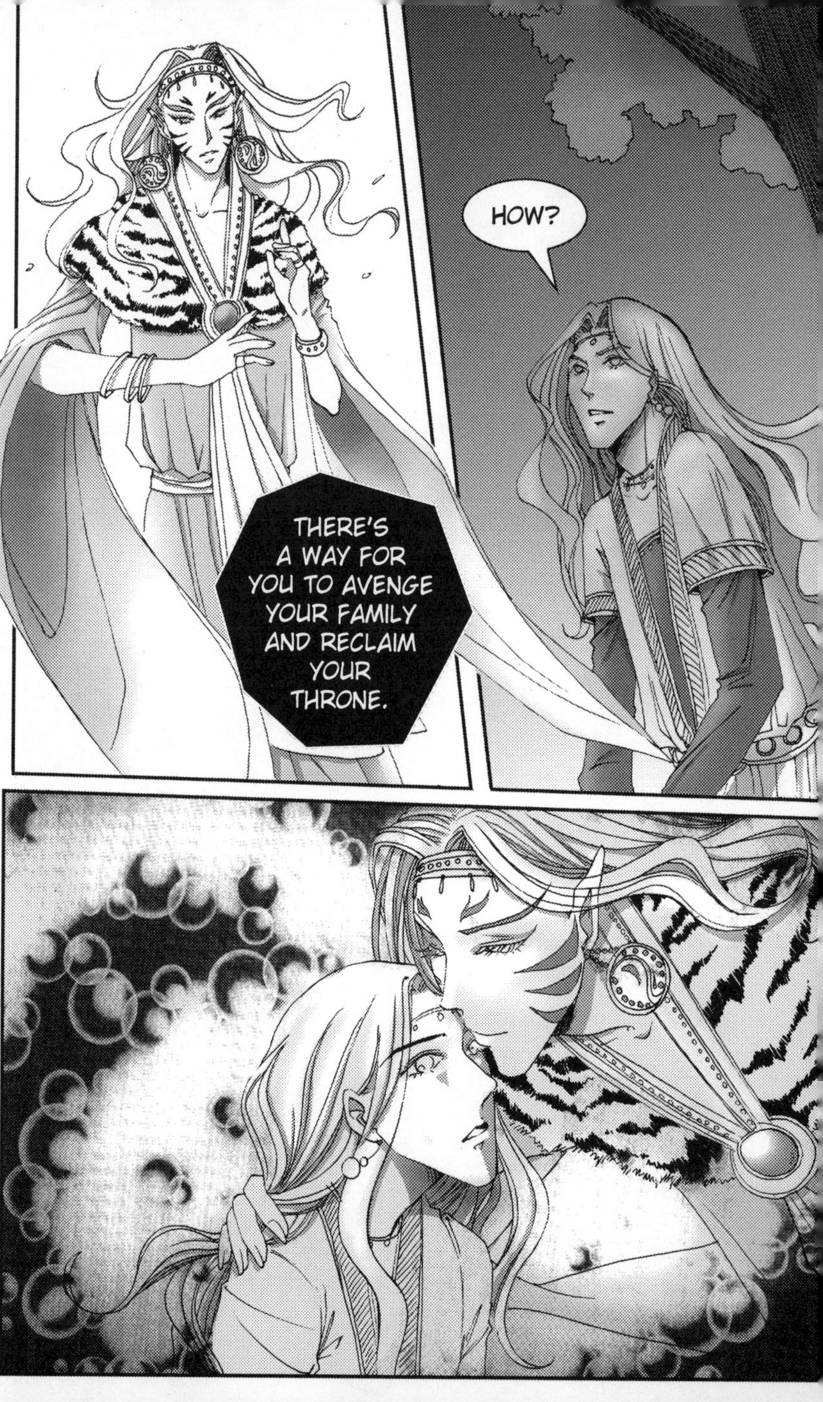
THERE'S A WAY FOR YOU TO AVENGE YOUR FAMILY AND RECLAIM YOUR THRONE.
HOW?

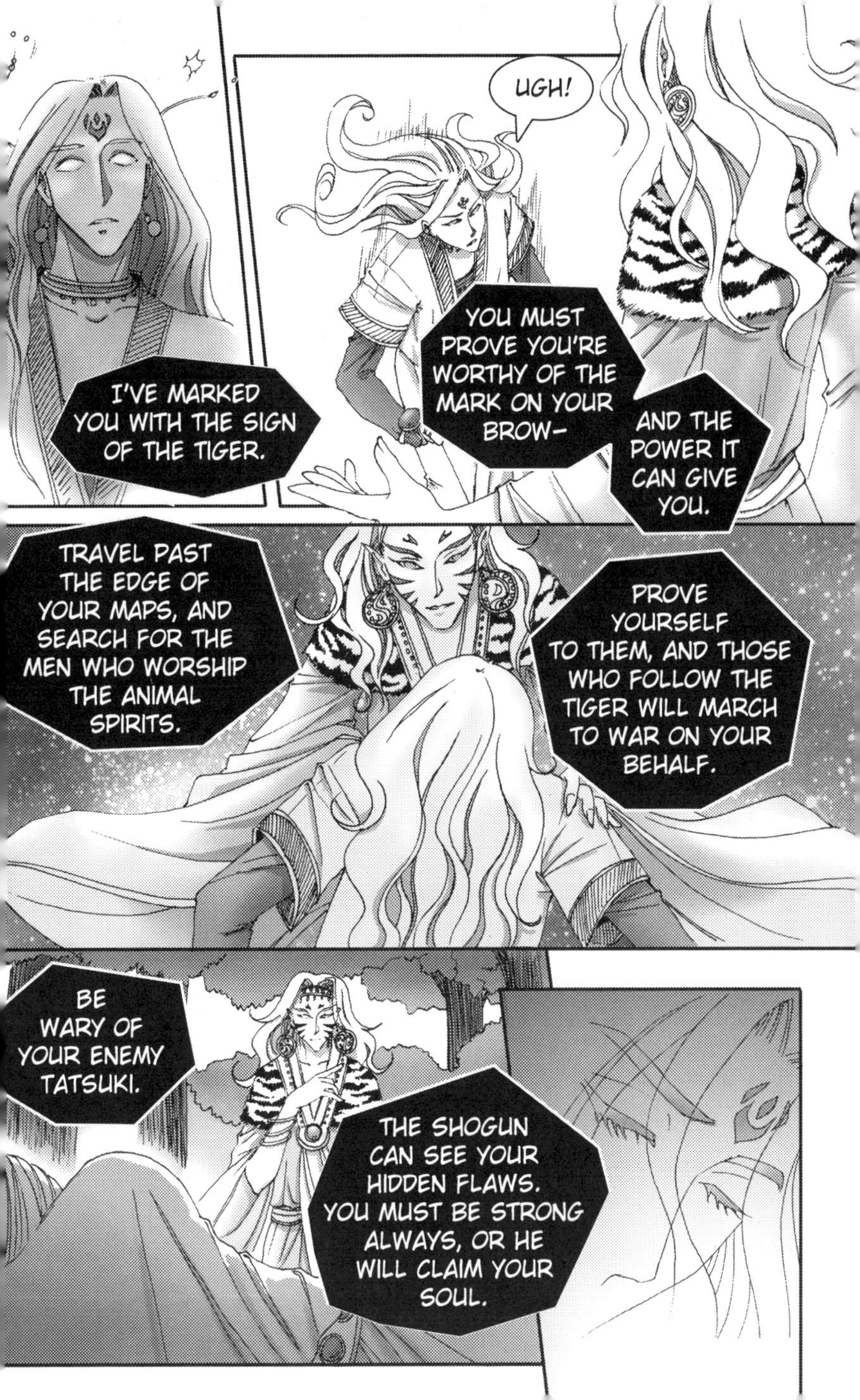
I'VE MARKED YOU WITH THE SIGN OF THE TIGER.
UGH!
YOU MUST PROVE YOU'RE WORTHY OF THE MARK ON YOUR BROW-
AND THE POWER IT CAN GIVE YOU.
TRAVEL PAST THE EDGE OF YOUR MAPS, AND SEARCH FOR THE MEN WHO WORSHIP THE ANIMAL SPIRITS.
PROVE YOURSELF TO THEM, AND THOSE WHO FOLLOW THE TIGER WILL MARCH TO WAR ON YOUR BEHALF.
BE WARY OF YOUR ENEMY TATSUKI.
THE SHOGUN CAN SEE YOUR HIDDEN FLAWS. YOU MUST BE STRONG ALWAYS, OR HE WILL CLAIM YOUR SOUL.

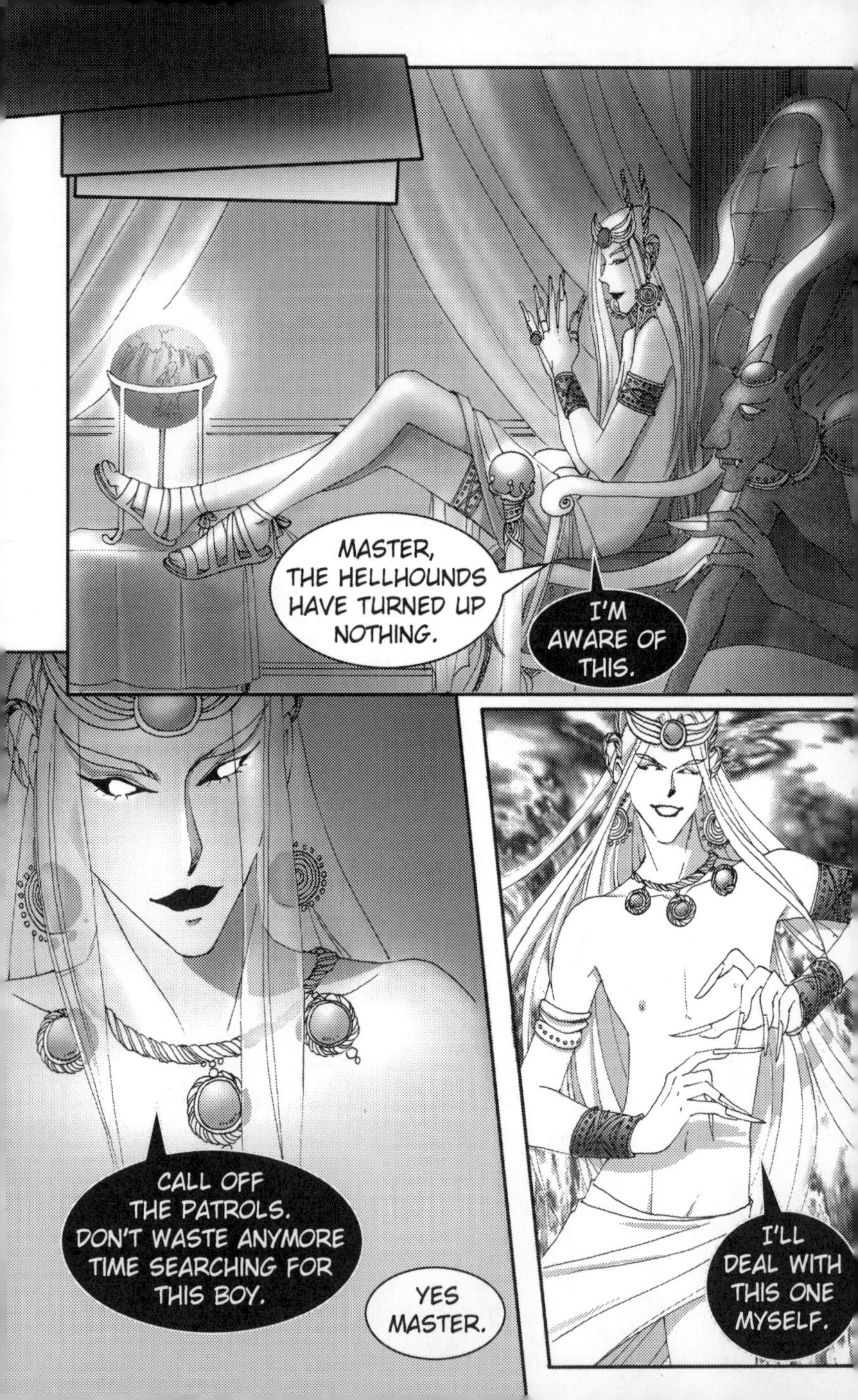
MASTER, THE HELLHOUNDS HAVE TURNED UP NOTHING.
I'M AWARE OF THIS.
CALL OFF THE PATROLS. DON'T WASTE ANYMORE TIME SEARCHING FOR THIS BOY.
YES MASTER.
I'LL DEAL WITH THIS ONE MYSELF.

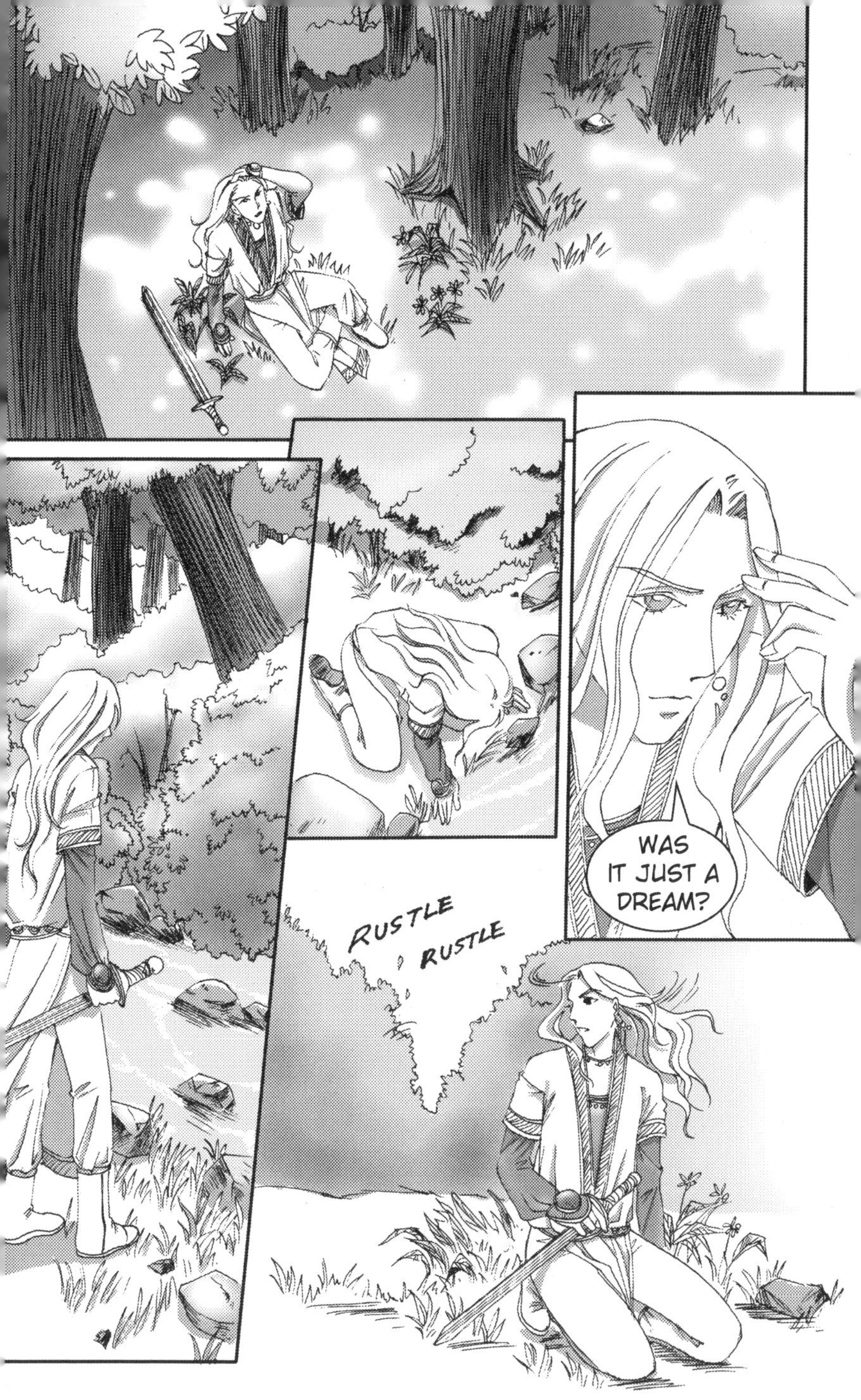
WAS IT JUST A DREAM?
RUSTLE
RUSTLE

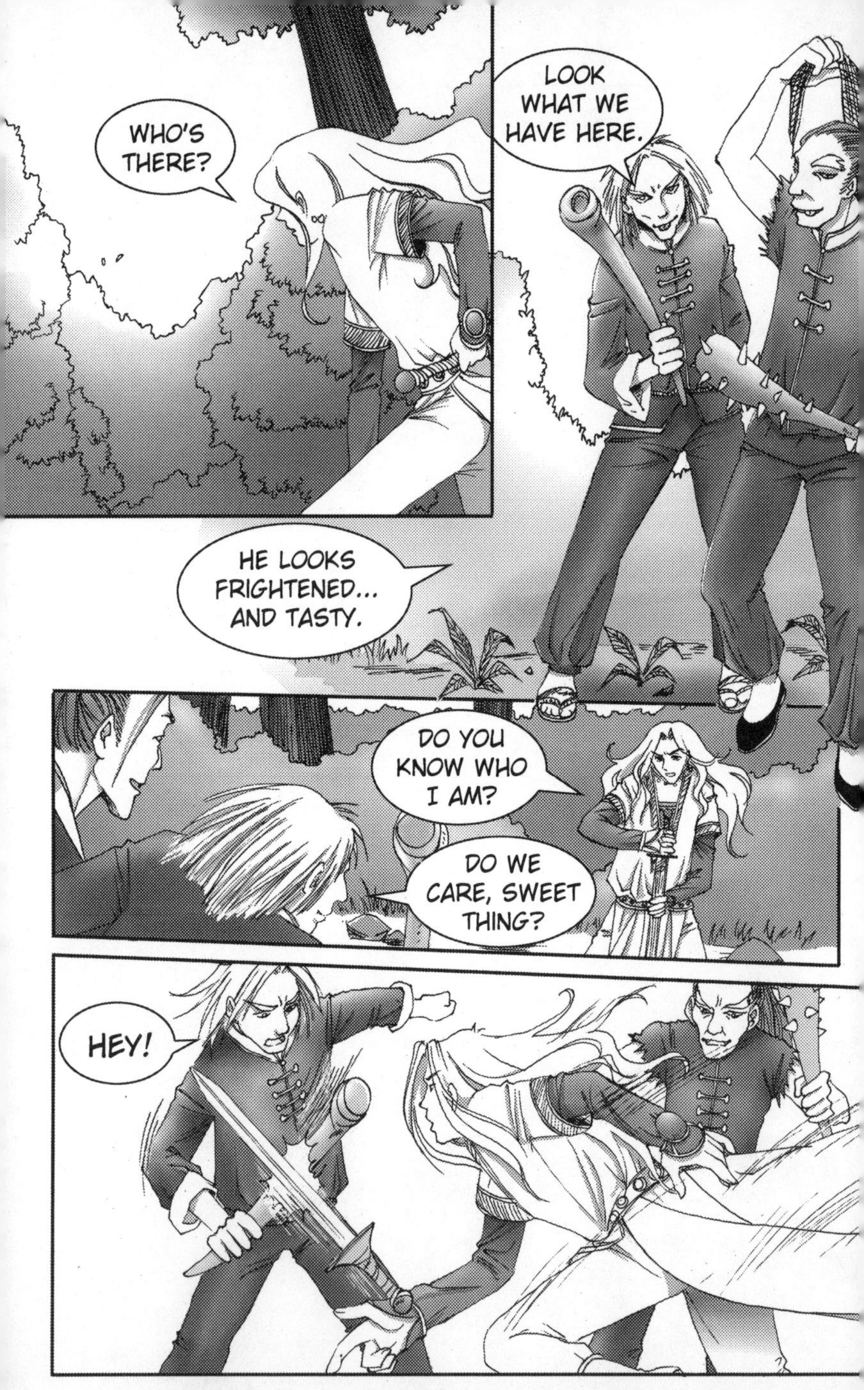
WHO'S THERE?
LOOK WHAT WE HAVE HERE.
HE LOOKS FRIGHTENED... AND TASTY.
DO YOU KNOW WHO I AM?
DO WE CARE, SWEET THING?
HEY!

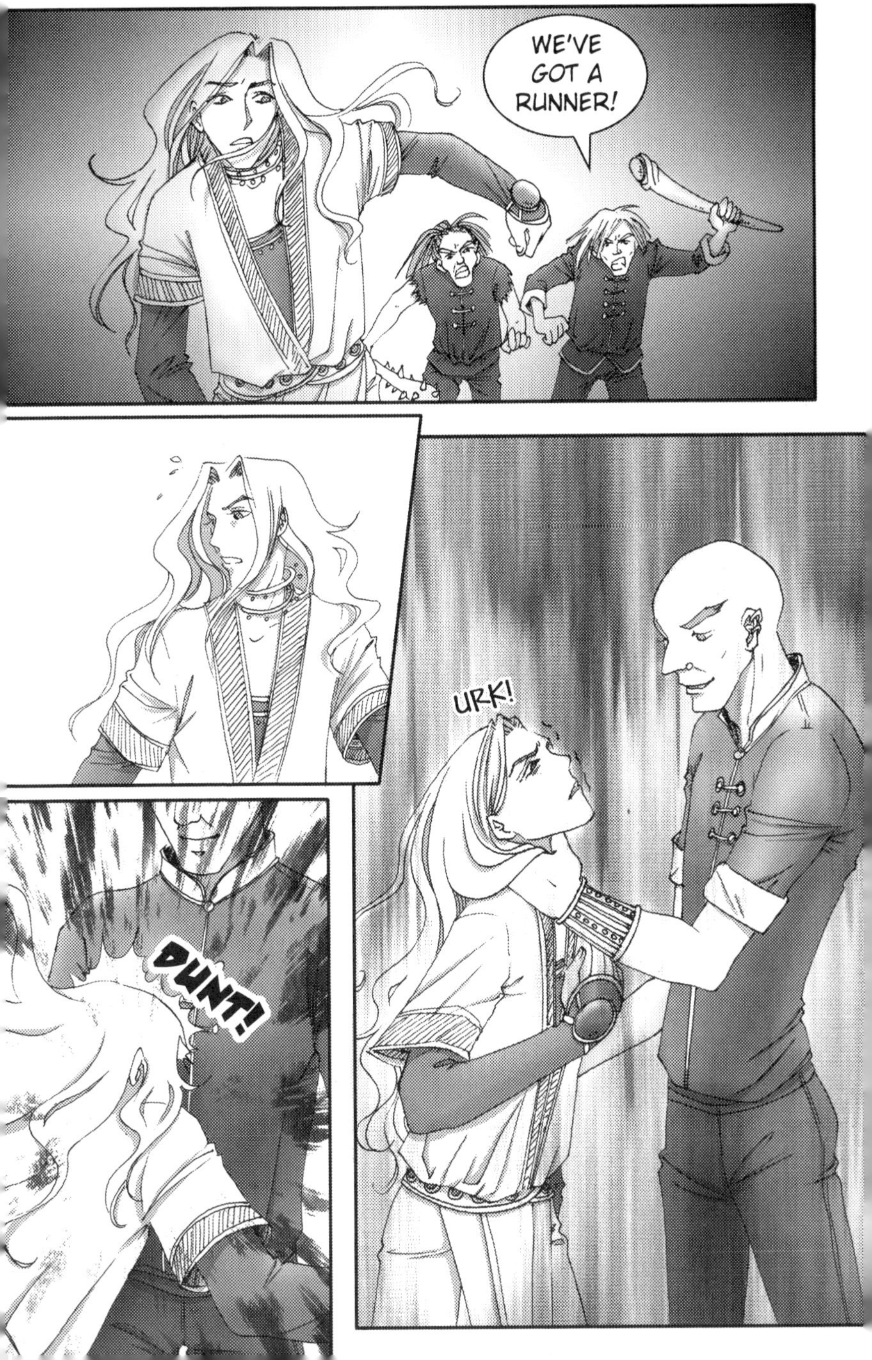
WE'VE GOT A RUNNER!
DUNT!
URK!

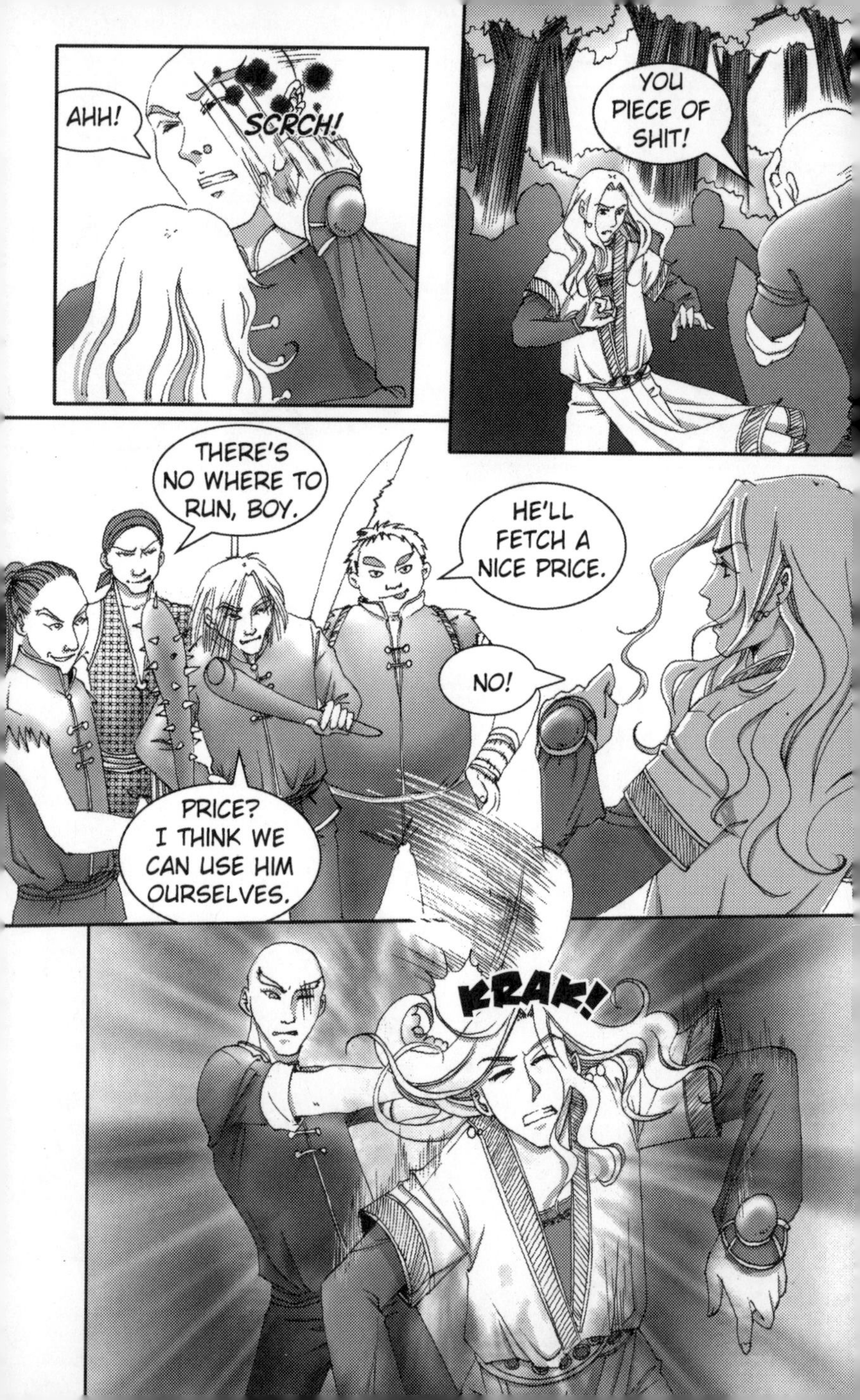
AHH!
SCRCH!
YOU PIECE OF SHIT!
THERE'S NO WHERE TO RUN, BOY.
HE'LL FETCH A NICE PRICE.
NO!
PRICE? I THINK WE CAN USE HIM OURSELVES.
KRAK!

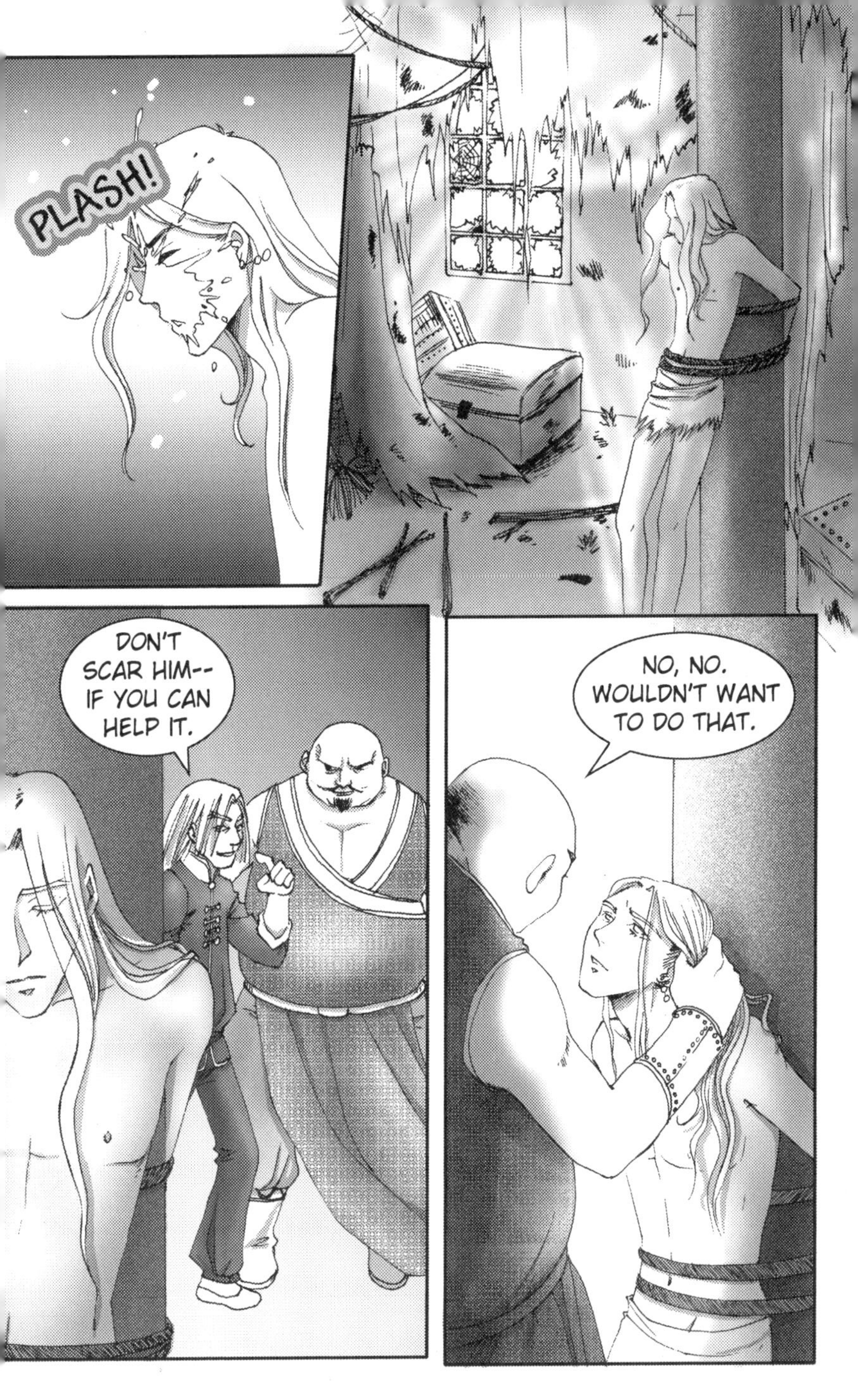
PLASH!
DON'T SCAR HIM-- IF YOU CAN HELP IT.
NO, NO. WOULDN'T WANT TO DO THAT.

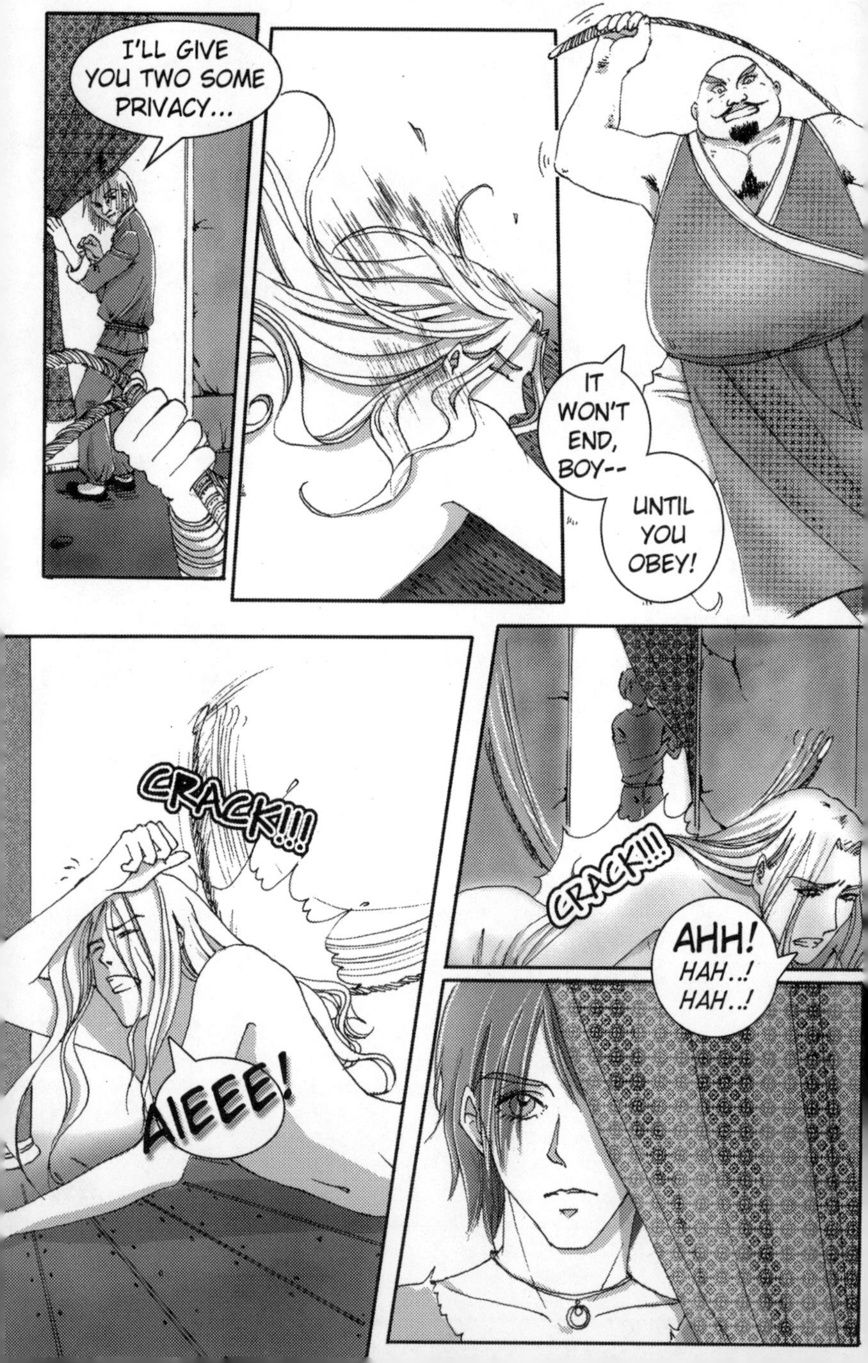
I'LL GIVE YOU TWO SOME PRIVACY...
IT WON'T END, BOY--
UNTIL YOU OBEY!
CRACK!!!
AIEEE!
CRACK!!!
AHH! HAH..! HAH..!

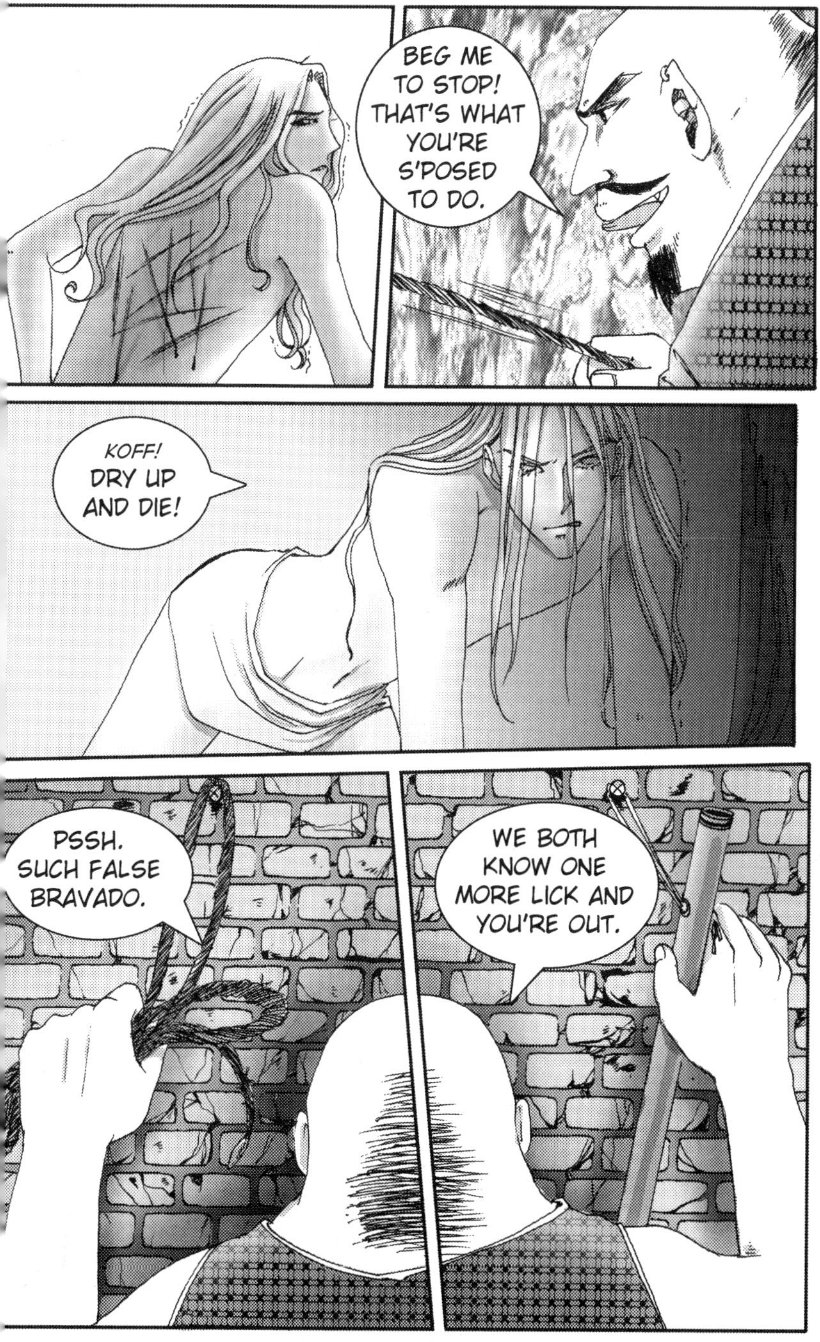
BEG ME TO STOP! THAT'S WHAT YOU'RE S'POSED TO DO.
KOFF! DRY UP AND DIE!
PSSH. SUCH FALSE BRAVADO.
WE BOTH KNOW ONE MORE LICK AND YOU'RE OUT.

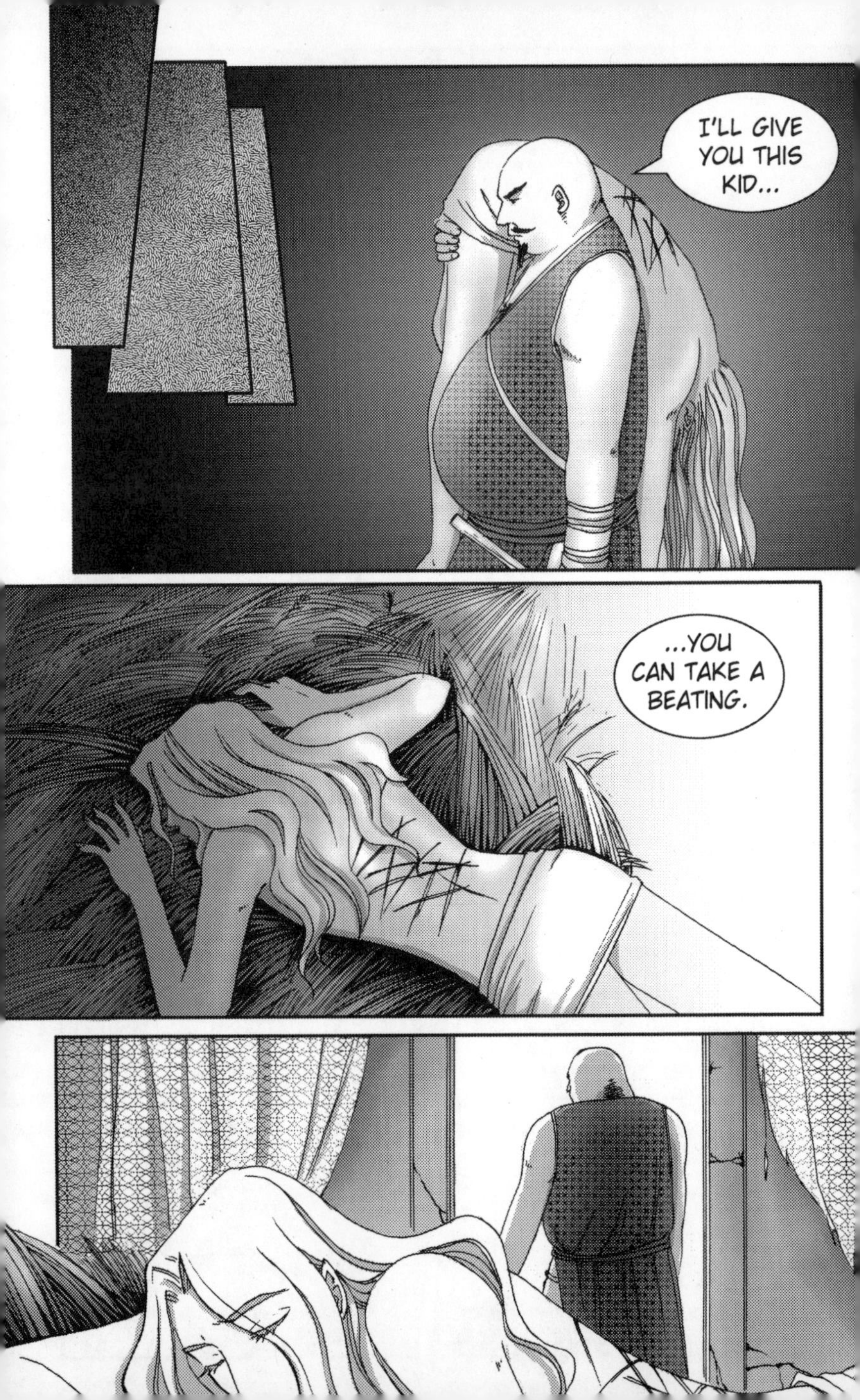
I'LL GIVE YOU THIS KID...
...YOU CAN TAKE A BEATING.

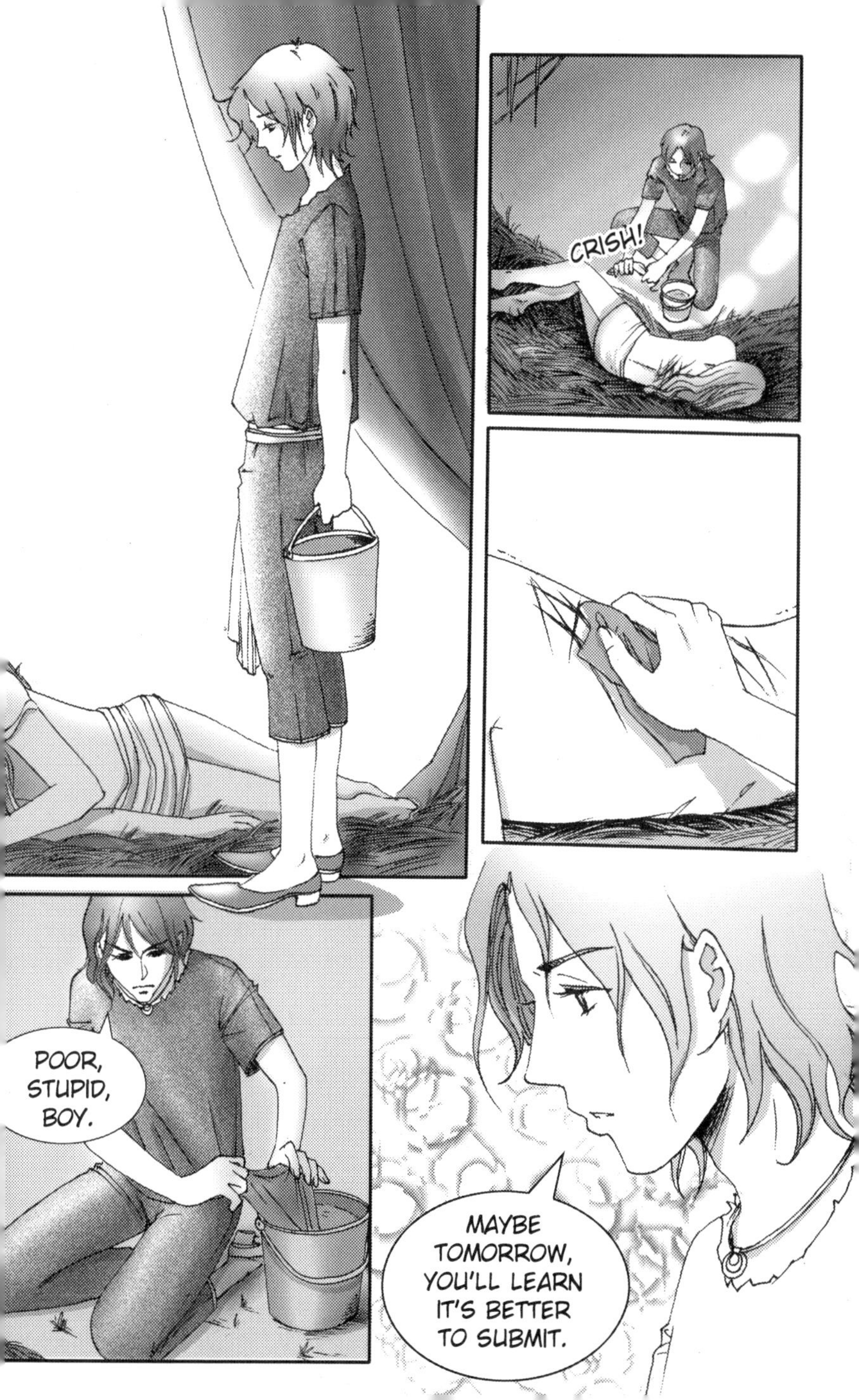
CRISH!
POOR, STUPID, BOY.
MAYBE TOMORROW, YOU'LL LEARN IT'S BETTER TO SUBMIT.

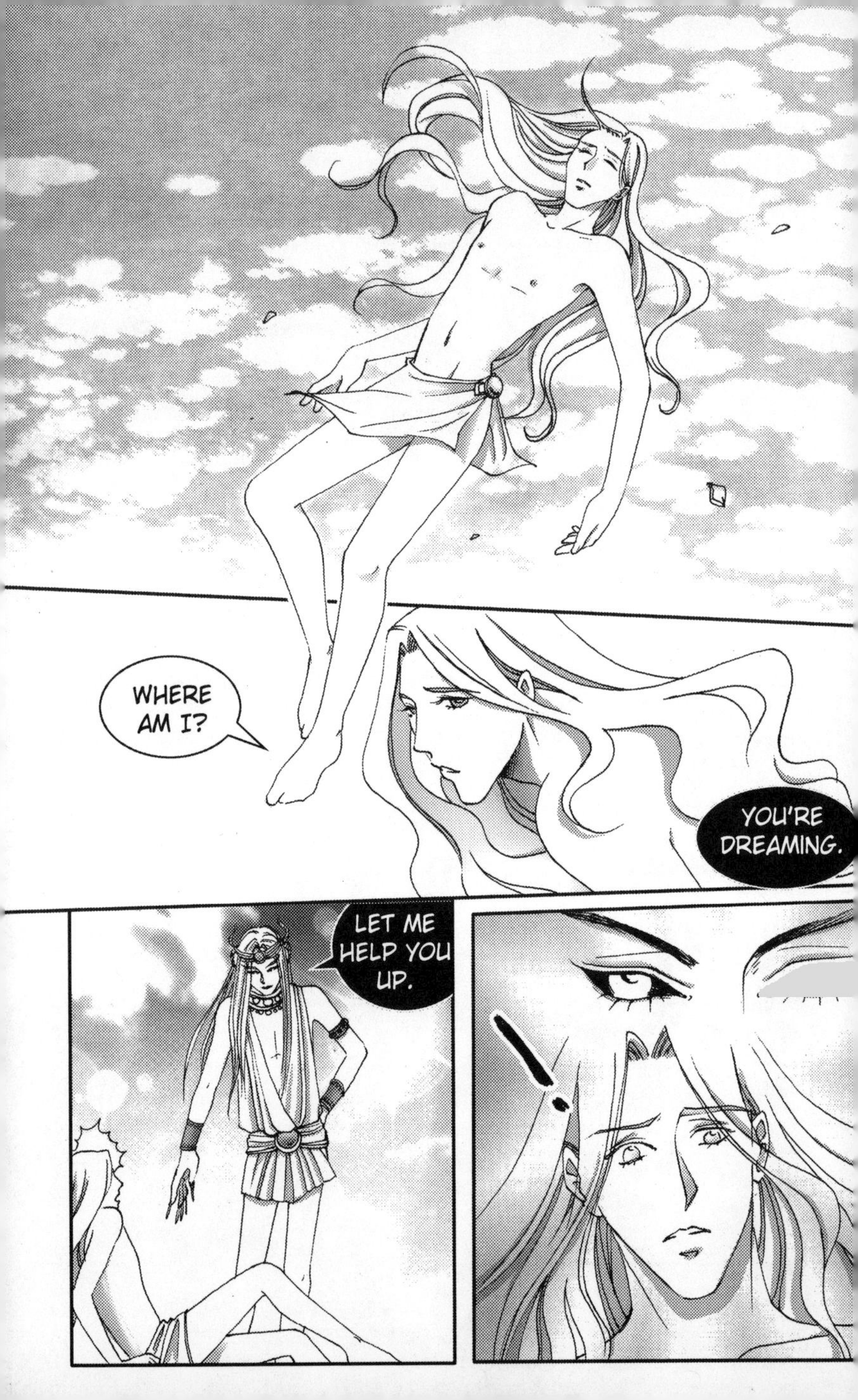
WHERE AM I?
YOU'RE DREAMING.
LET ME HELP YOU UP.
!

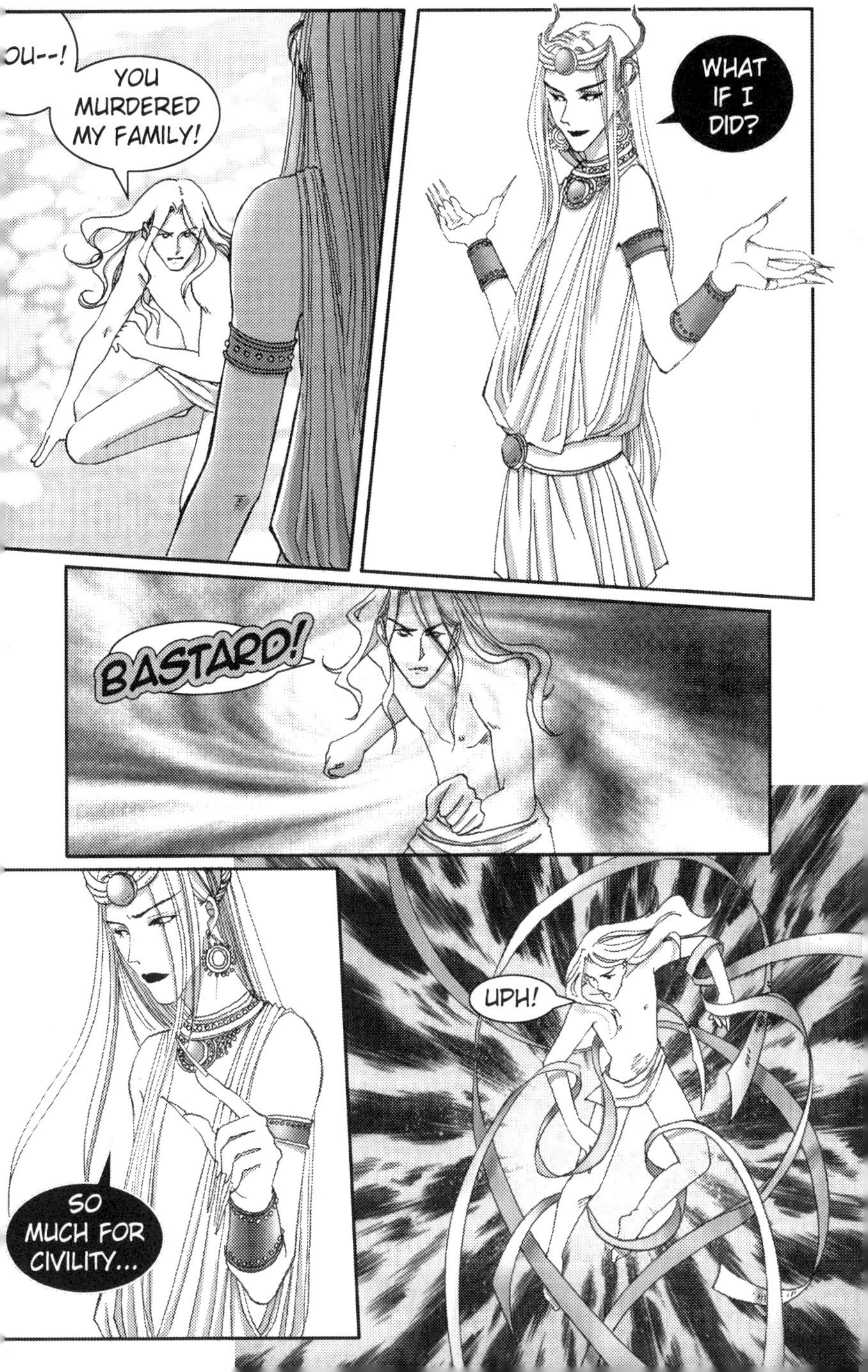
OU--!
YOU MURDERED MY FAMILY!
WHAT IF I DID?
BASTARD!
SO MUCH FOR CIVILITY...
UPH!

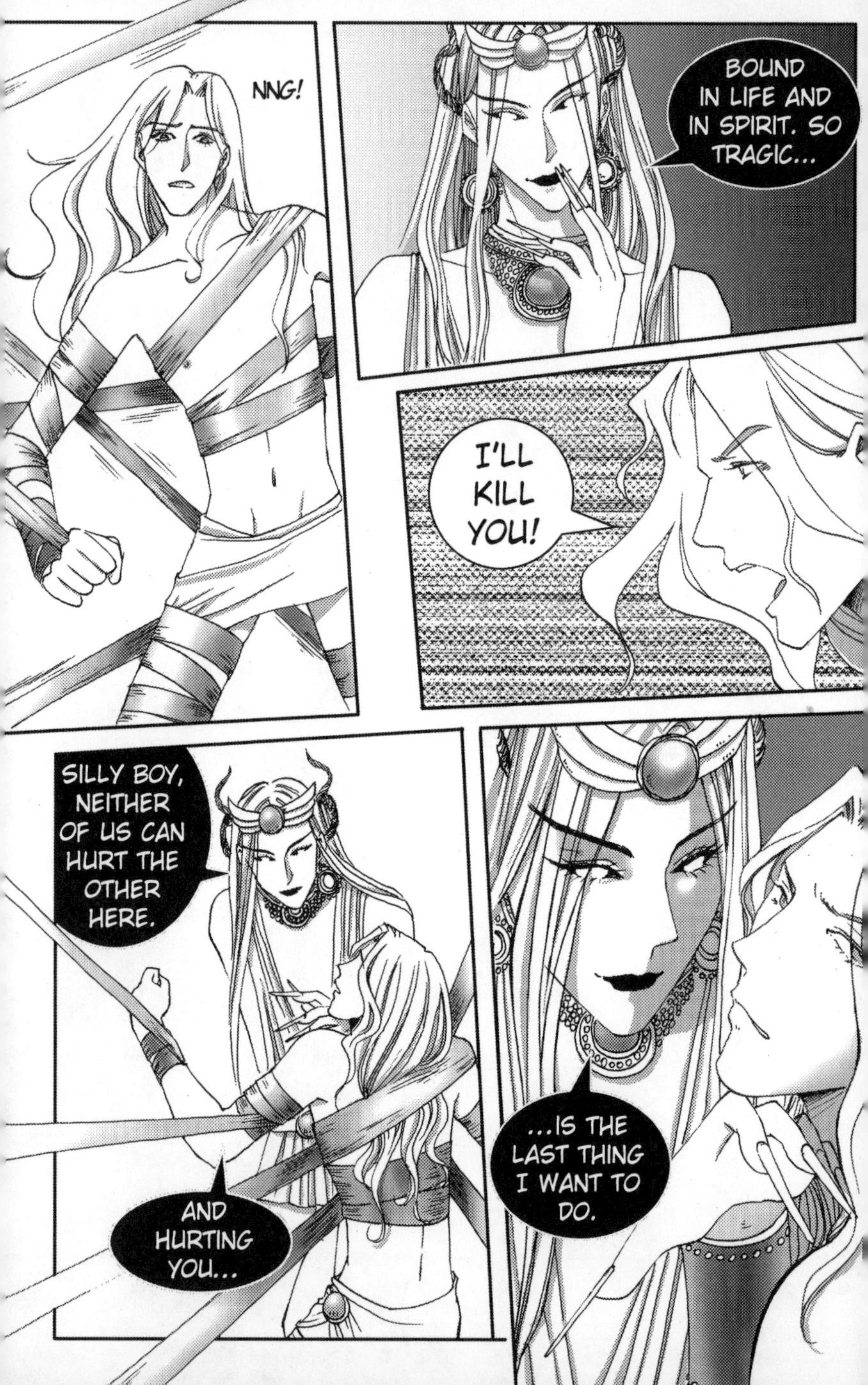
NNG!
BOUND IN LIFE AND IN SPIRIT. SO TRAGIC...
I'LL KILL YOU!
SILLY BOY, NEITHER OF US CAN HURT THE OTHER HERE.
AND HURTING YOU...
...IS THE LAST THING I WANT TO DO.

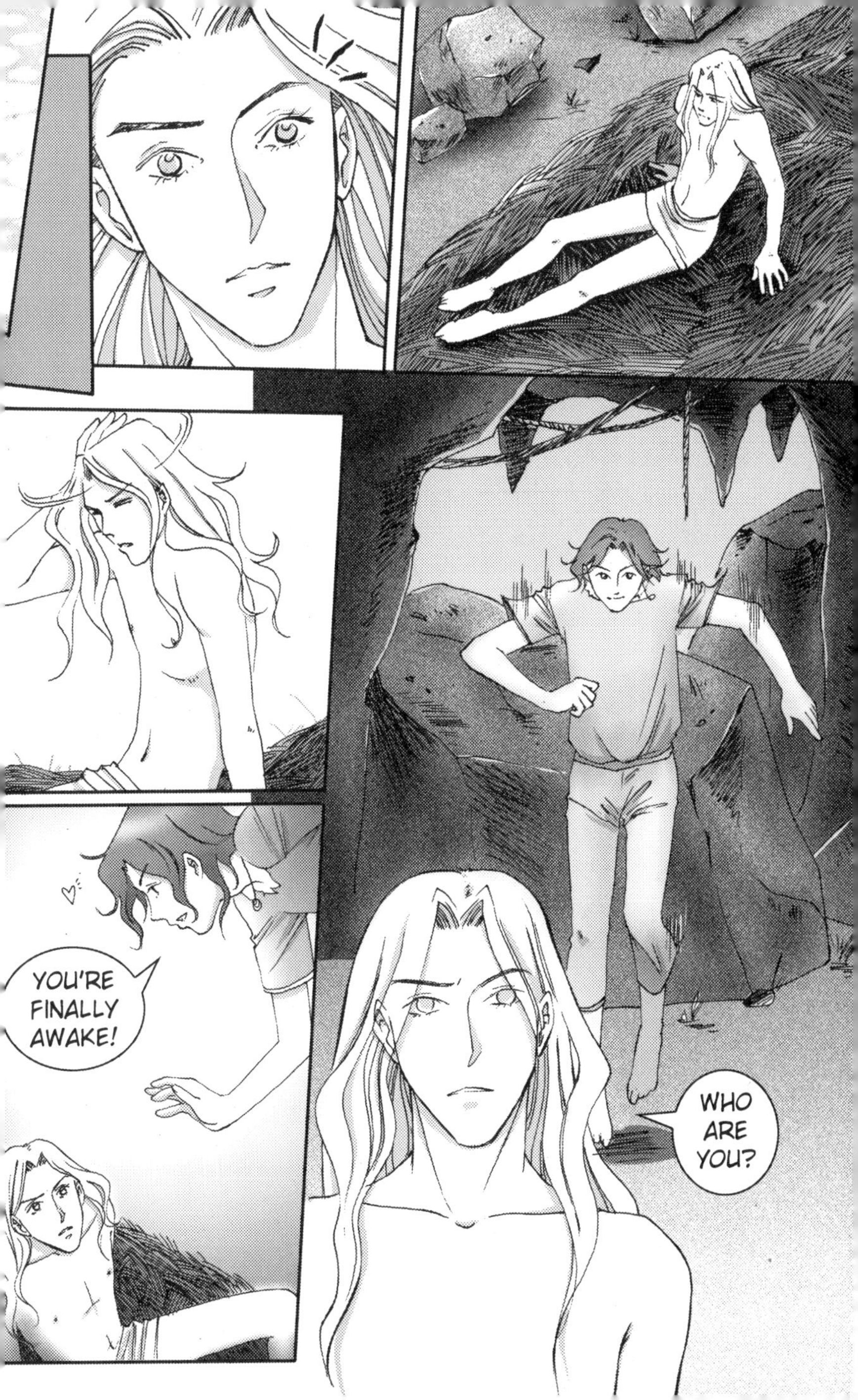
YOU'RE FINALLY AWAKE!
WHO ARE YOU?

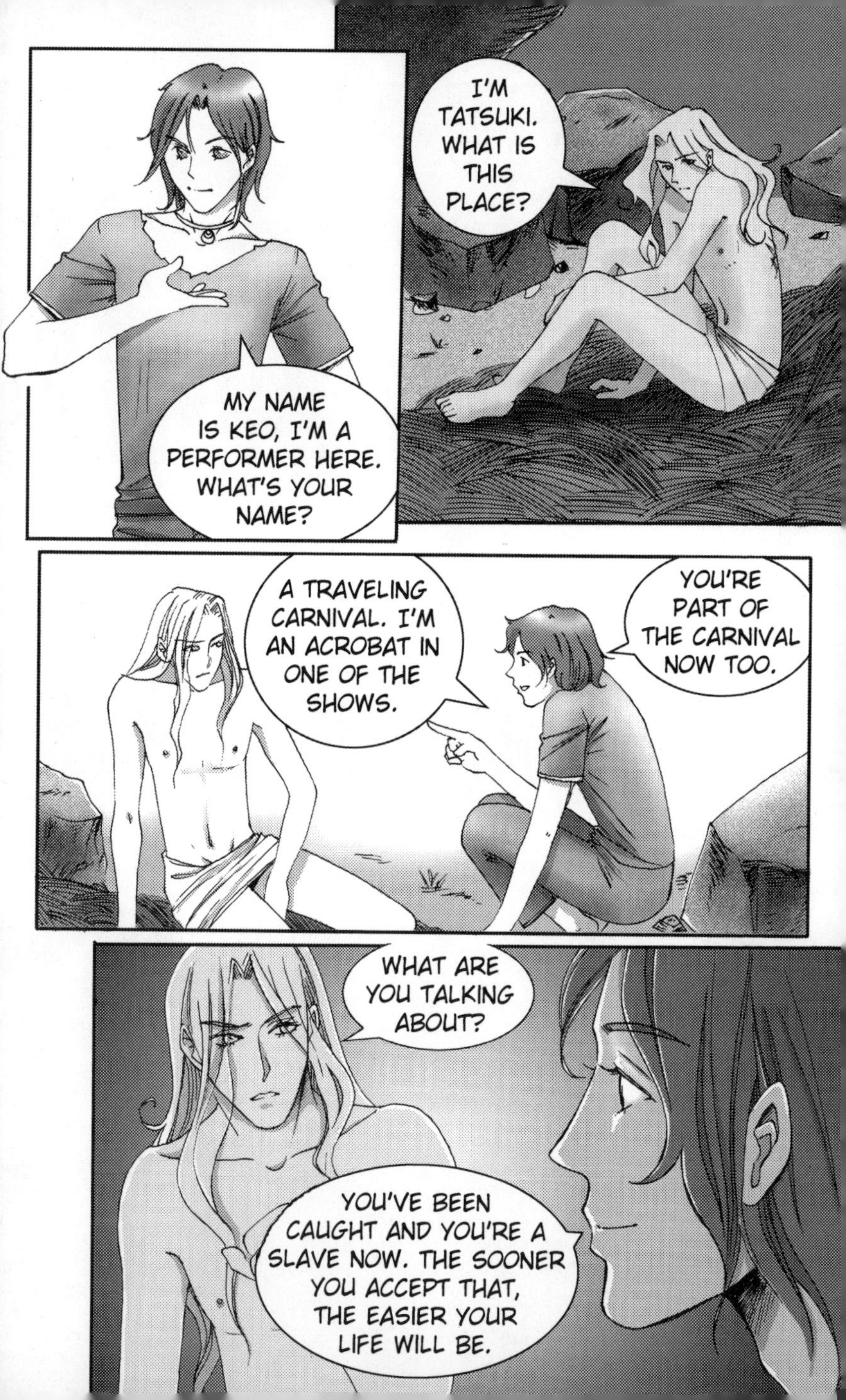
MY NAME IS KEO, I'M A PERFORMER HERE. WHAT'S YOUR NAME?
I'M TATSUKI. WHAT IS THIS PLACE?
A TRAVELING CARNIVAL. I'M AN ACROBAT IN ONE OF THE SHOWS.
YOU'RE PART OF THE CARNIVAL NOW TOO.
WHAT ARE YOU TALKING ABOUT?
YOU'VE BEEN CAUGHT AND YOU'RE A SLAVE NOW. THE SOONER YOU ACCEPT THAT, THE EASIER YOUR LIFE WILL BE.

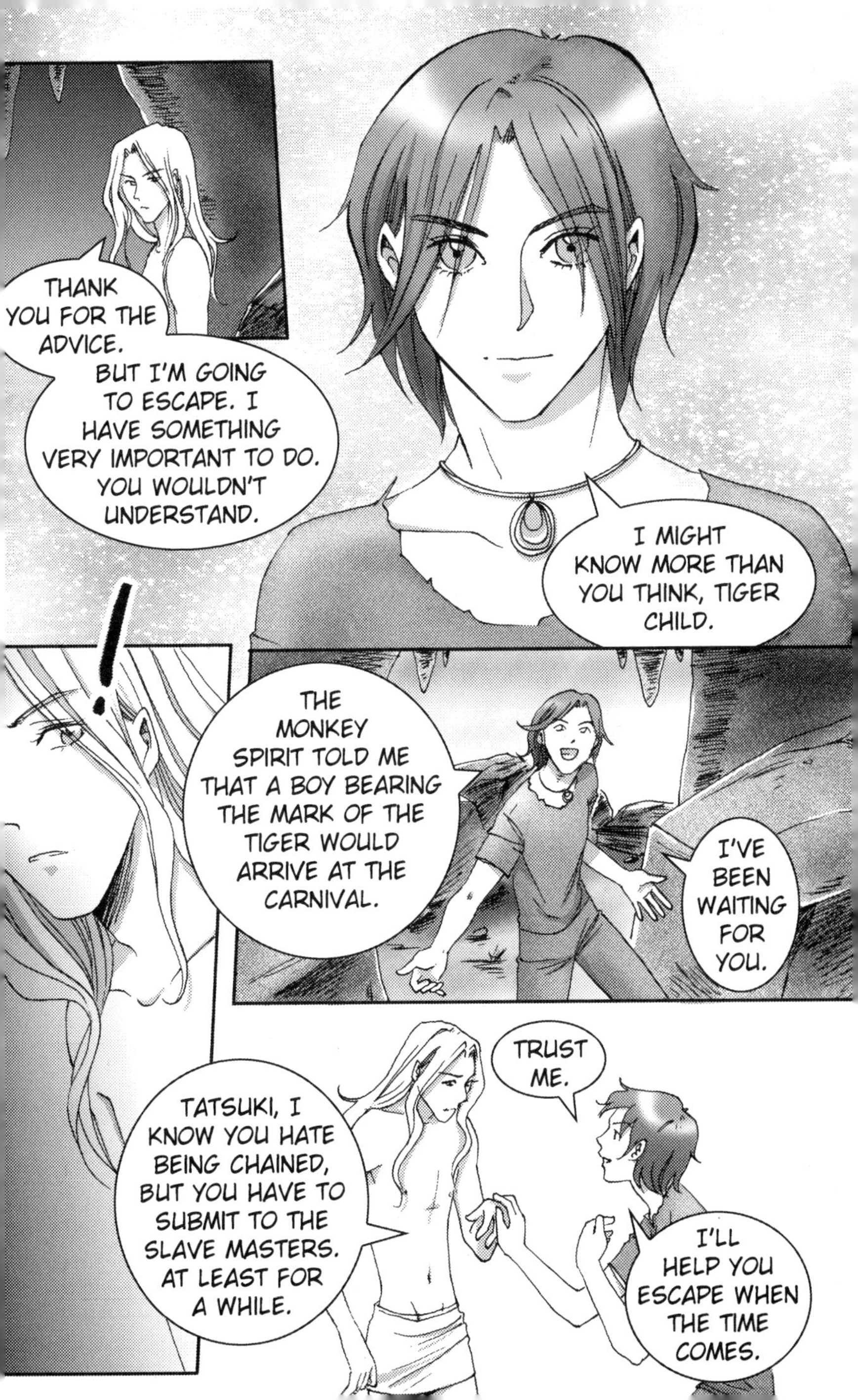
THANK YOU FOR THE ADVICE.
BUT I'M GOING TO ESCAPE. I HAVE SOMETHING VERY IMPORTANT TO DO. YOU WOULDN'T UNDERSTAND.
I MIGHT KNOW MORE THAN YOU THINK, TIGER CHILD.
!
THE MONKEY SPIRIT TOLD ME THAT A BOY BEARING THE MARK OF THE TIGER WOULD ARRIVE AT THE CARNIVAL.
I'VE BEEN WAITING FOR YOU.
TRUST ME.
TATSUKI, I KNOW YOU HATE BEING CHAINED, BUT YOU HAVE TO SUBMIT TO THE SLAVE MASTERS. AT LEAST FOR A WHILE.
I'LL HELP YOU ESCAPE WHEN THE TIME COMES.

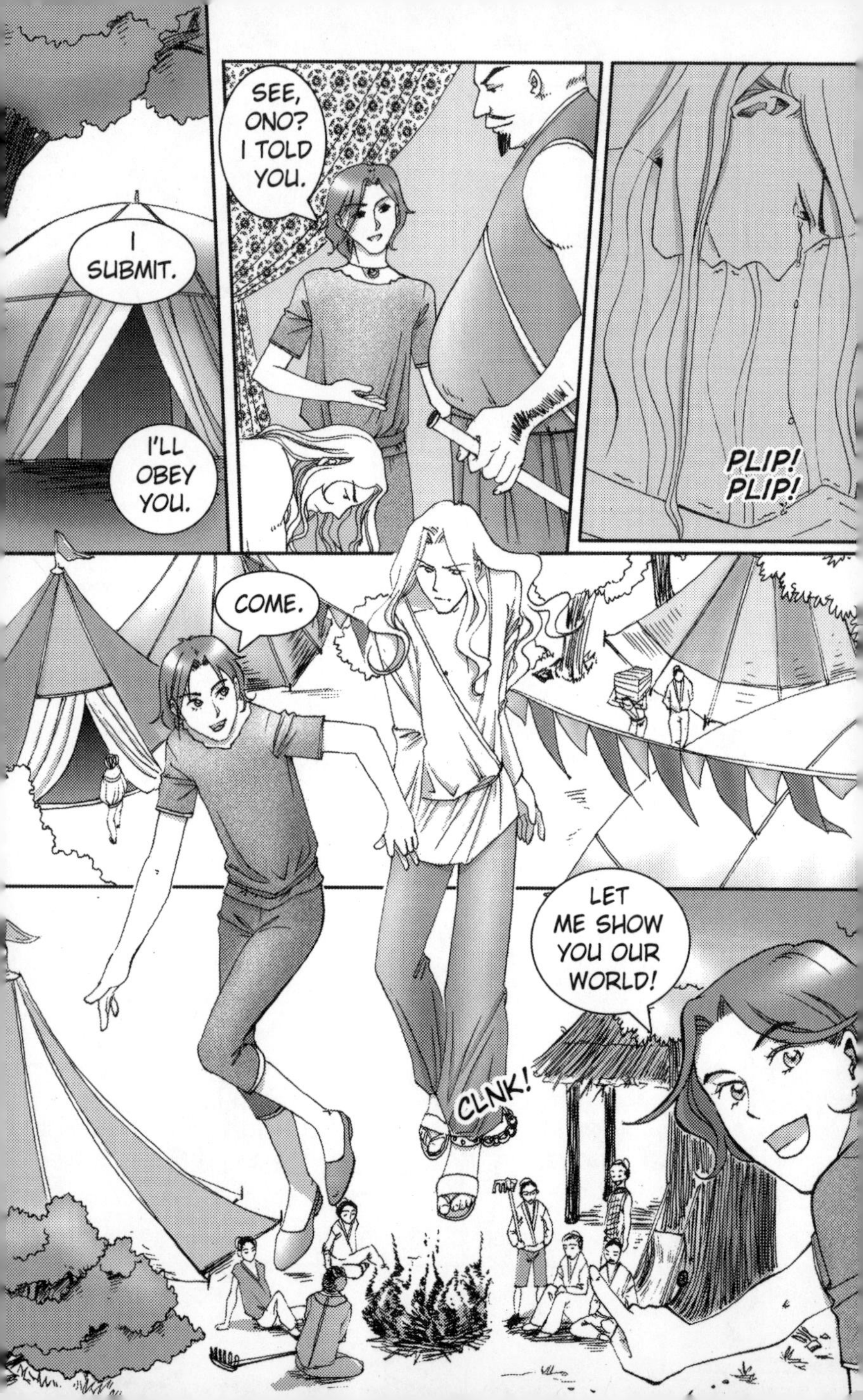
I SUBMIT.
I'LL OBEY YOU.
SEE, ONO? I TOLD YOU.
PLIP! PLIP!
COME.
LET ME SHOW YOU OUR WORLD!
CLNK!

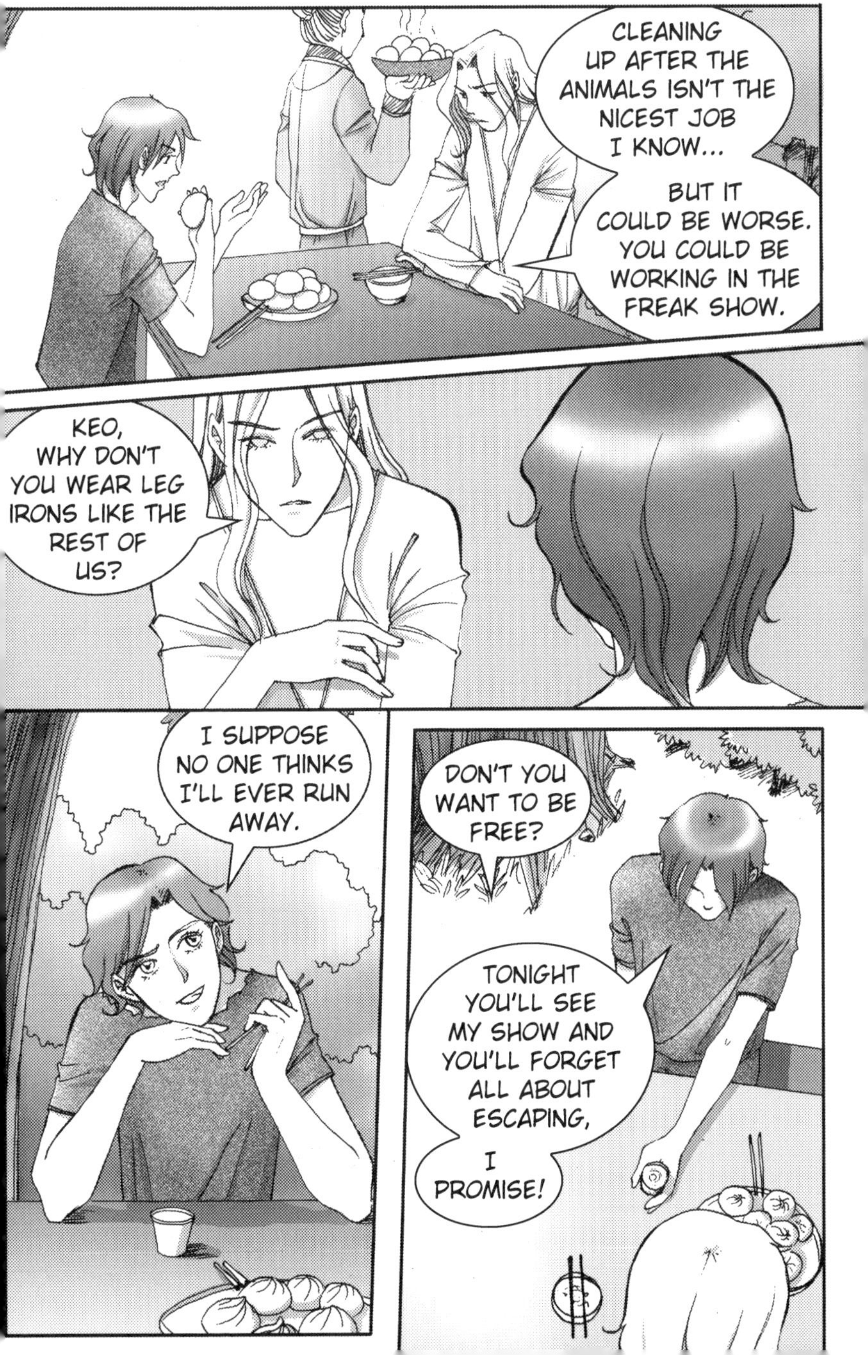
CLEANING UP AFTER THE ANIMALS ISN'T THE NICEST JOB I KNOW...
BUT IT COULD BE WORSE. YOU COULD BE WORKING IN THE FREAK SHOW.
KEO, WHY DON'T YOU WEAR LEG IRONS LIKE THE REST OF US?
I SUPPOSE NO ONE THINKS I'LL EVER RUN AWAY.
DON'T YOU WANT TO BE FREE?
TONIGHT YOU'LL SEE MY SHOW AND YOU'LL FORGET ALL ABOUT ESCAPING,
I PROMISE!

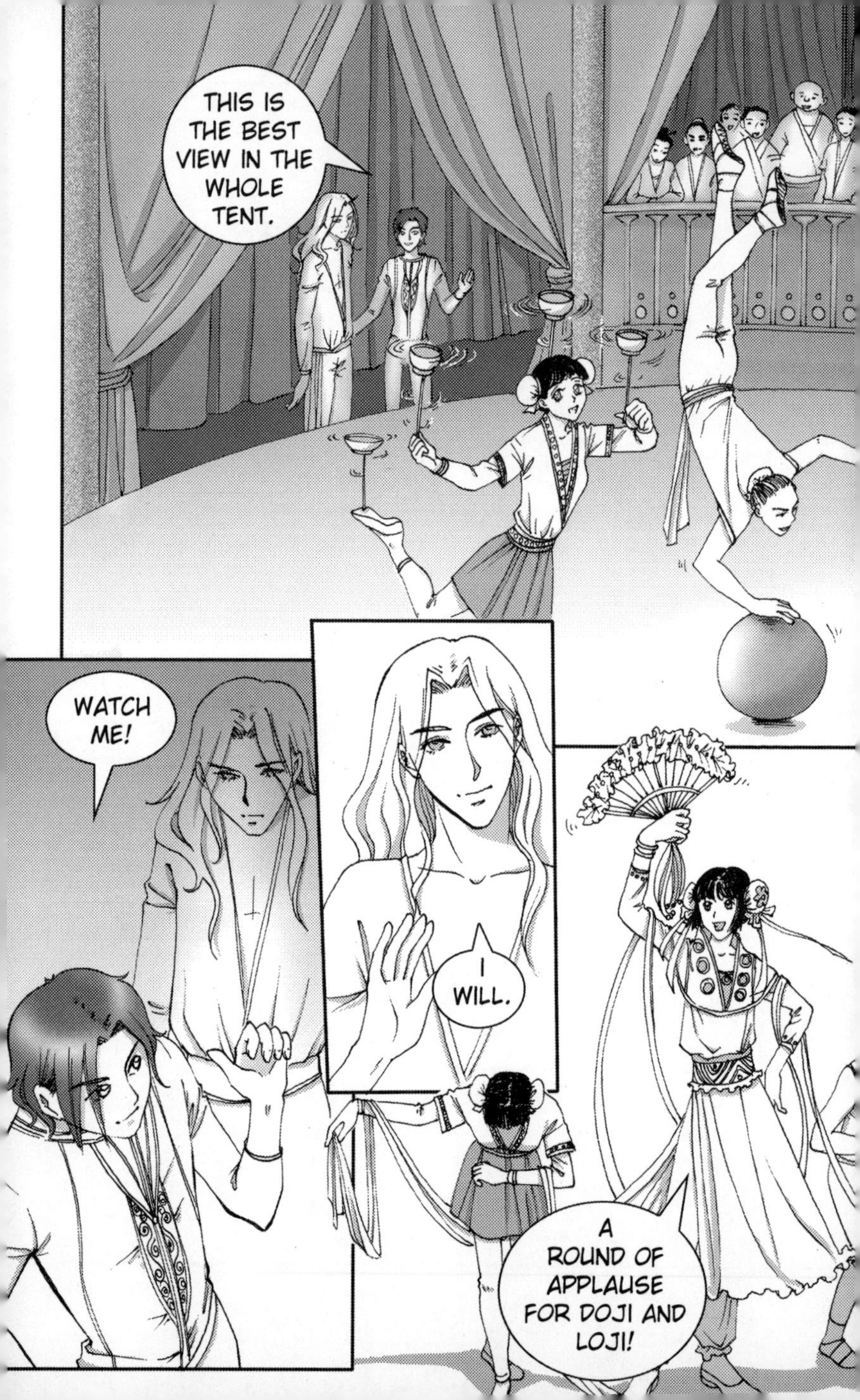
THIS IS THE BEST VIEW IN THE WHOLE TENT.
WATCH ME!
I WILL.
A ROUND OF APPLAUSE FOR DOJI AND LOJI!

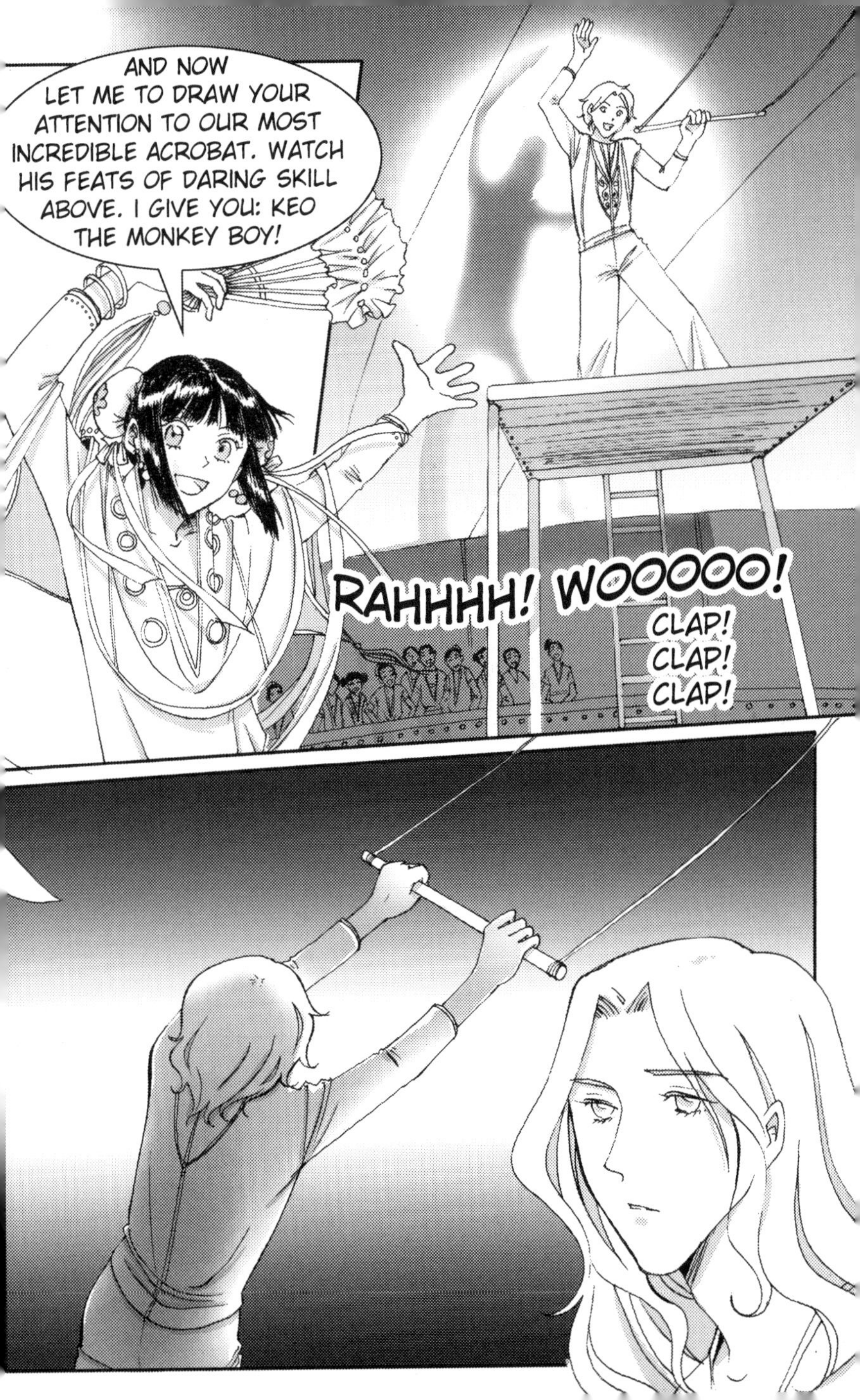
AND NOW LET ME TO DRAW YOUR ATTENTION TO OUR MOST INCREDIBLE ACROBAT. WATCH HIS FEATS OF DARING SKILL ABOVE. I GIVE YOU: KEO THE MONKEY BOY!
RAHHHH! WOOOOO!
CLAP! CLAP! CLAP!

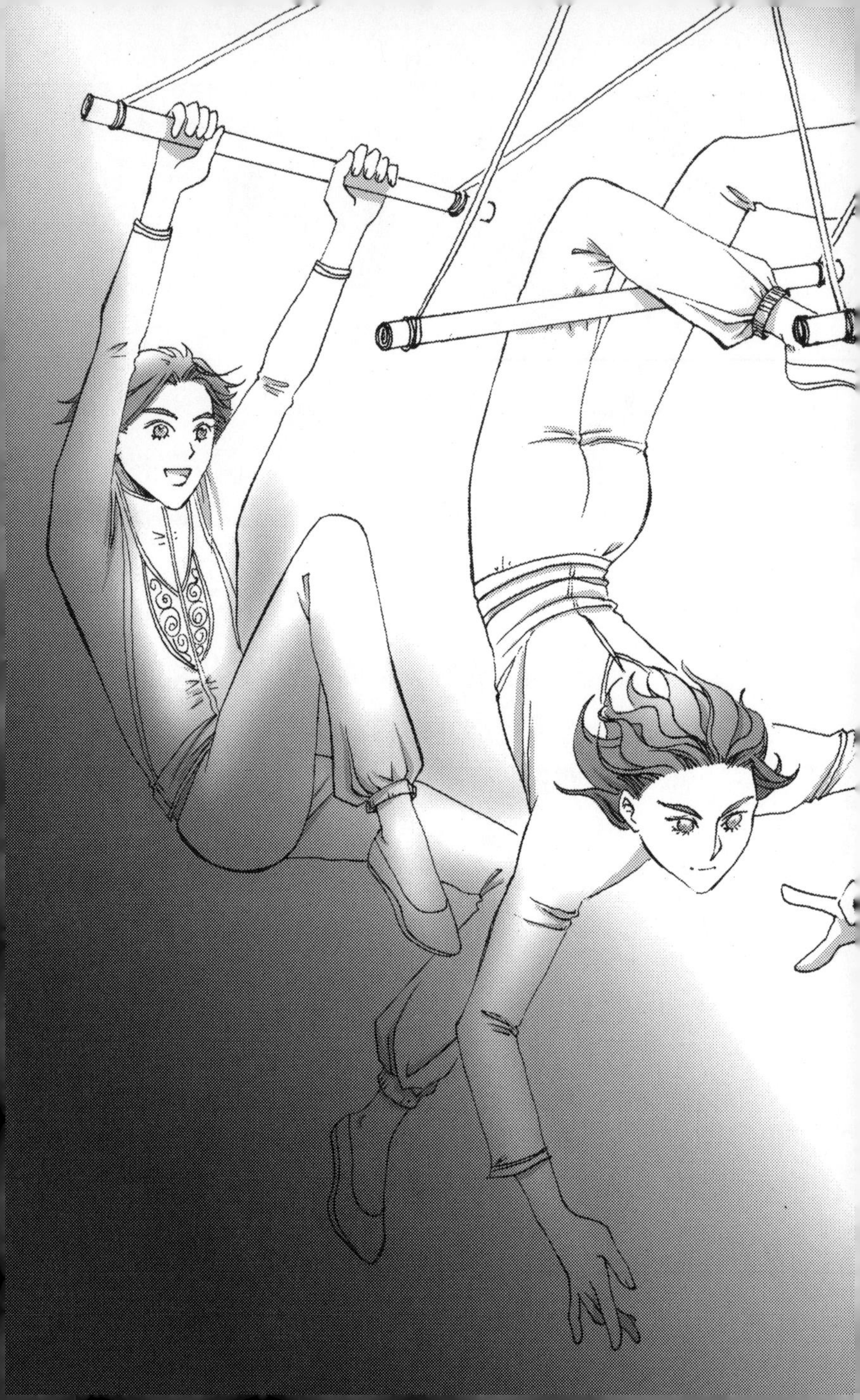

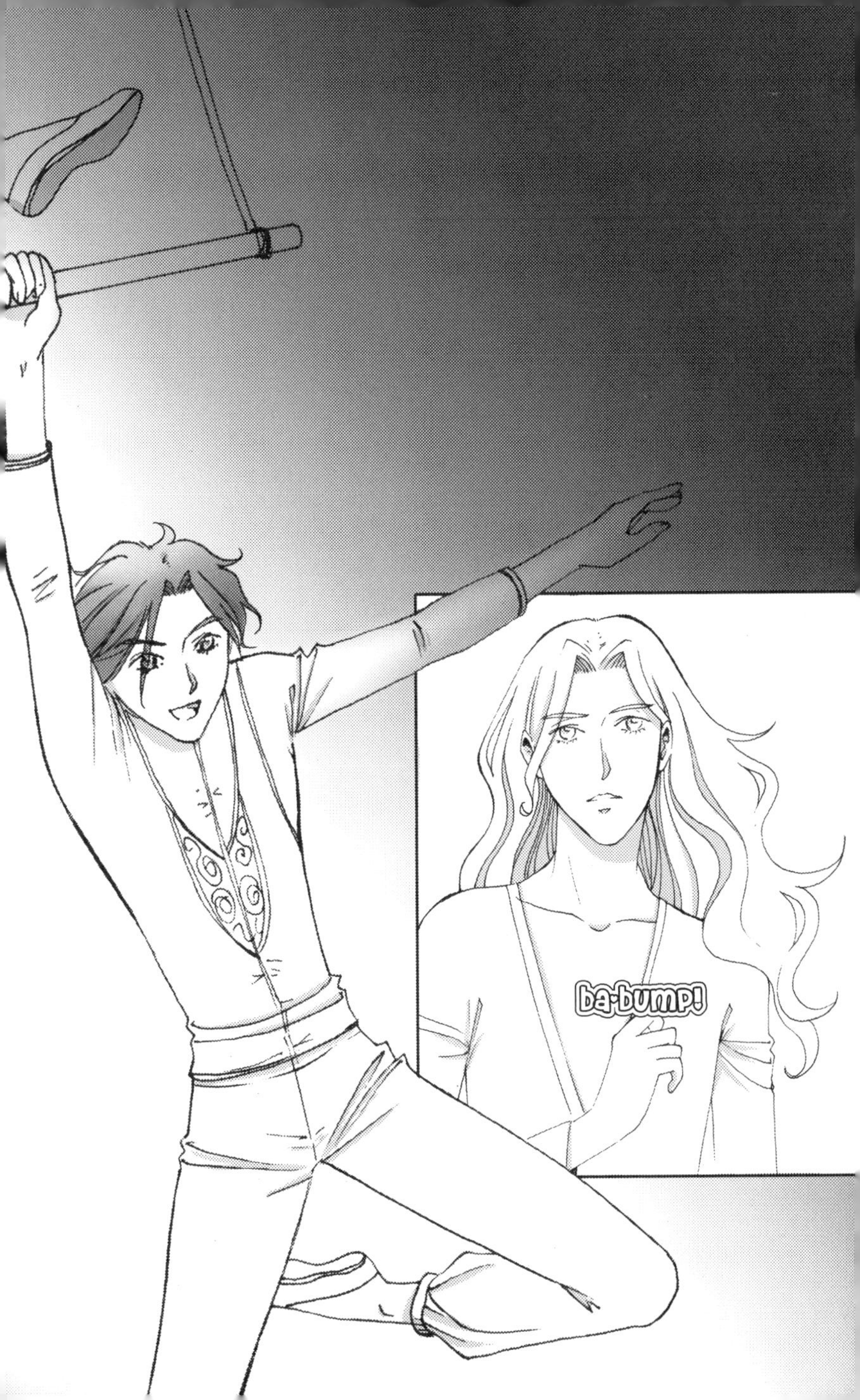
ba-bump!

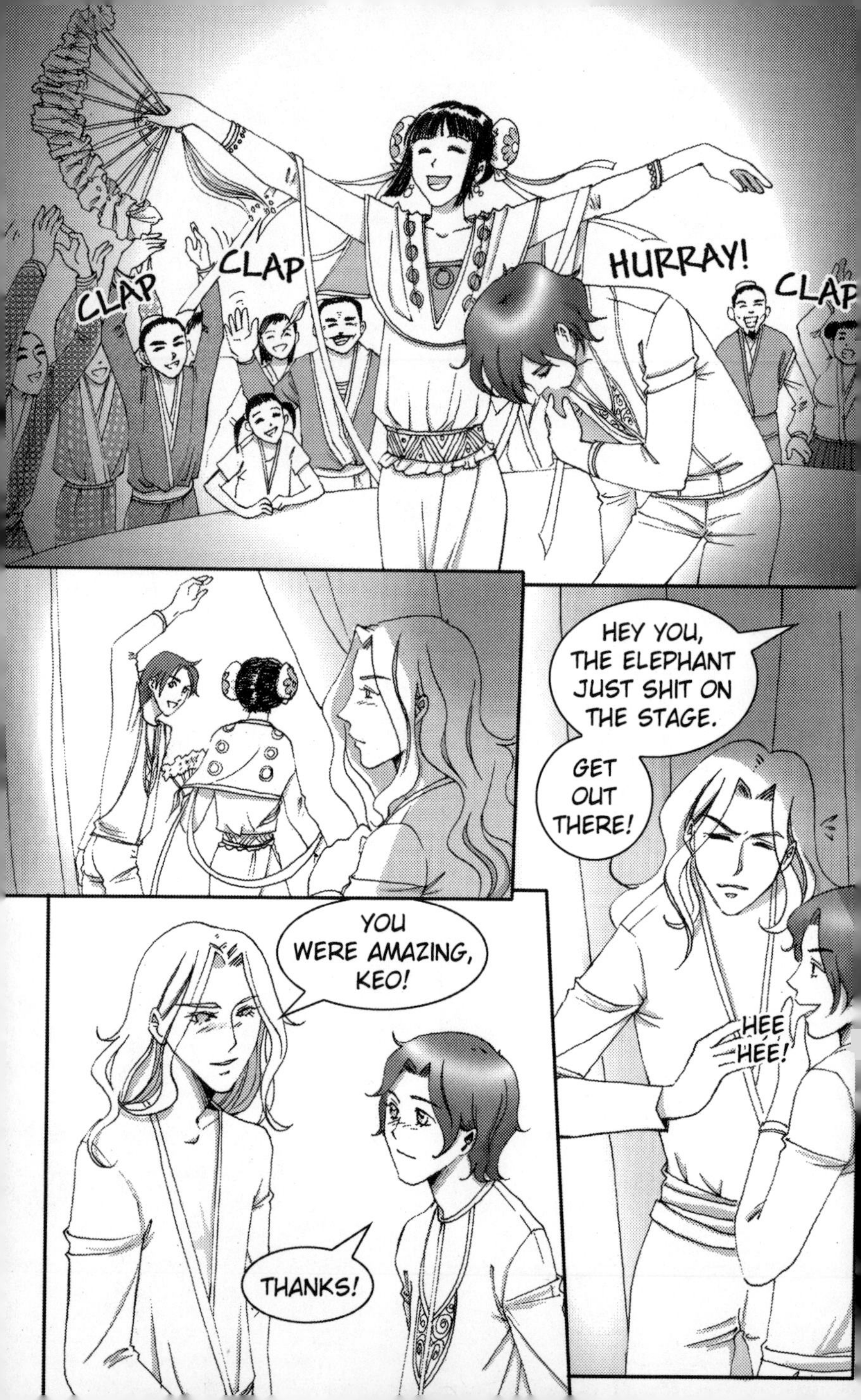
CLAP
CLAP
HURRAY!
CLAP
HEY YOU, THE ELEPHANT JUST SHIT ON THE STAGE.
GET OUT THERE!
HEE HEE!
YOU WERE AMAZING, KEO!
THANKS!

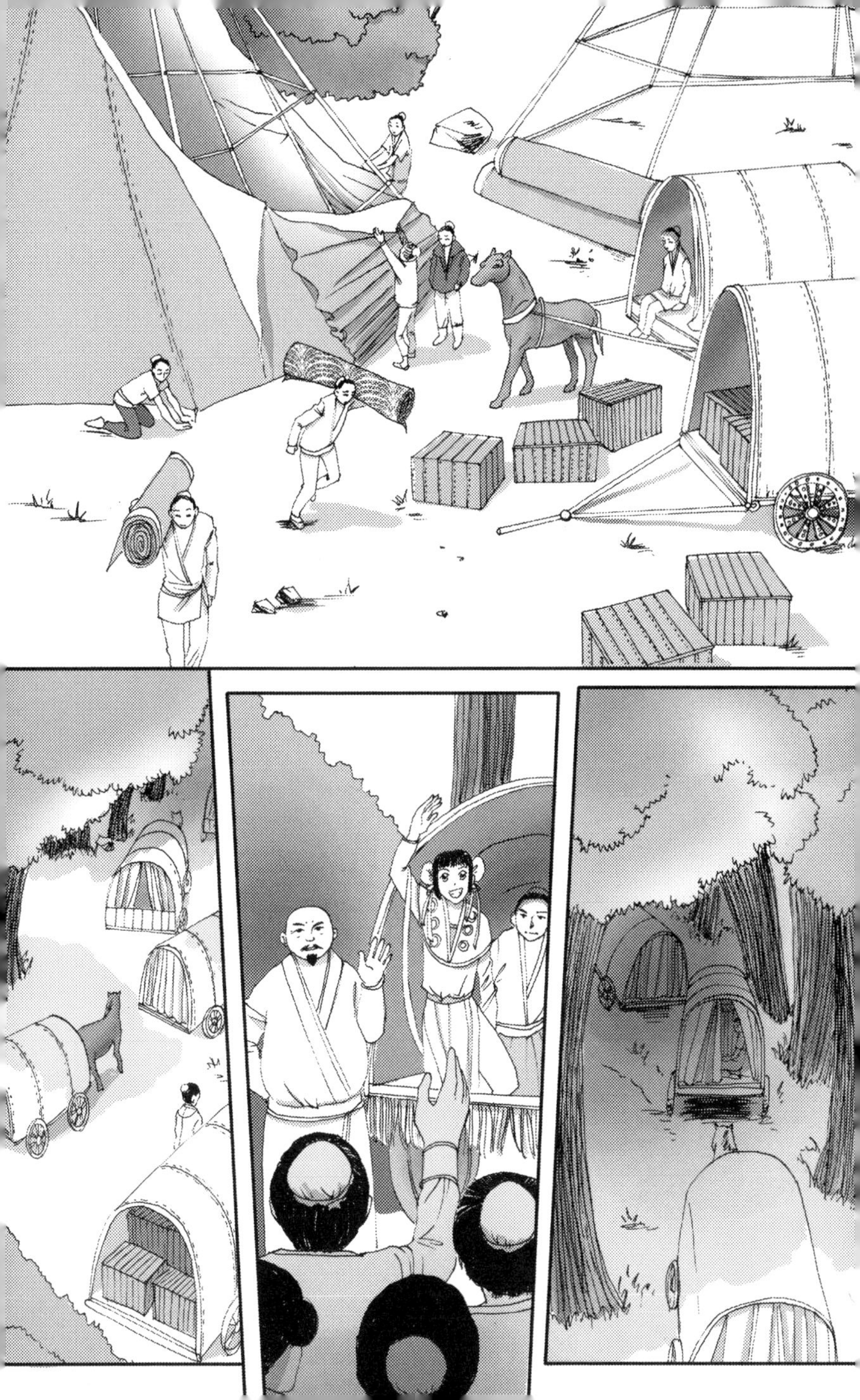

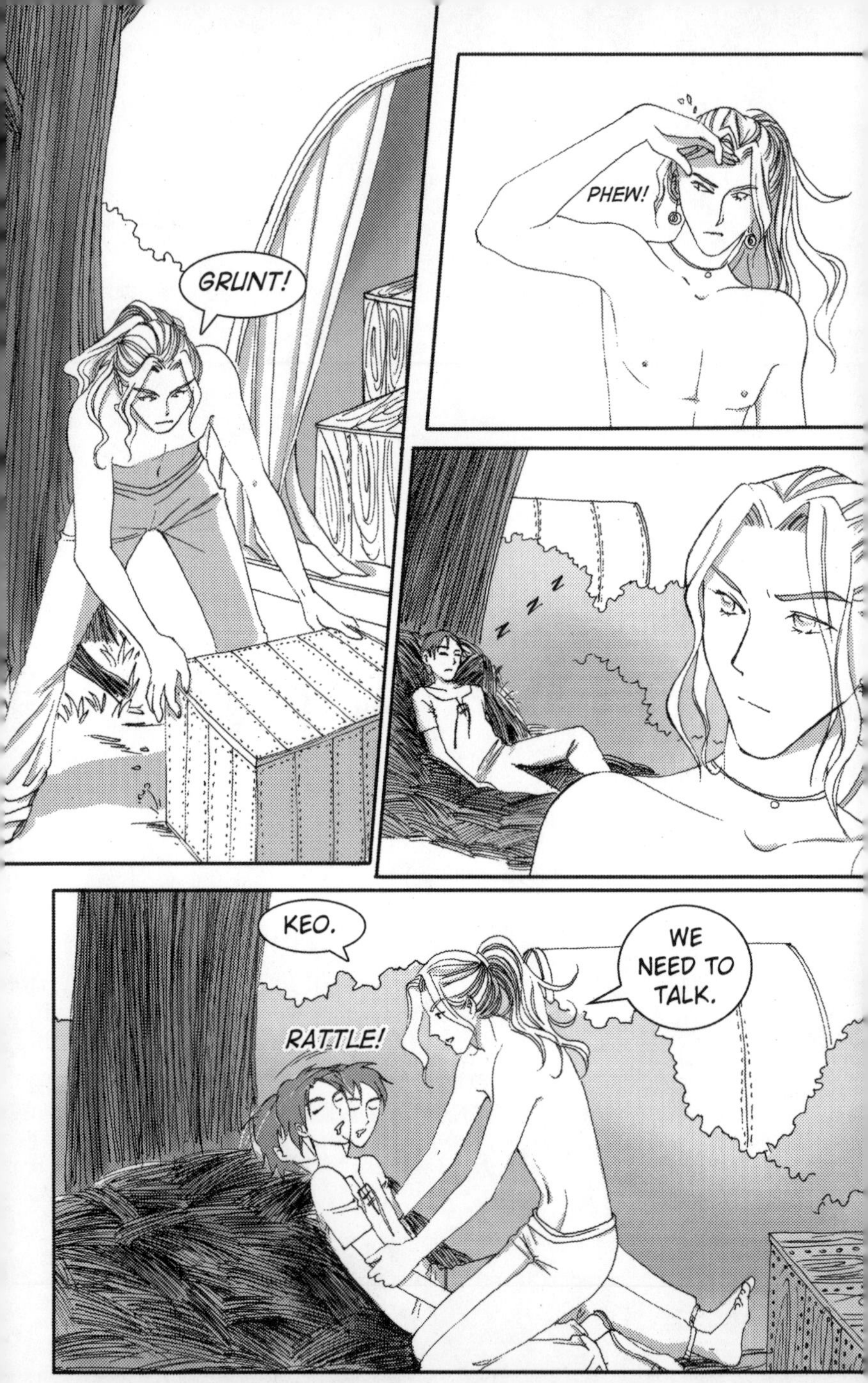
GRUNT!
PHEW!
KEO.
WE NEED TO TALK.
RATTLE!

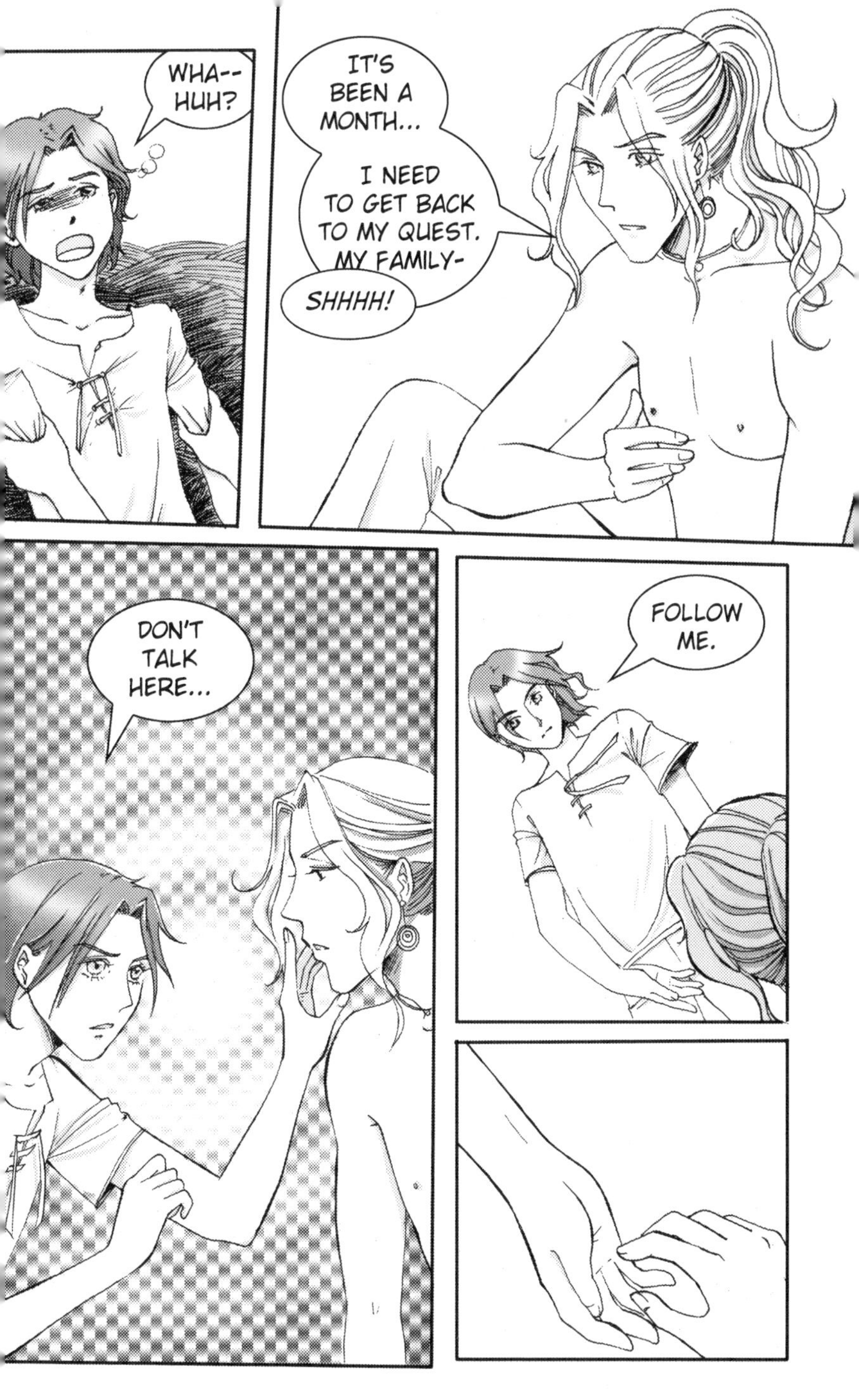
WHA-- HUH?
IT'S BEEN A MONTH...
I NEED TO GET BACK TO MY QUEST. MY FAMILY-
SHHHH!
DON'T TALK HERE...
FOLLOW ME.

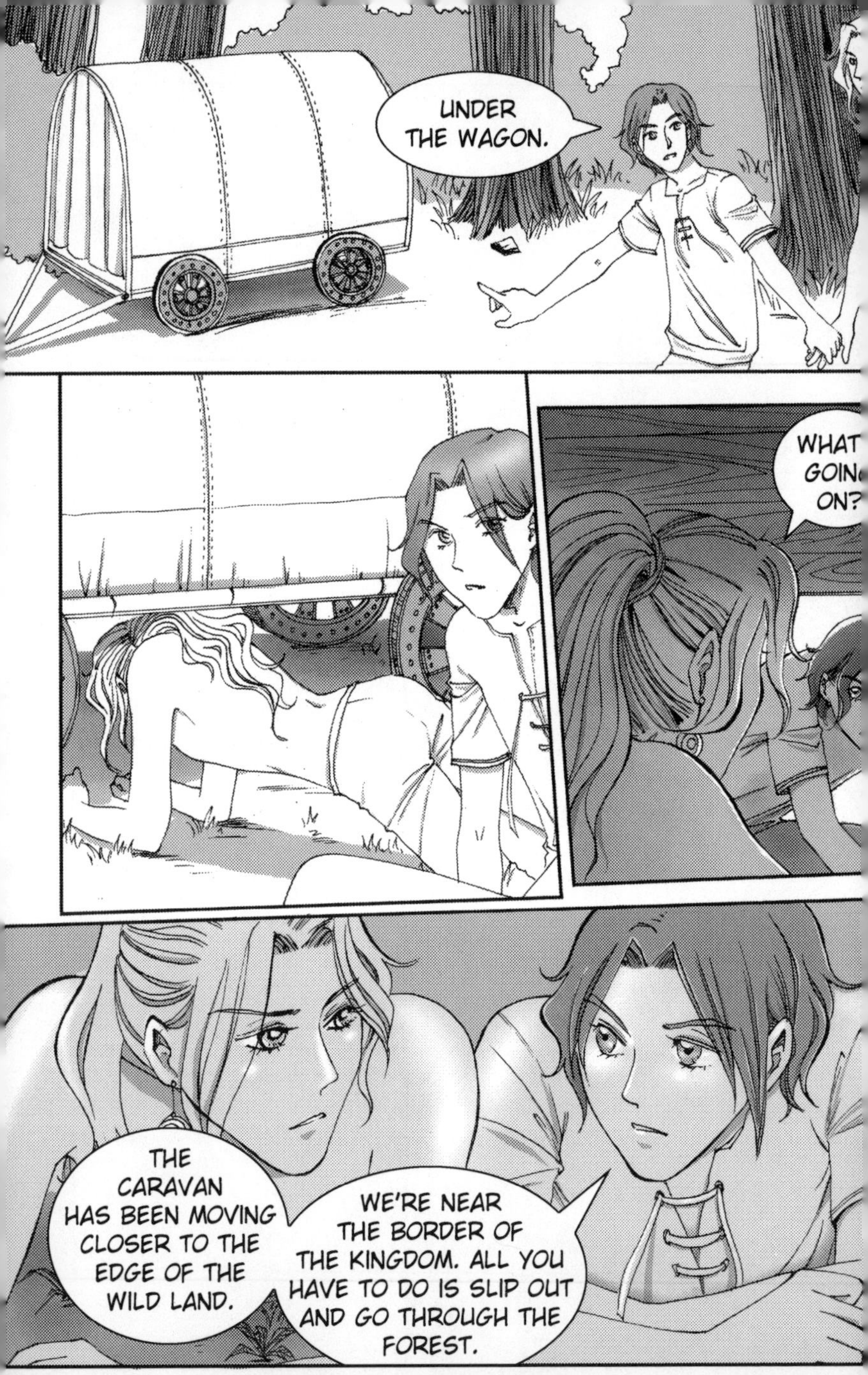
UNDER THE WAGON.
WHAT GOIN ON?
THE CARAVAN HAS BEEN MOVING CLOSER TO THE EDGE OF THE WILD LAND.
WE'RE NEAR THE BORDER OF THE KINGDOM. ALL YOU HAVE TO DO IS SLIP OUT AND GO THROUGH THE FOREST.

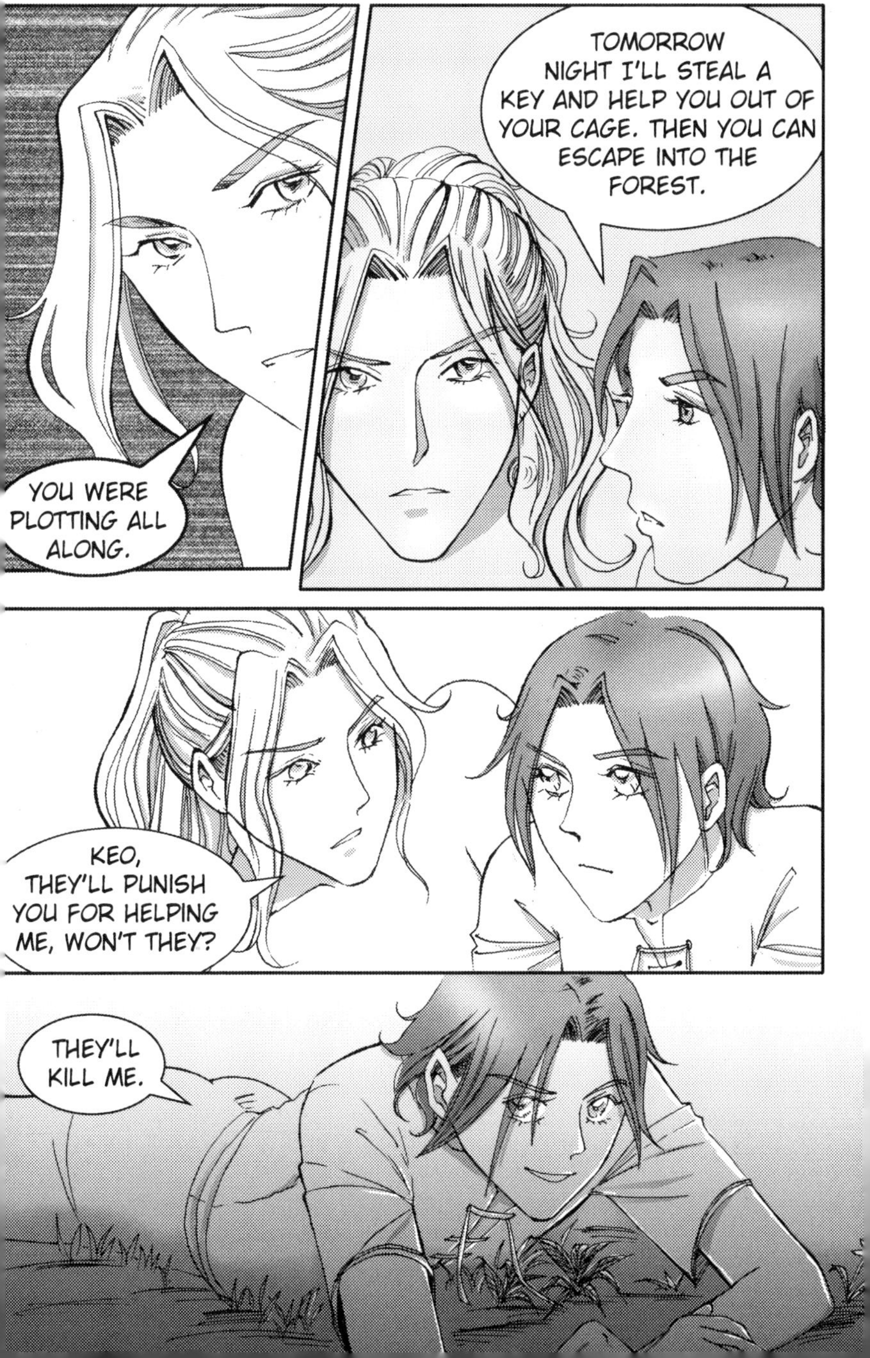
TOMORROW NIGHT I'LL STEAL A KEY AND HELP YOU OUT OF YOUR CAGE. THEN YOU CAN ESCAPE INTO THE FOREST.
YOU WERE PLOTTING ALL ALONG.
KEO, THEY'LL PUNISH YOU FOR HELPING ME, WON'T THEY?
THEY'LL KILL ME.

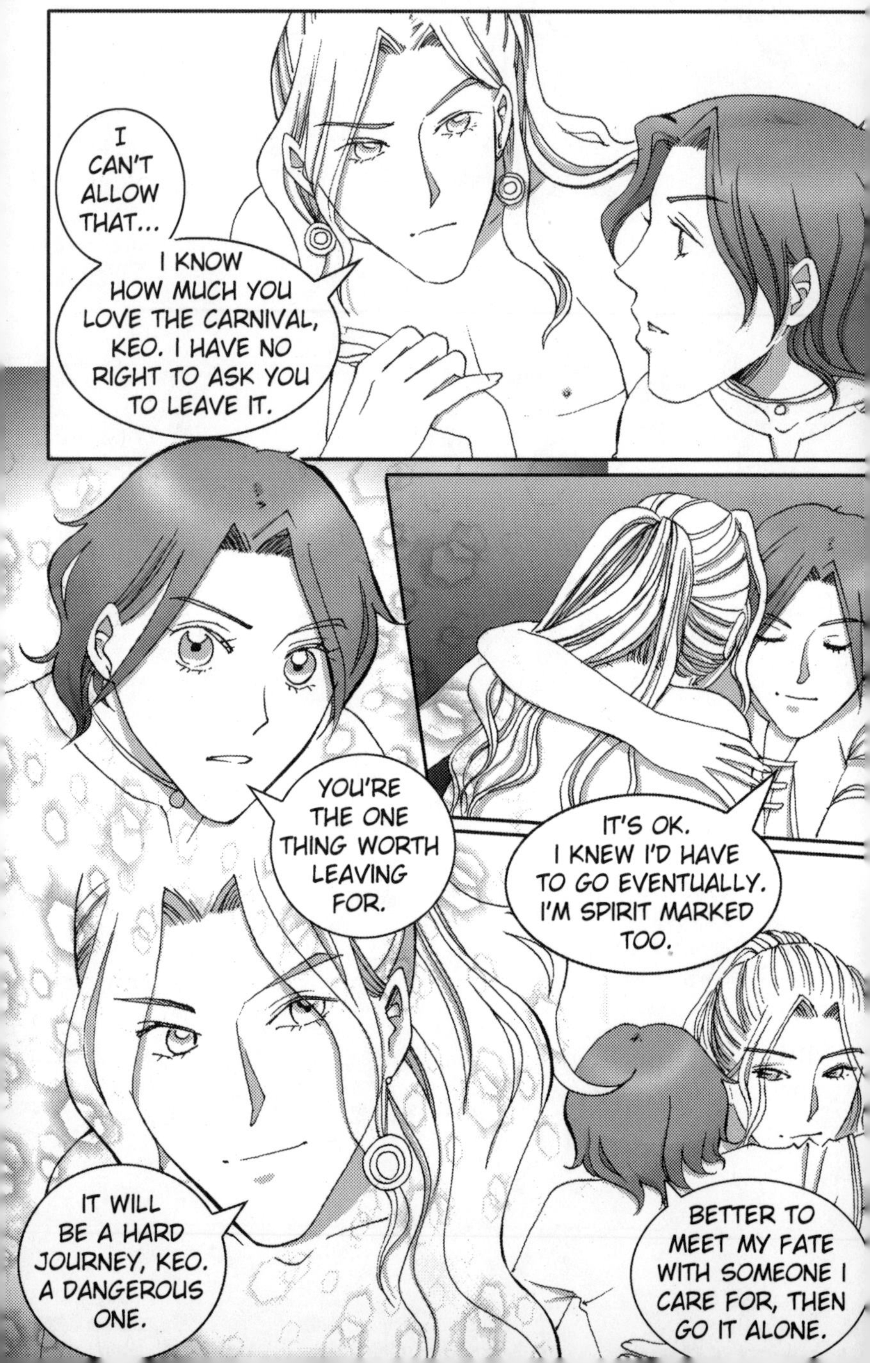
I CAN'T ALLOW THAT...
I KNOW HOW MUCH YOU LOVE THE CARNIVAL, KEO. I HAVE NO RIGHT TO ASK YOU TO LEAVE IT.
YOU'RE THE ONE THING WORTH LEAVING FOR.
IT'S OK. I KNEW I'D HAVE TO GO EVENTUALLY. I'M SPIRIT MARKED TOO.
IT WILL BE A HARD JOURNEY, KEO. A DANGEROUS ONE.
BETTER TO MEET MY FATE WITH SOMEONE I CARE FOR, THEN GO IT ALONE.

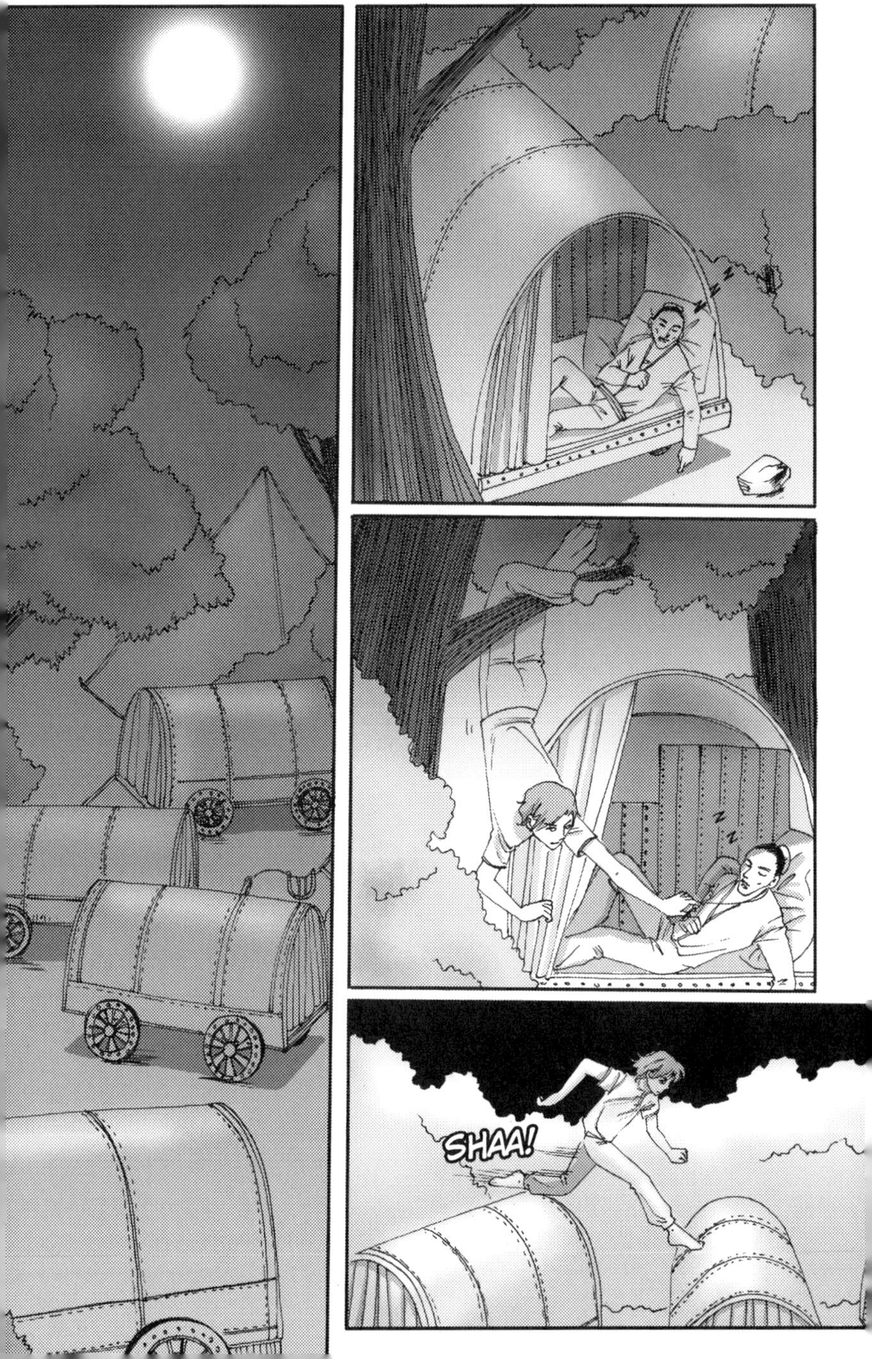
SHAA!

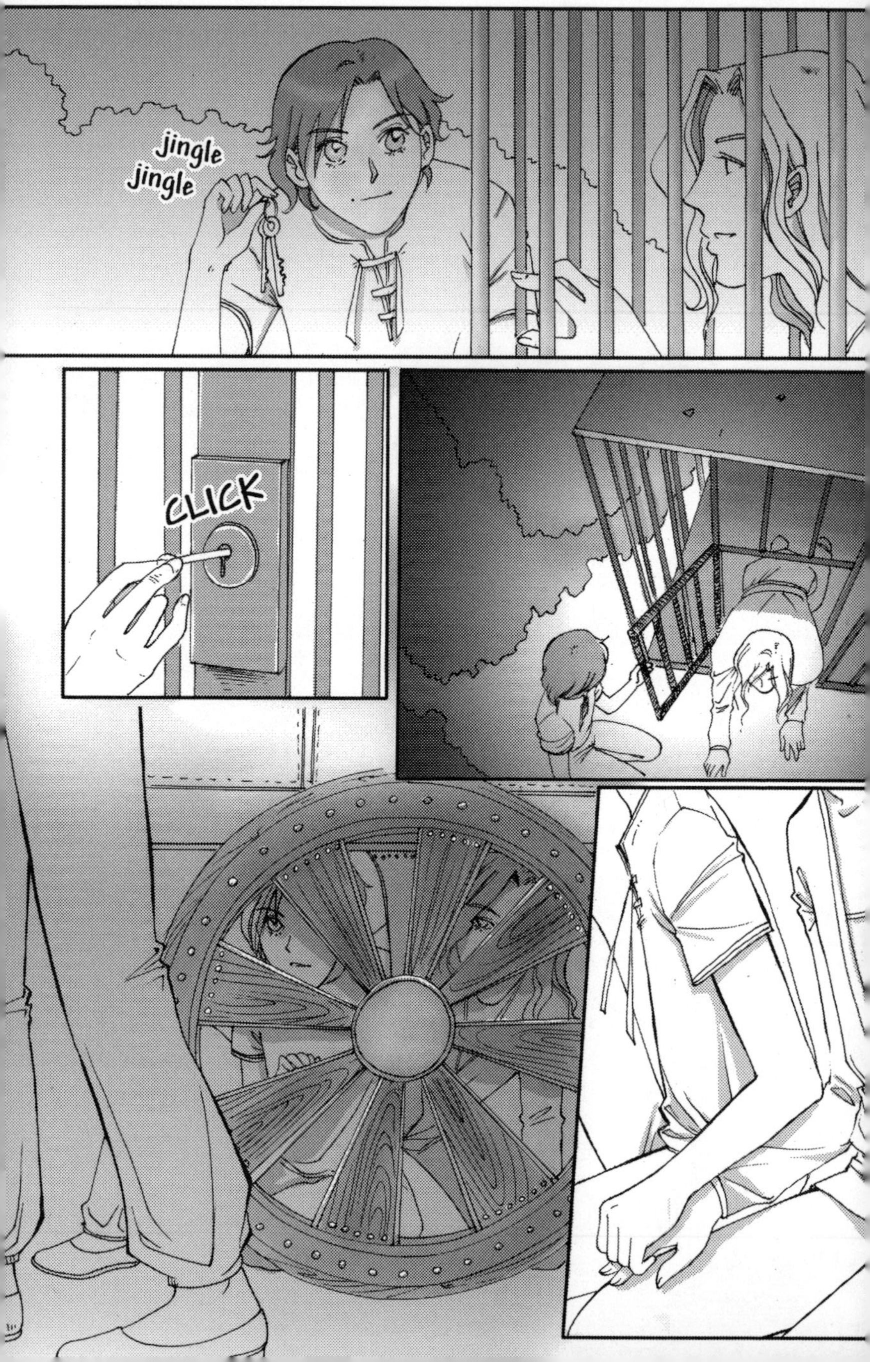
jingle
jingle
CLICK

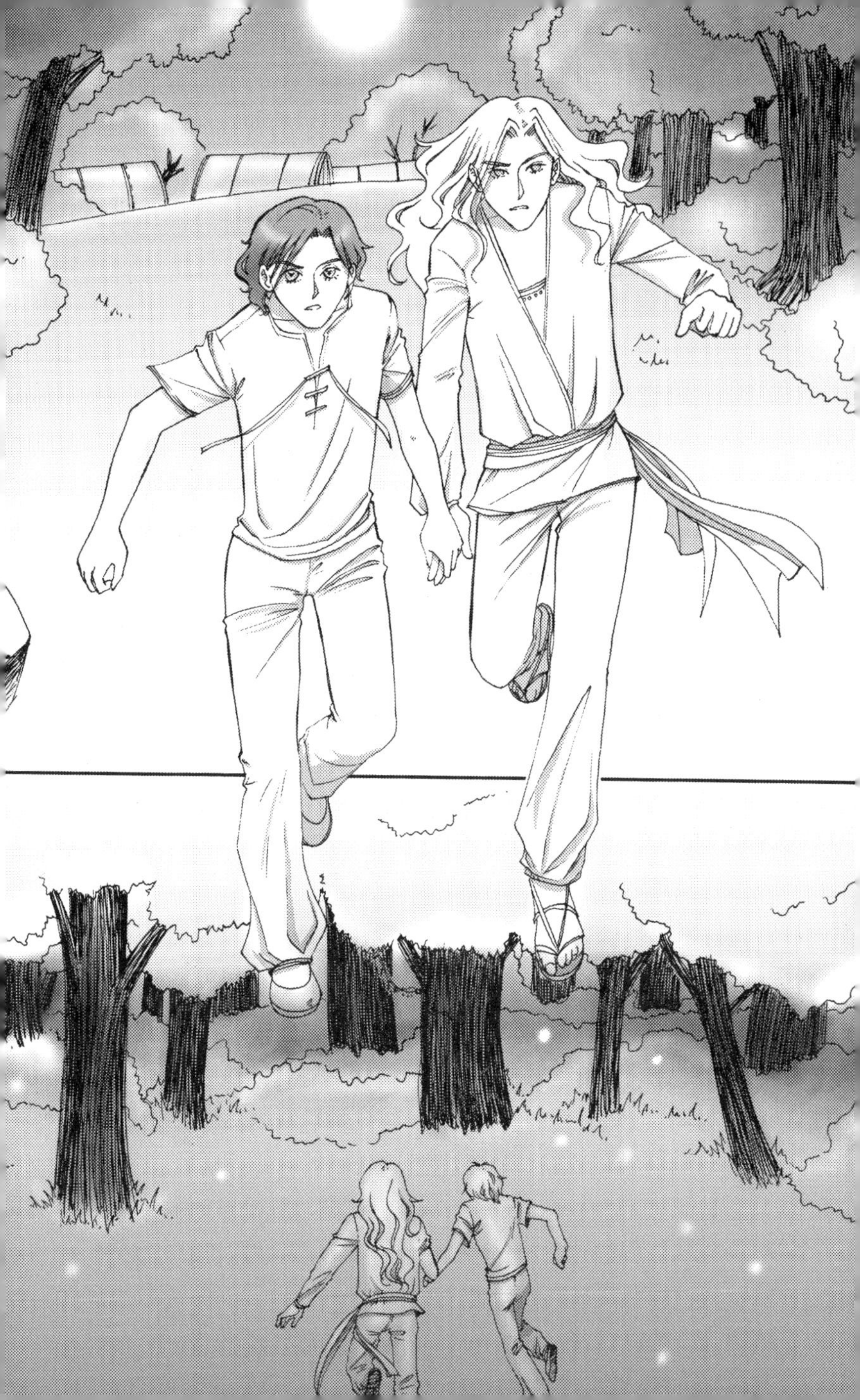

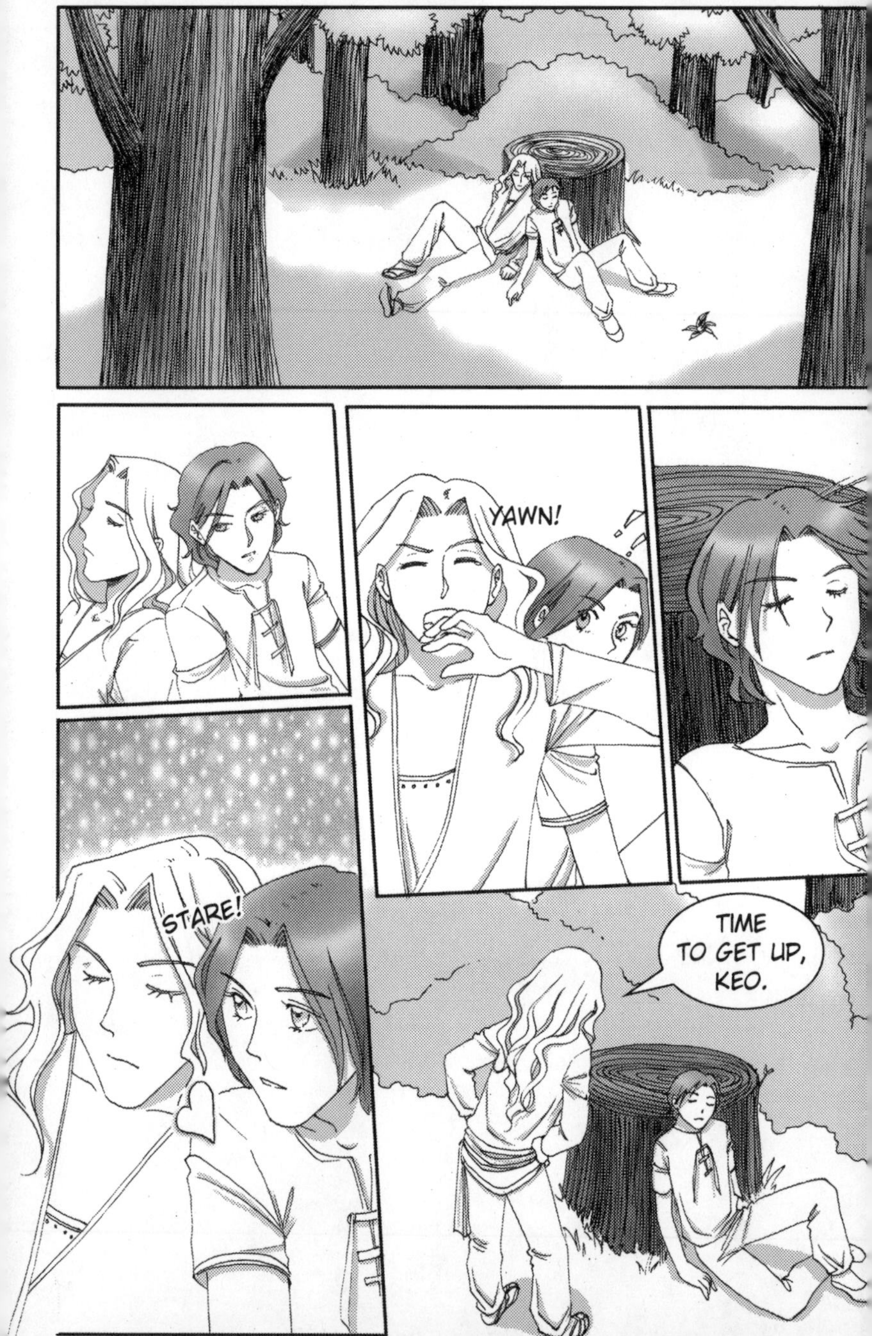
YAWN!
STARE!
TIME TO GET UP, KEO.

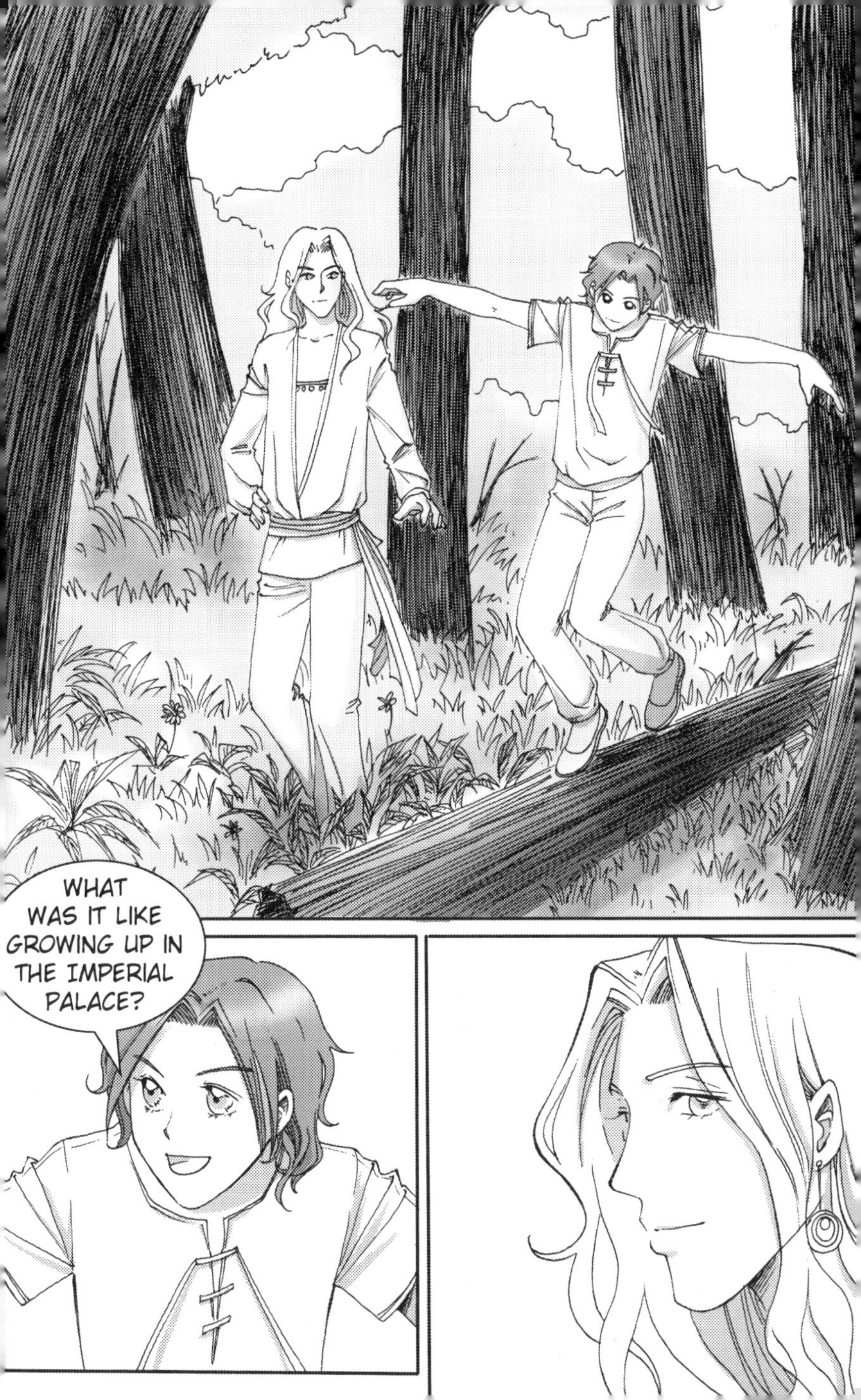
WHAT WAS IT LIKE GROWING UP IN THE IMPERIAL PALACE?

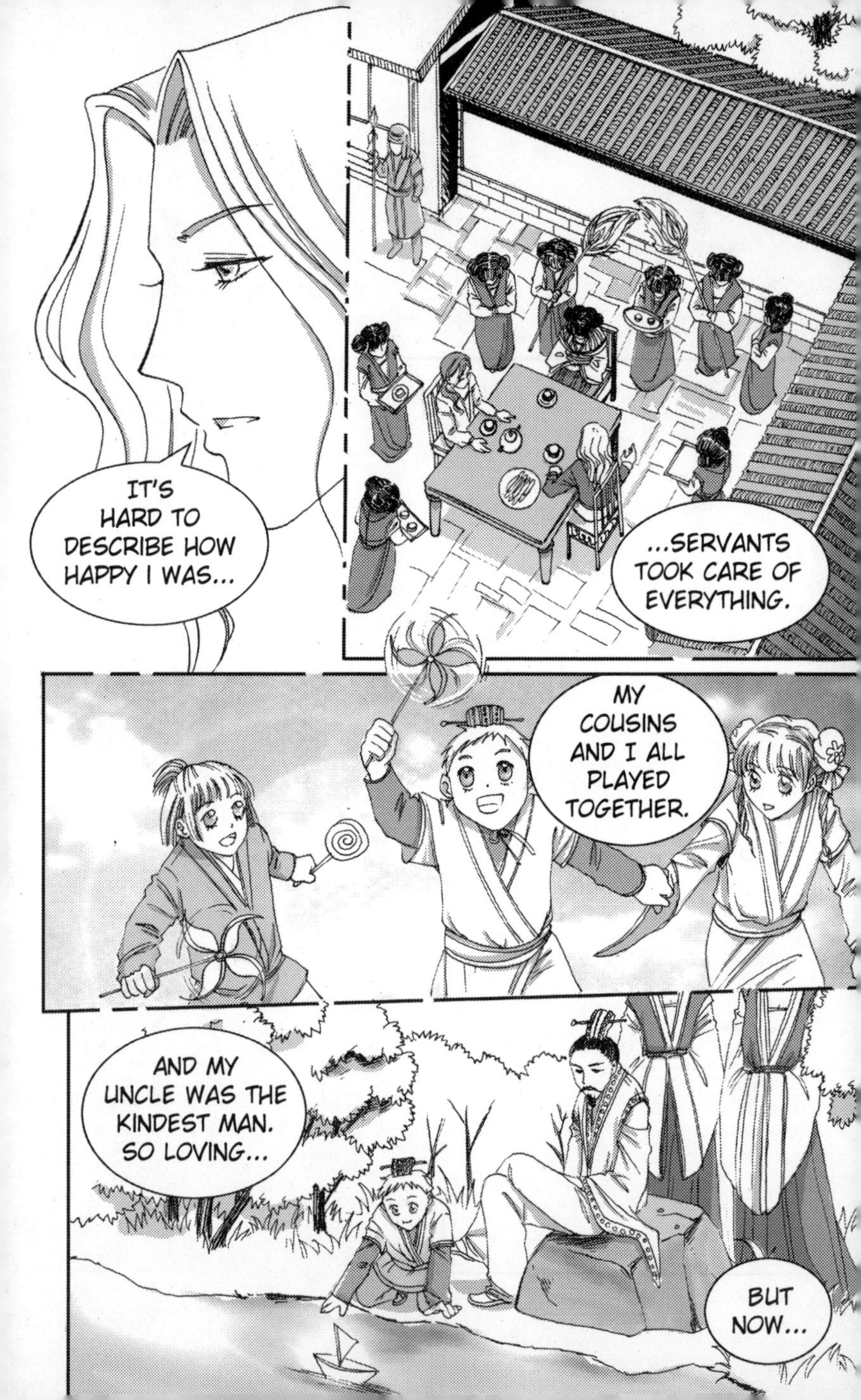

IT'S HARD TO DESCRIBE HOW HAPPY I WAS...
...SERVANTS TOOK CARE OF EVERYTHING.
MY COUSINS AND I ALL PLAYED TOGETHER.
AND MY UNCLE WAS THE KINDEST MAN. SO LOVING...
BUT NOW...

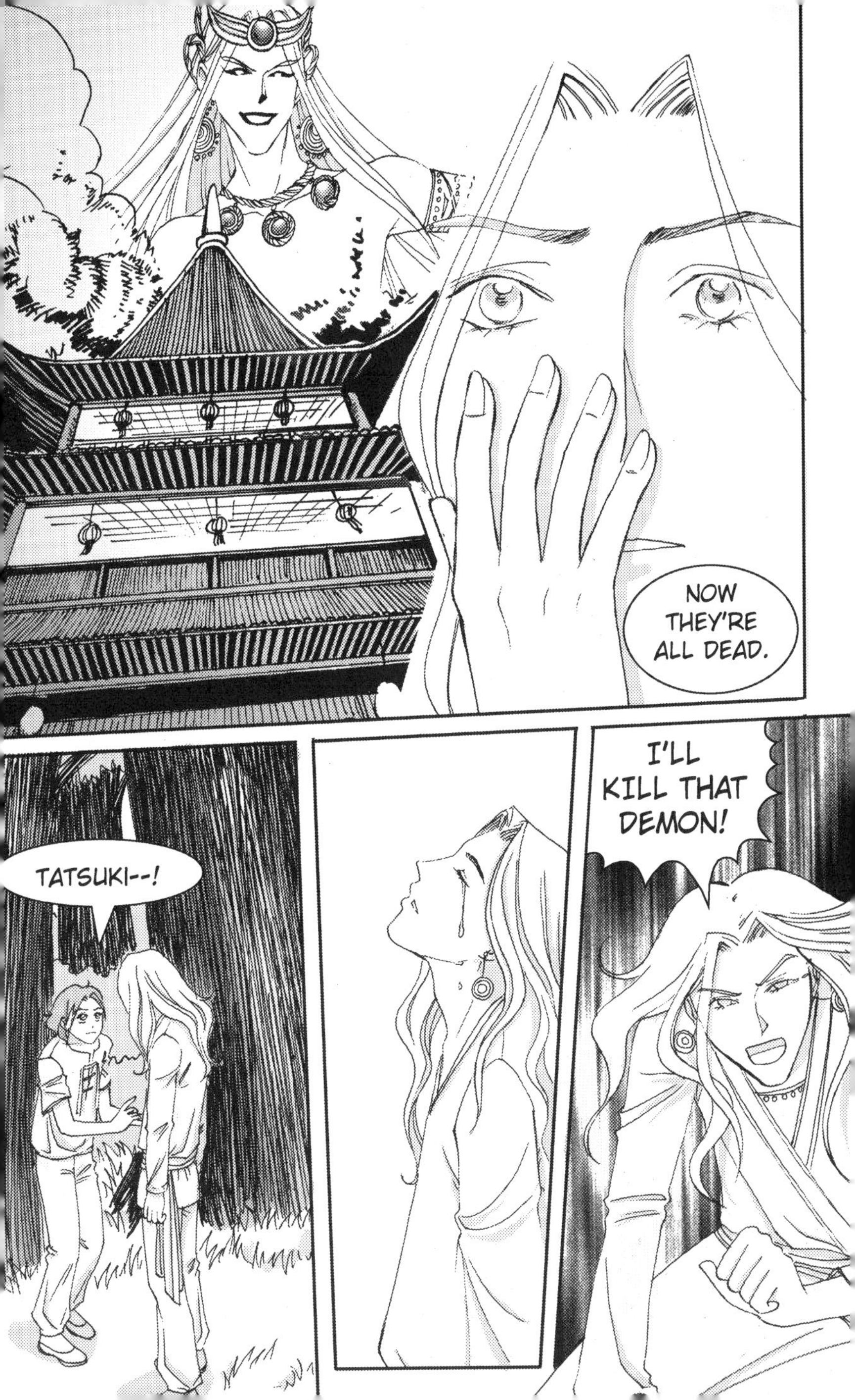
NOW THEY'RE ALL DEAD.
I'LL KILL THAT DEMON!
TATSUKI--!

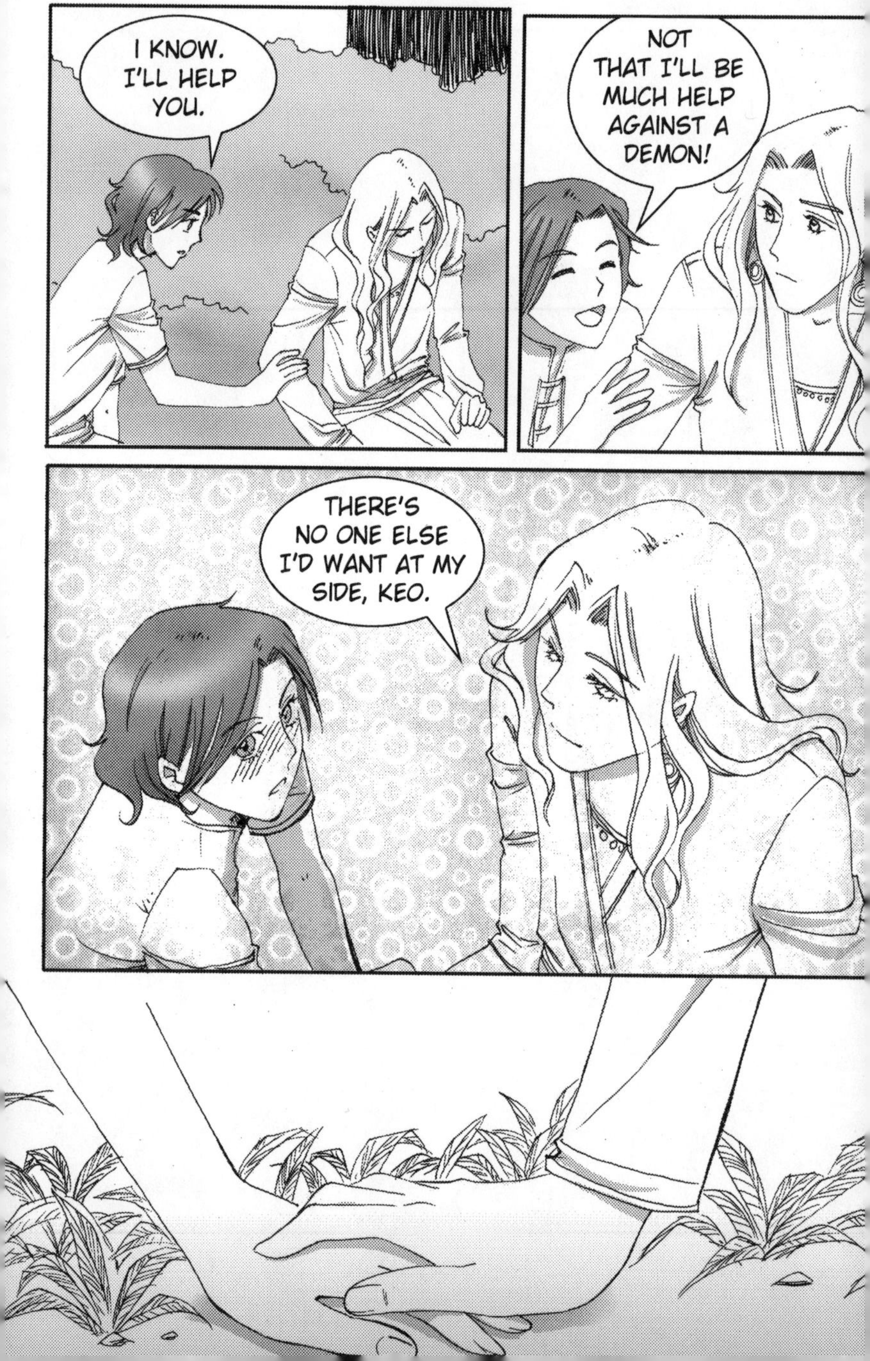
I KNOW. I'LL HELP YOU.
NOT THAT I'LL BE MUCH HELP AGAINST A DEMON!
THERE'S NO ONE ELSE I'D WANT AT MY SIDE, KEO.

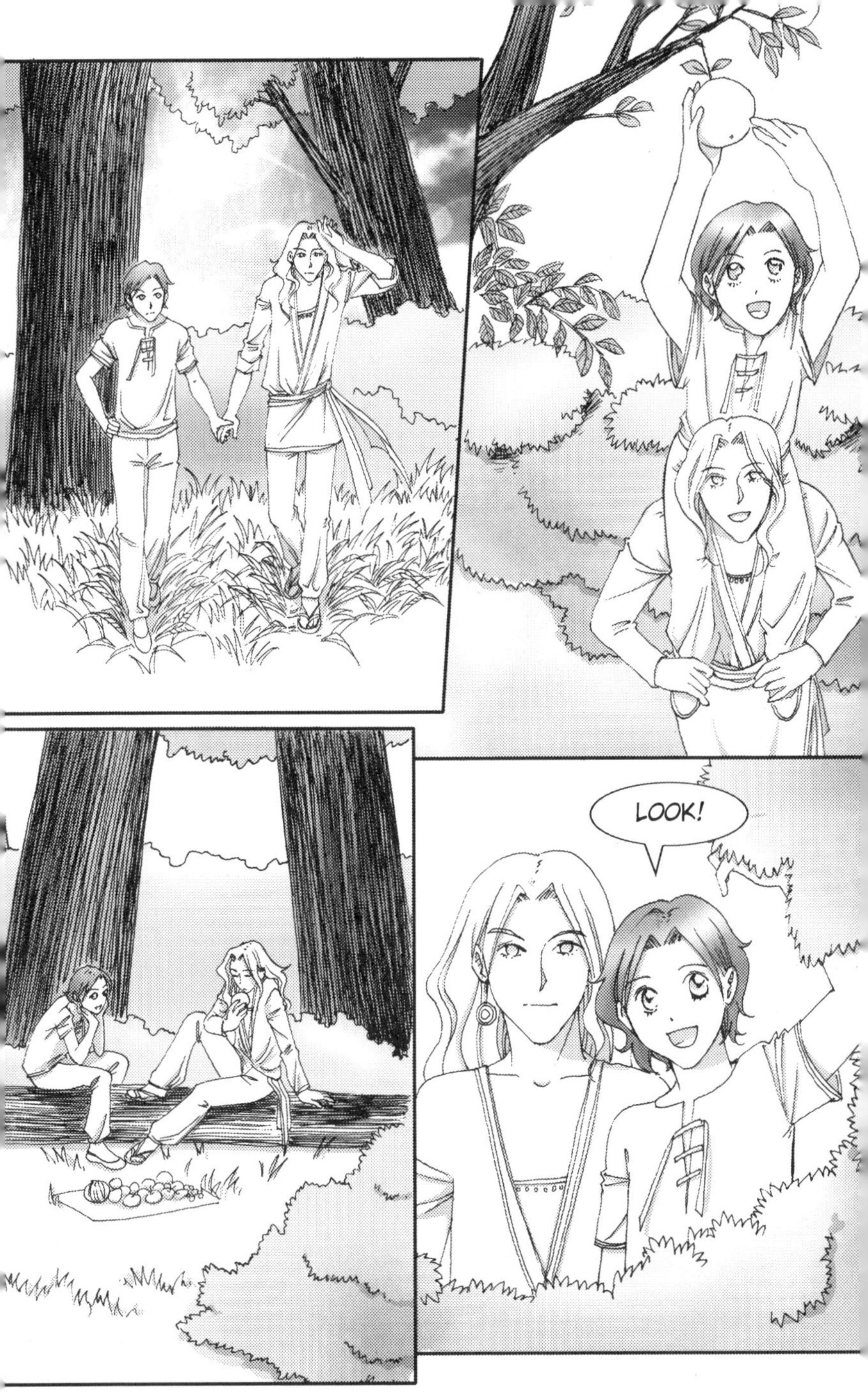
LOOK!

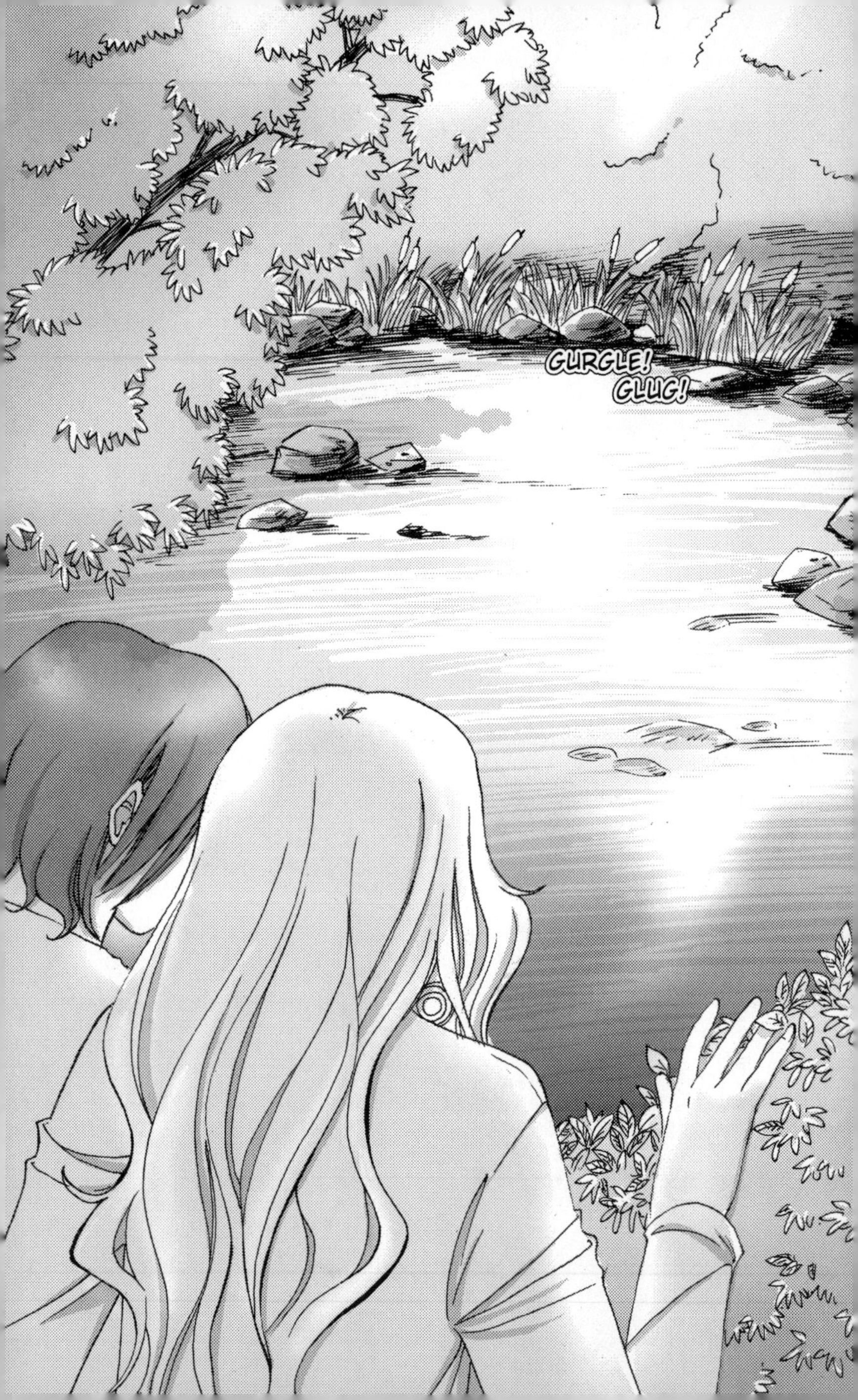
GURGLE!
GLUG!

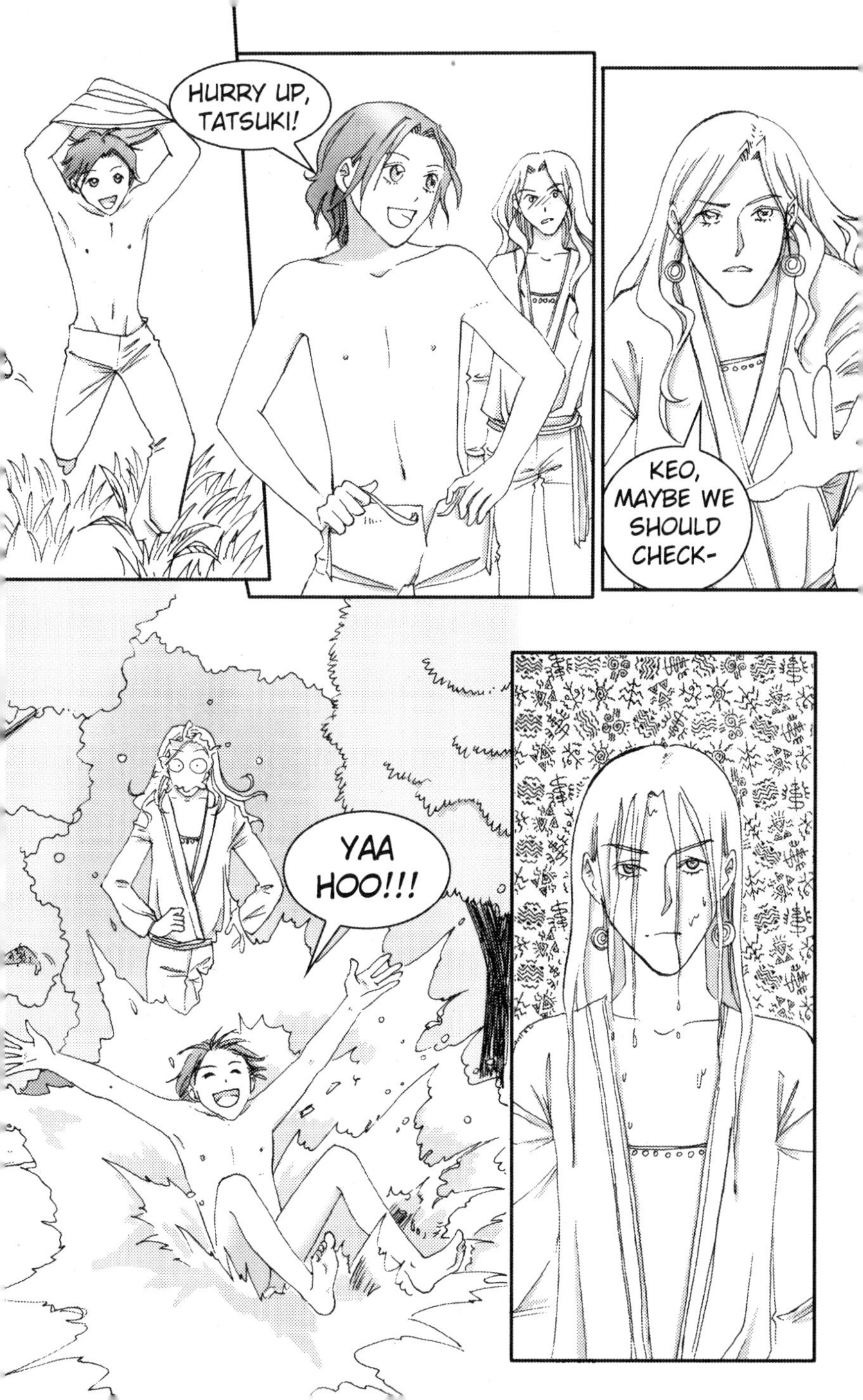
HURRY UP, TATSUKI!
KEO, MAYBE WE SHOULD CHECK-
YAA HOO!!!

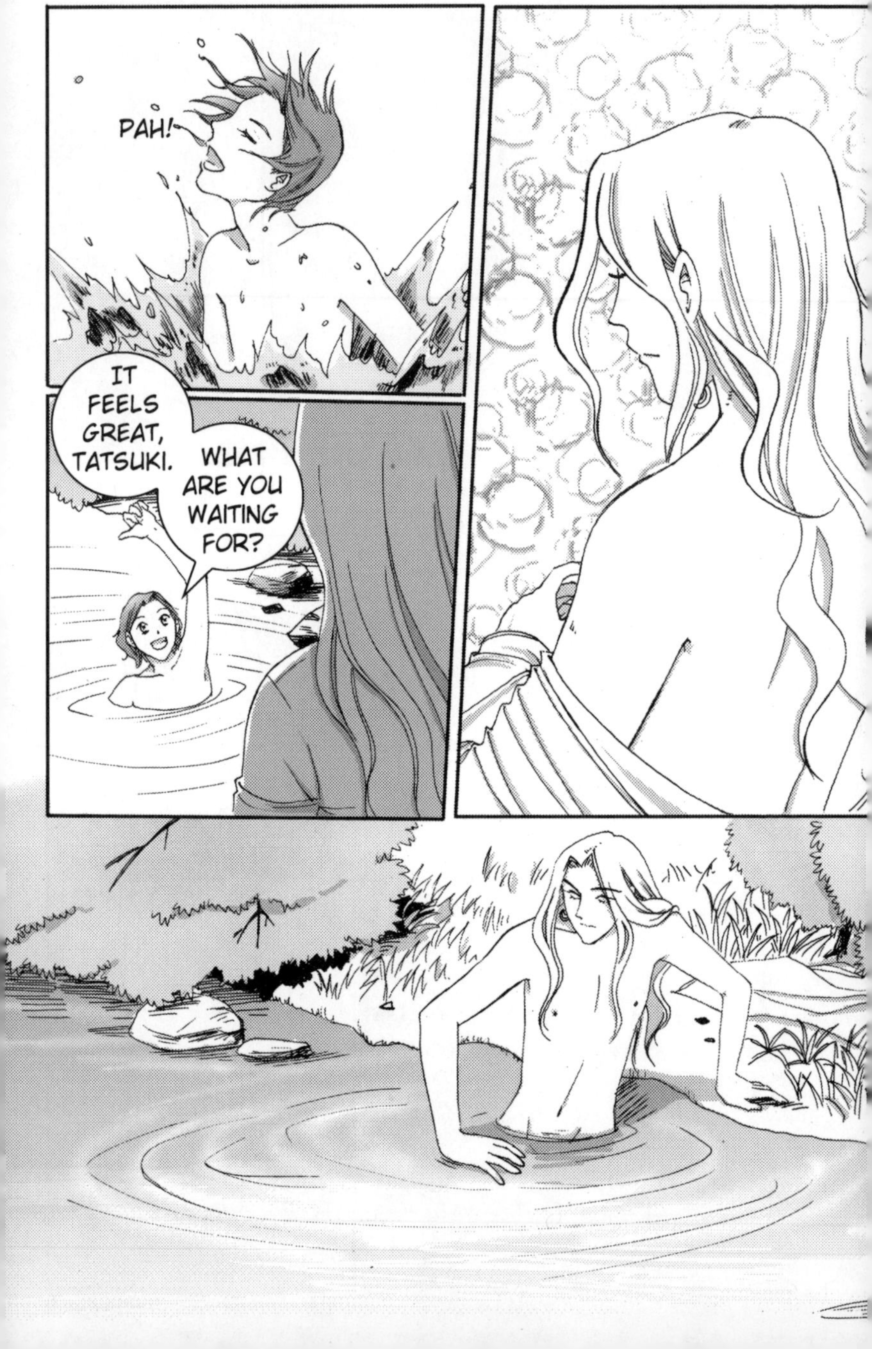
PAH!
IT FEELS GREAT, TATSUKI.
WHAT ARE YOU WAITING FOR?

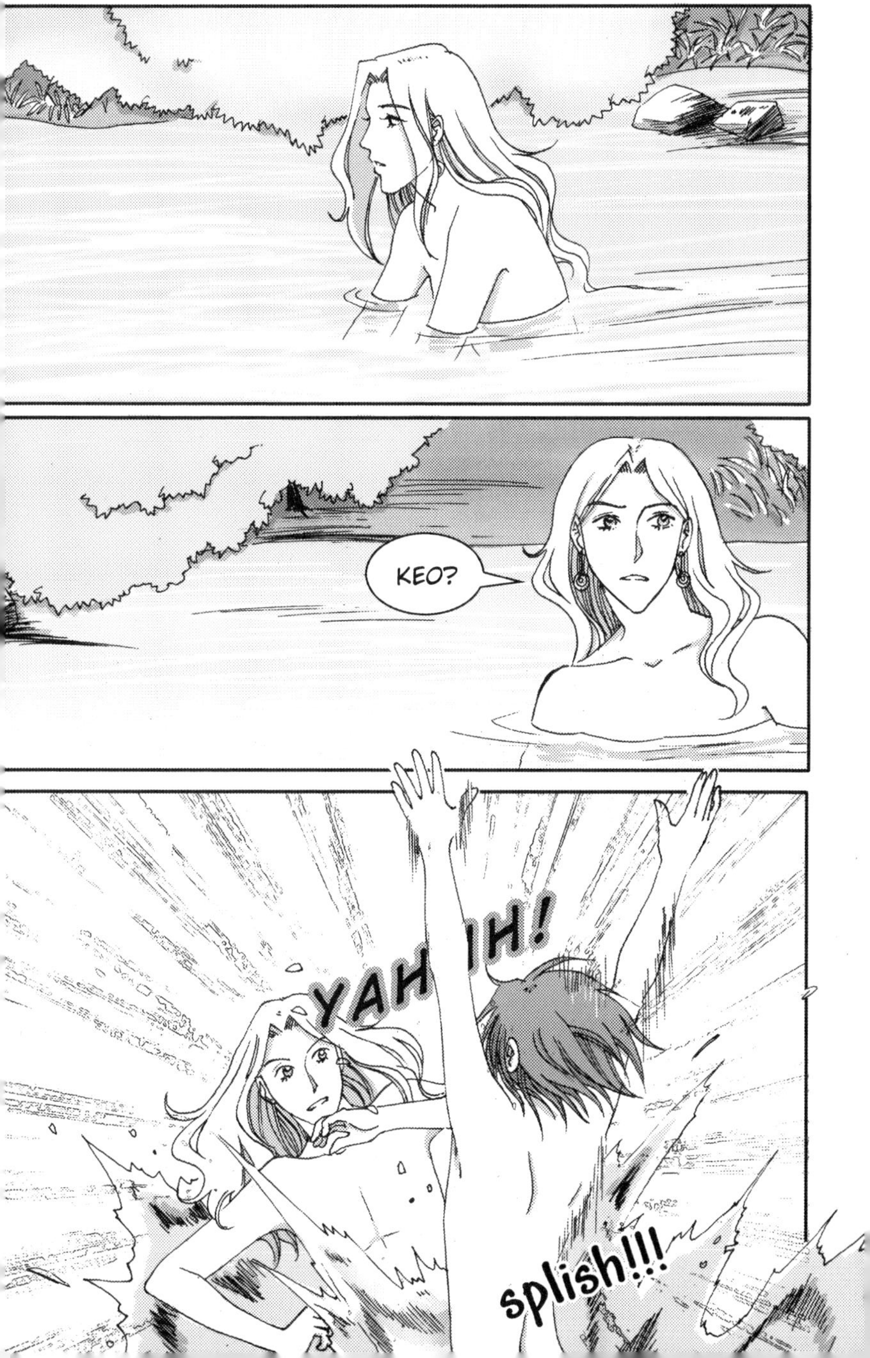
KEO?
YAHHH!
splish!!!

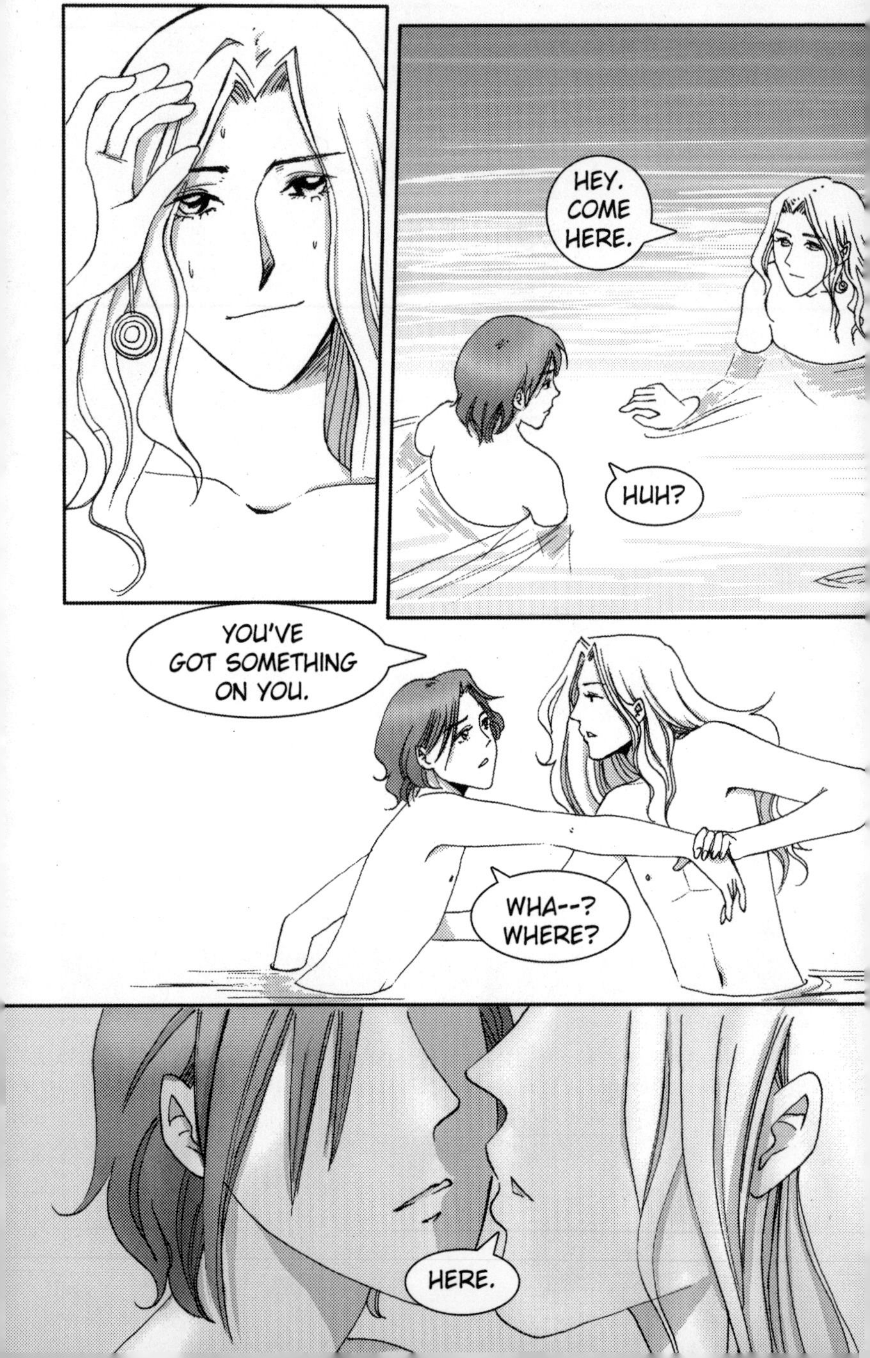
HEY. COME HERE.
HUH?
YOU'VE GOT SOMETHING ON YOU.
WHA--? WHERE?
HERE.

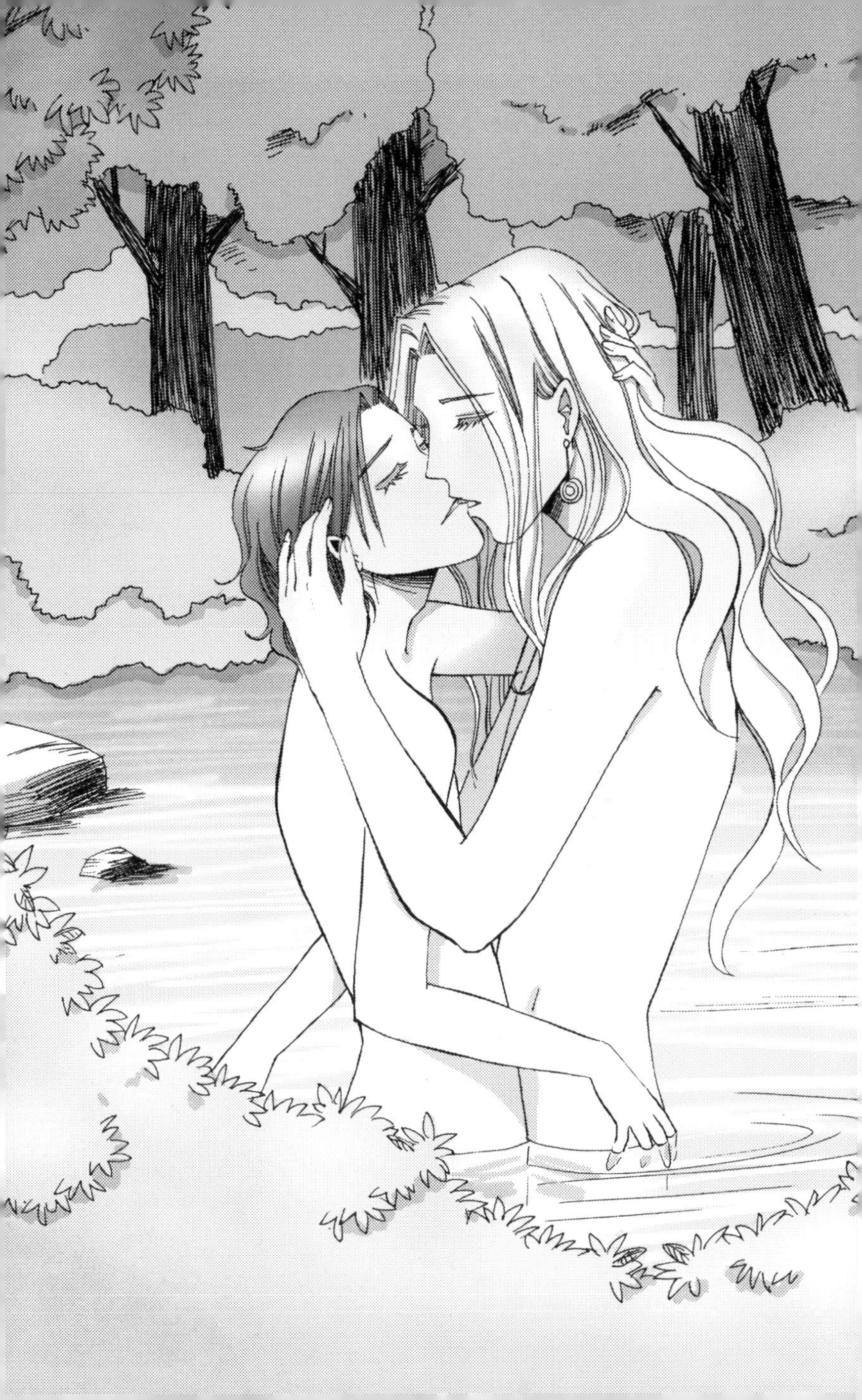

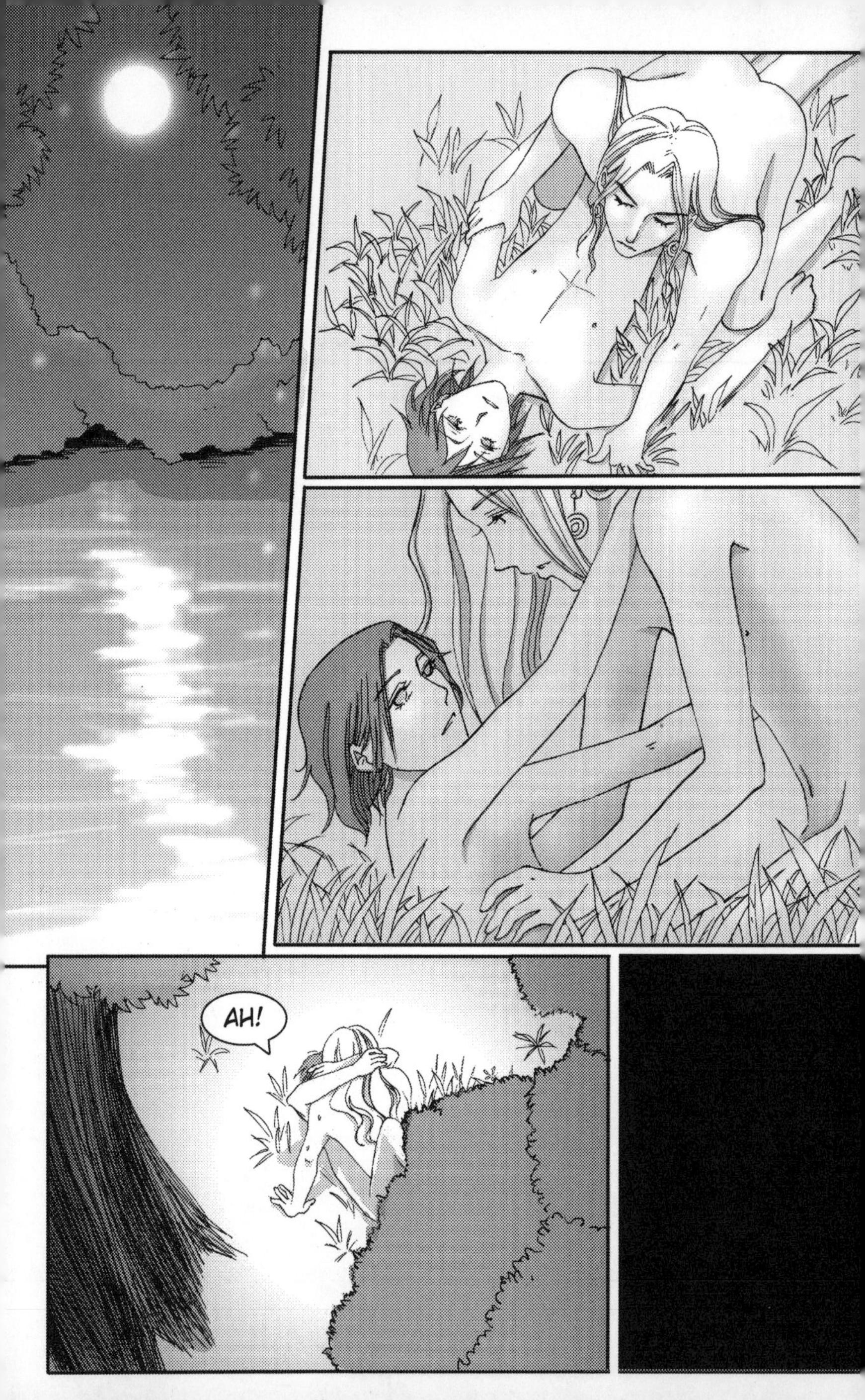
AH!

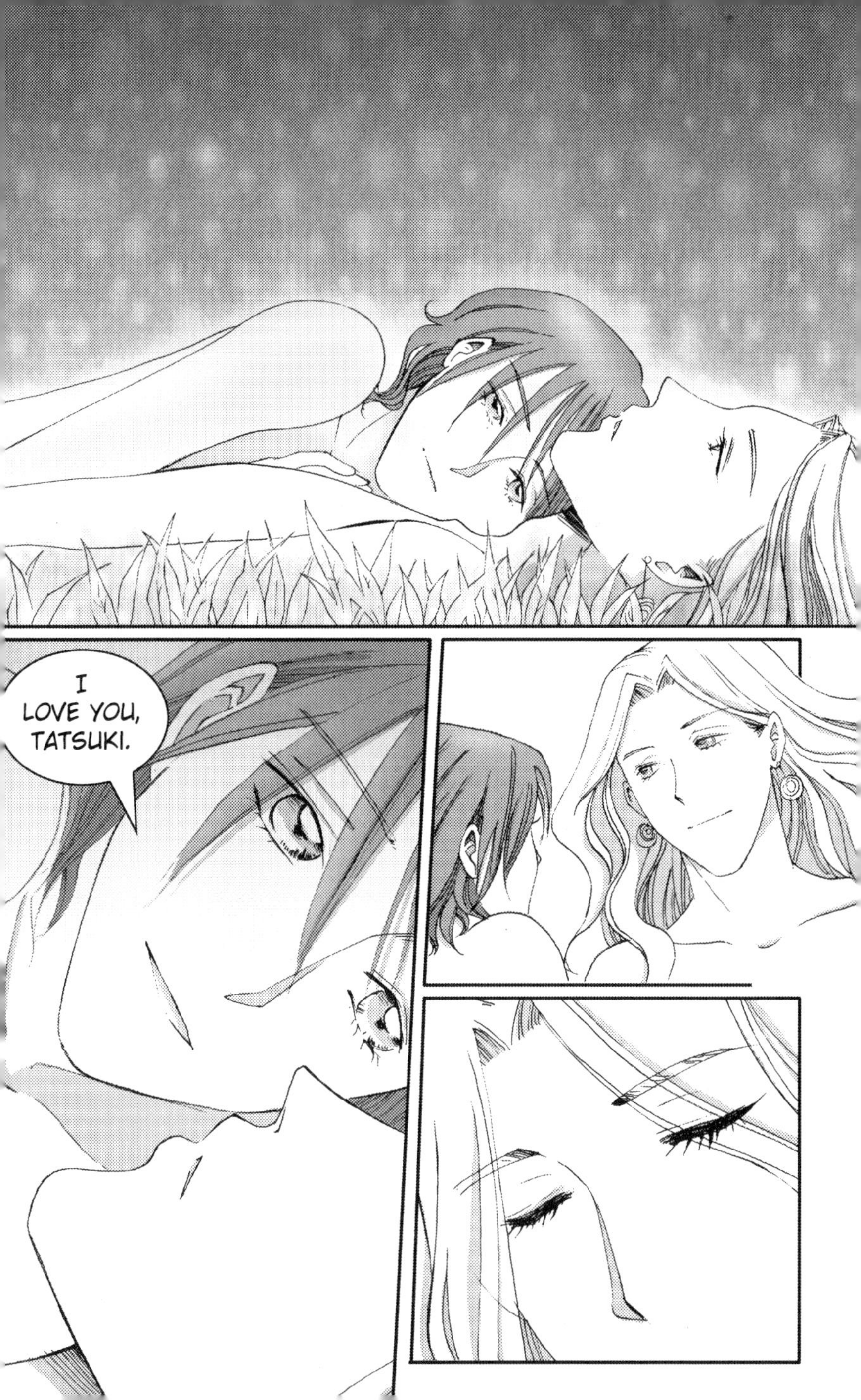
I LOVE YOU, TATSUKI.

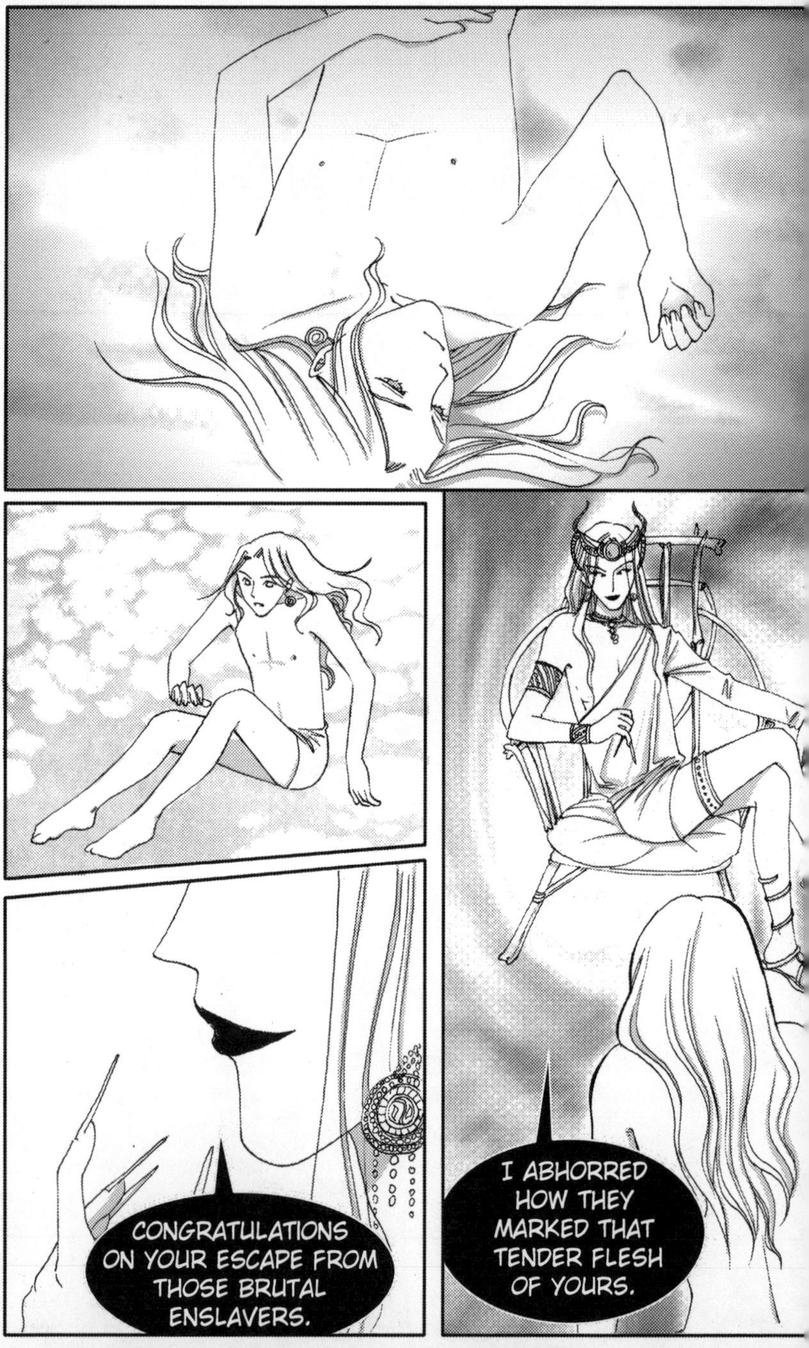
CONGRATULATIONS ON YOUR ESCAPE FROM THOSE BRUTAL ENSLAVERS.
I ABHORRED HOW THEY MARKED THAT TENDER FLESH OF YOURS.

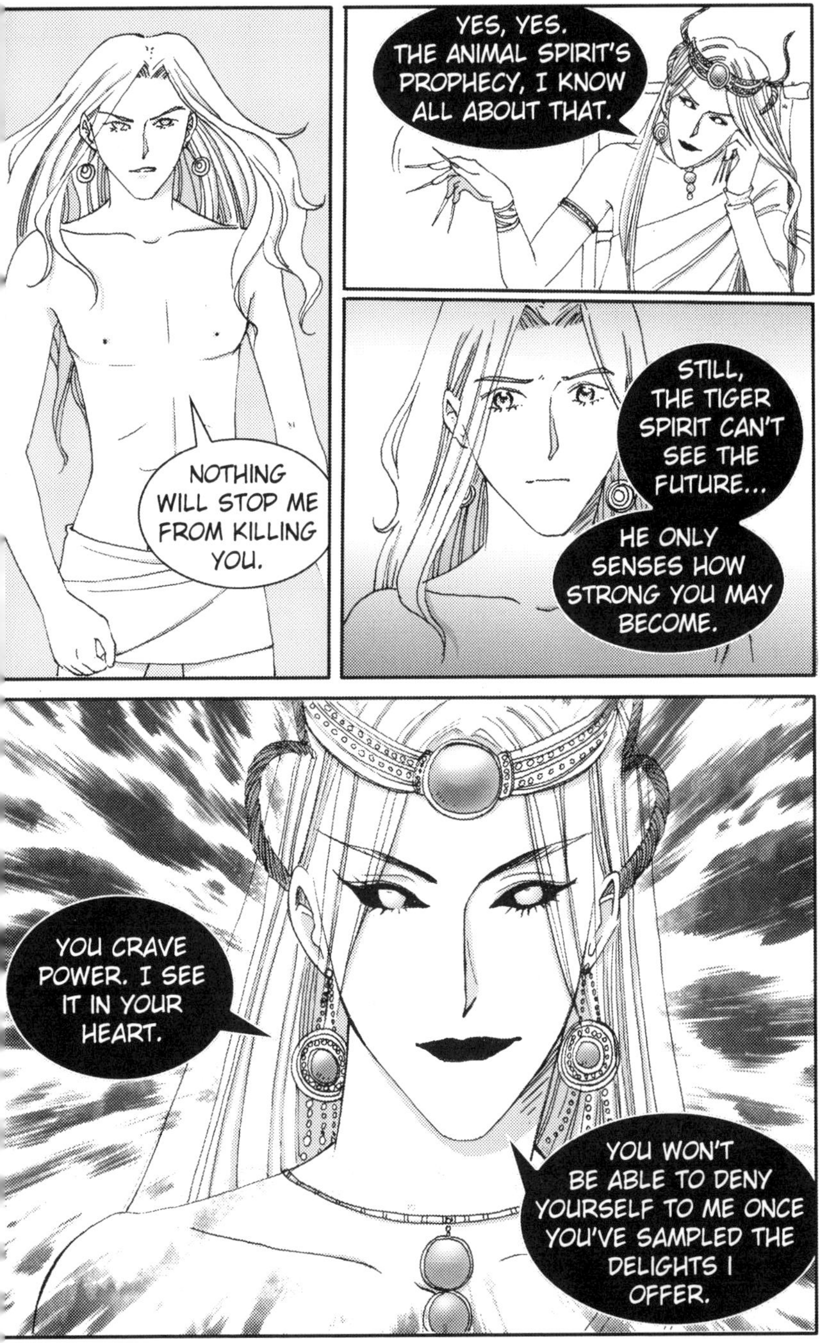
NOTHING WILL STOP ME FROM KILLING YOU.
YES, YES. THE ANIMAL SPIRIT'S PROPHECY, I KNOW ALL ABOUT THAT.
STILL, THE TIGER SPIRIT CAN'T SEE THE FUTURE...
HE ONLY SENSES HOW STRONG YOU MAY BECOME.
YOU CRAVE POWER. I SEE IT IN YOUR HEART.
YOU WON'T BE ABLE TO DENY YOURSELF TO ME ONCE YOU'VE SAMPLED THE DELIGHTS I OFFER.

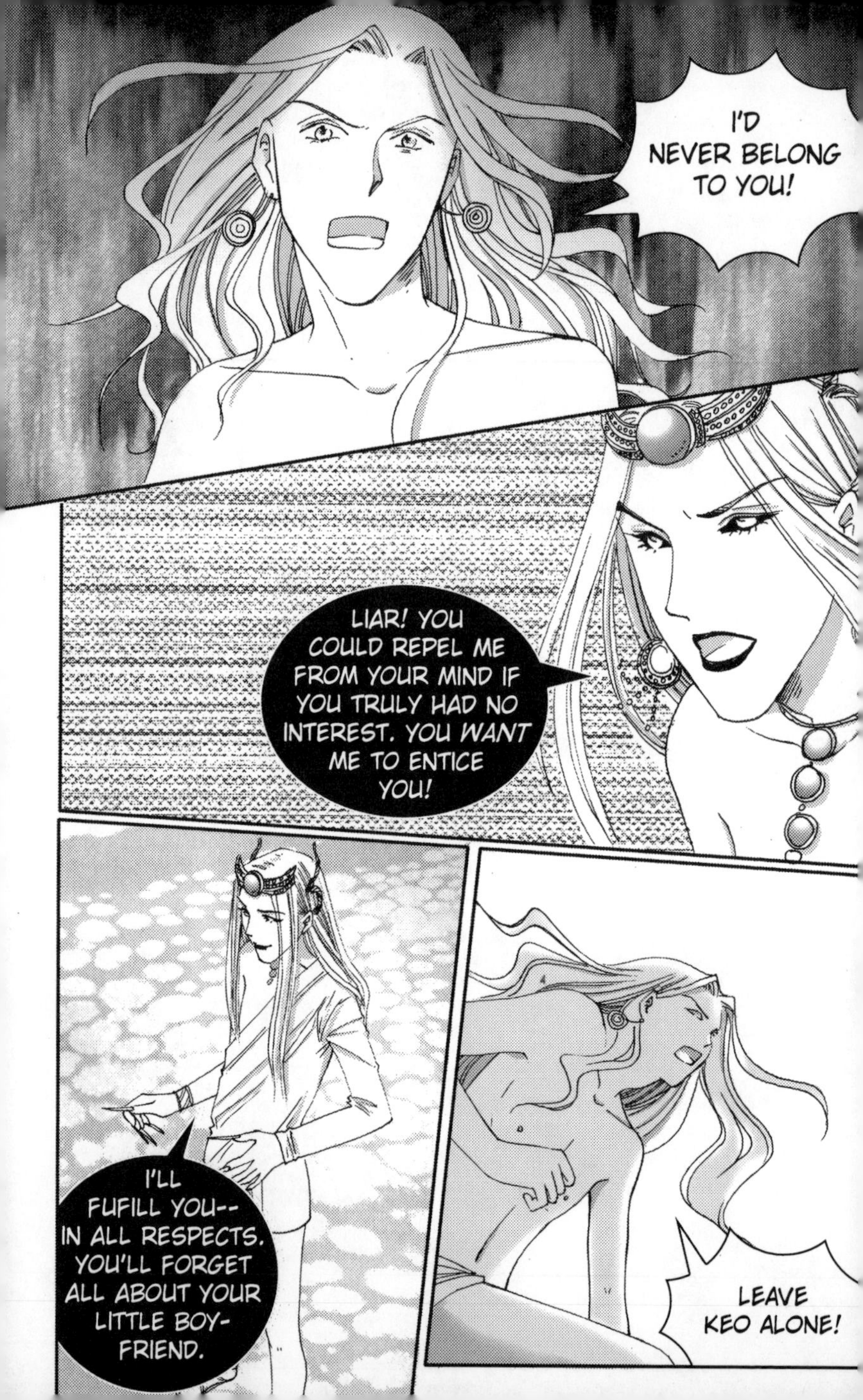
I'D NEVER BELONG TO YOU!
LIAR! YOU COULD REPEL ME FROM YOUR MIND IF YOU TRULY HAD NO INTEREST. YOU *WANT* ME TO ENTICE YOU!
I'LL FUFILL YOU-- IN ALL RESPECTS. YOU'LL FORGET ALL ABOUT YOUR LITTLE BOY-FRIEND.
LEAVE KEO ALONE!

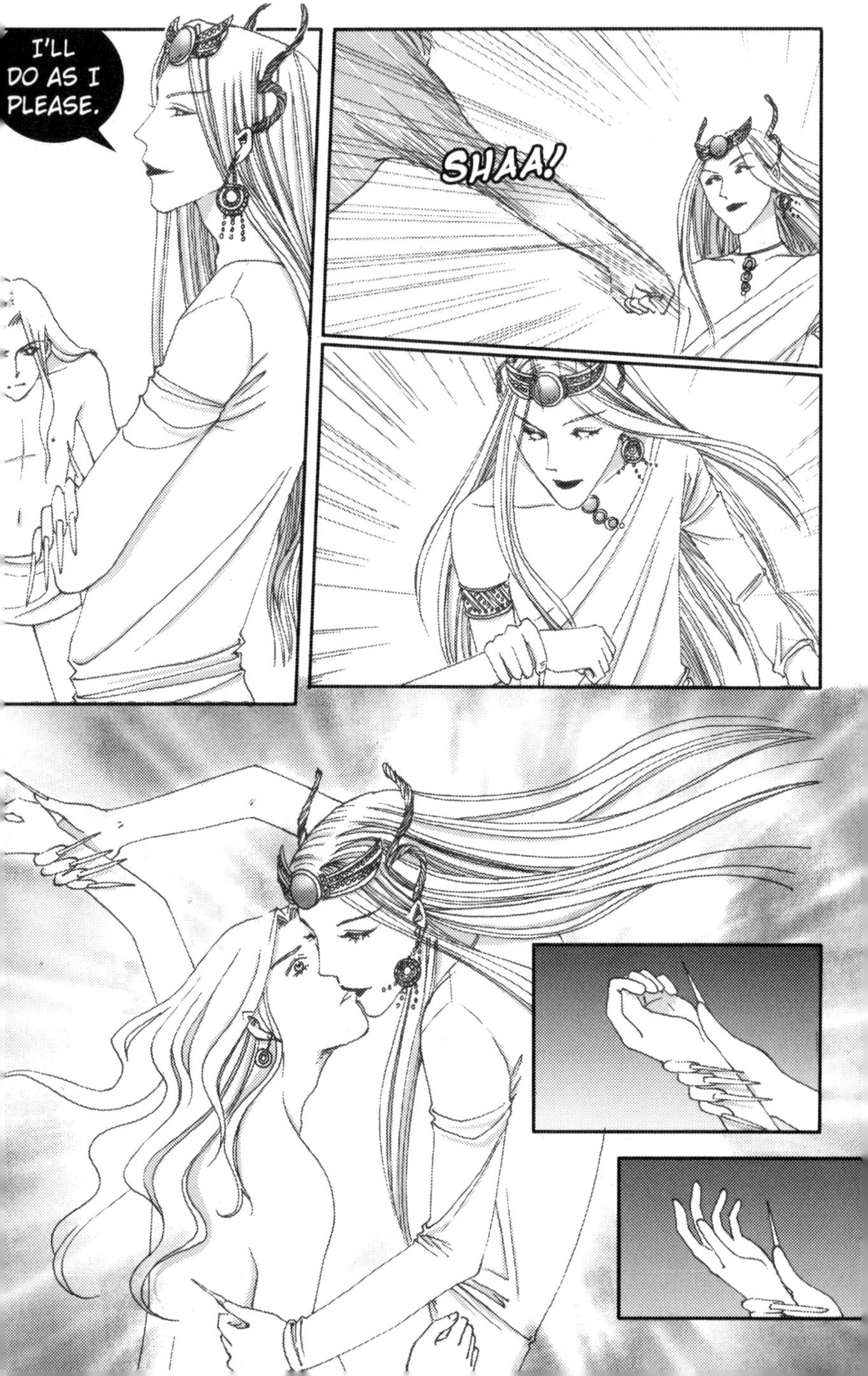
I'LL DO AS I PLEASE.
SHAA!

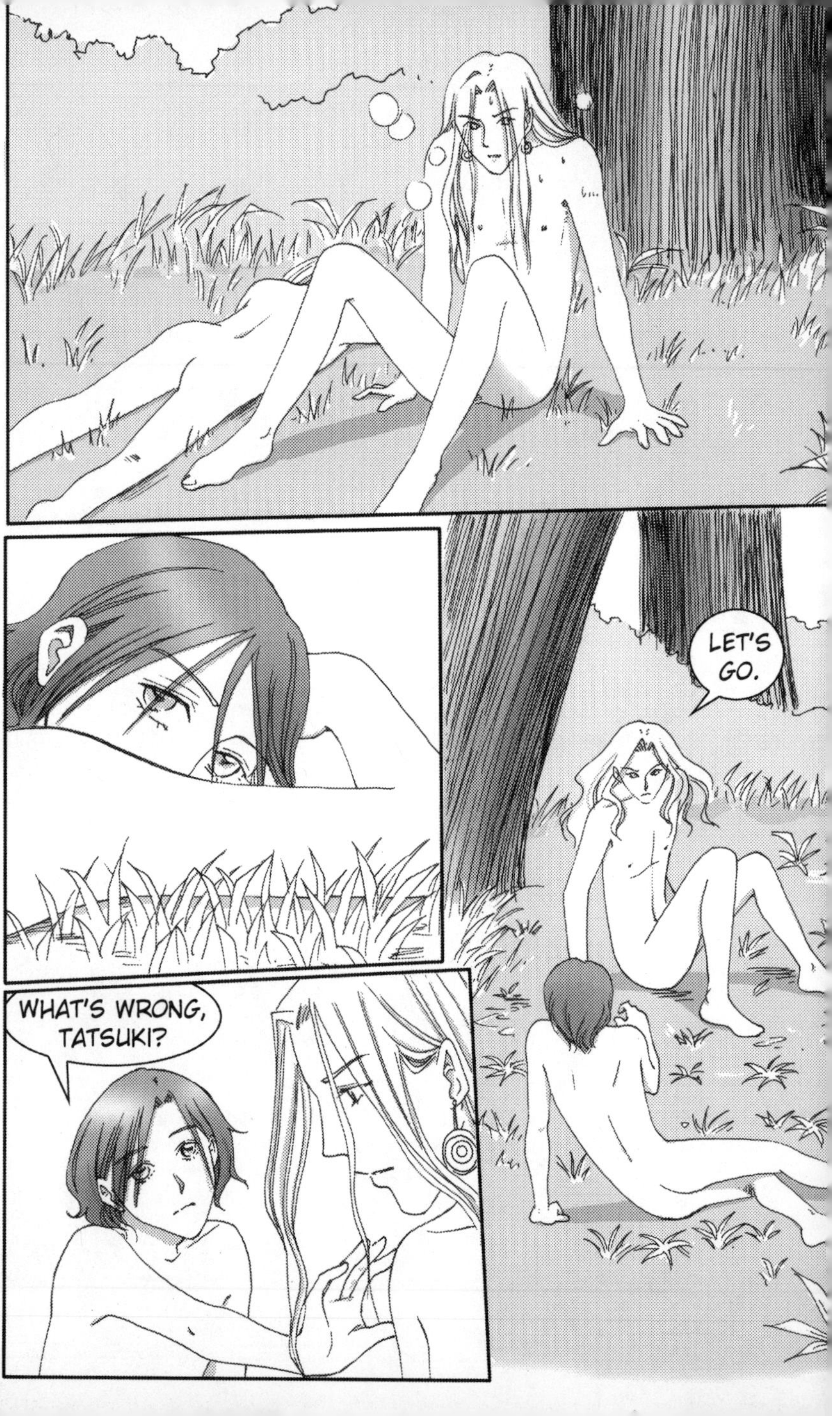
LET'S GO.
WHAT'S WRONG, TATSUKI?

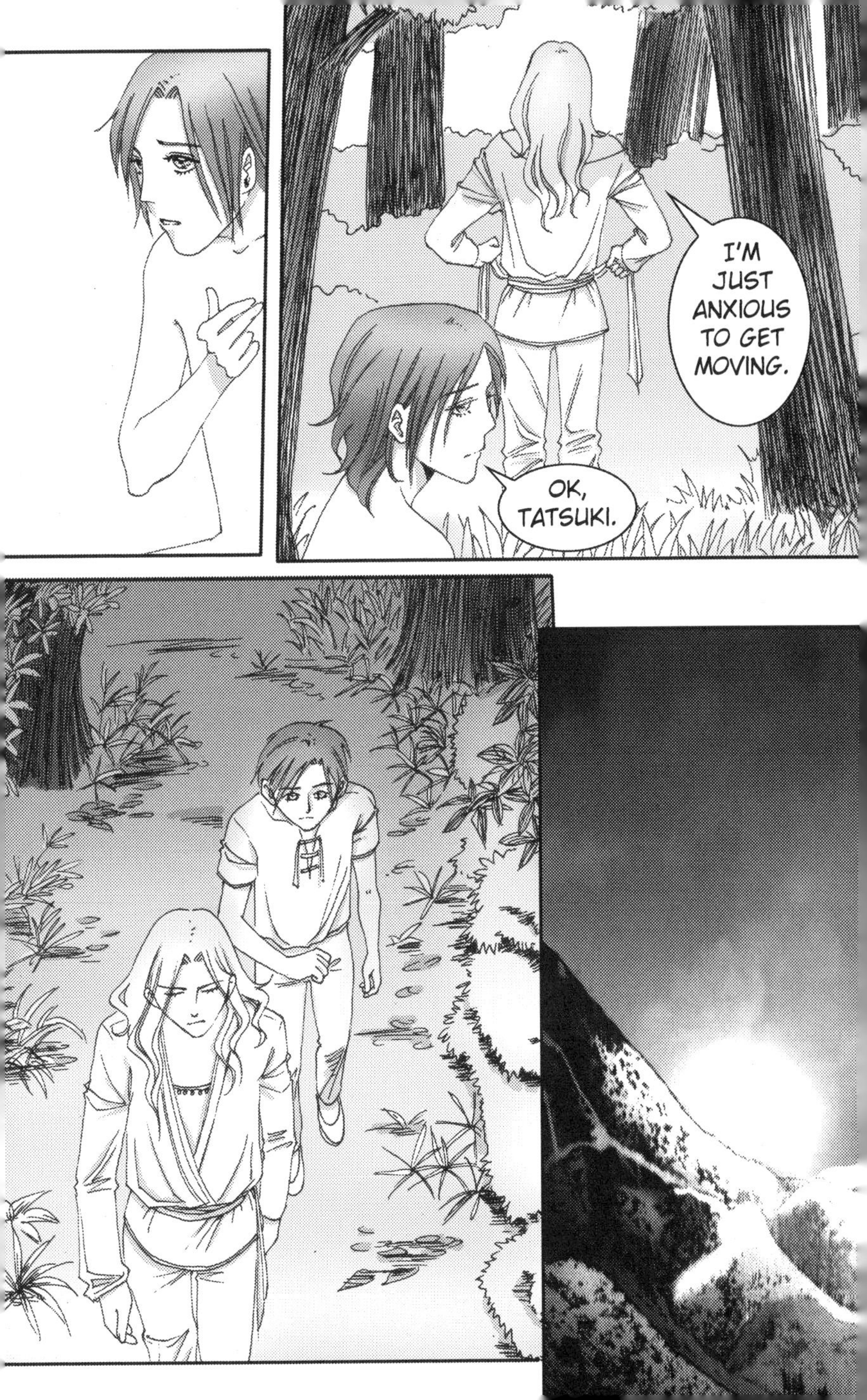
I'M JUST ANXIOUS TO GET MOVING.
OK, TATSUKI.

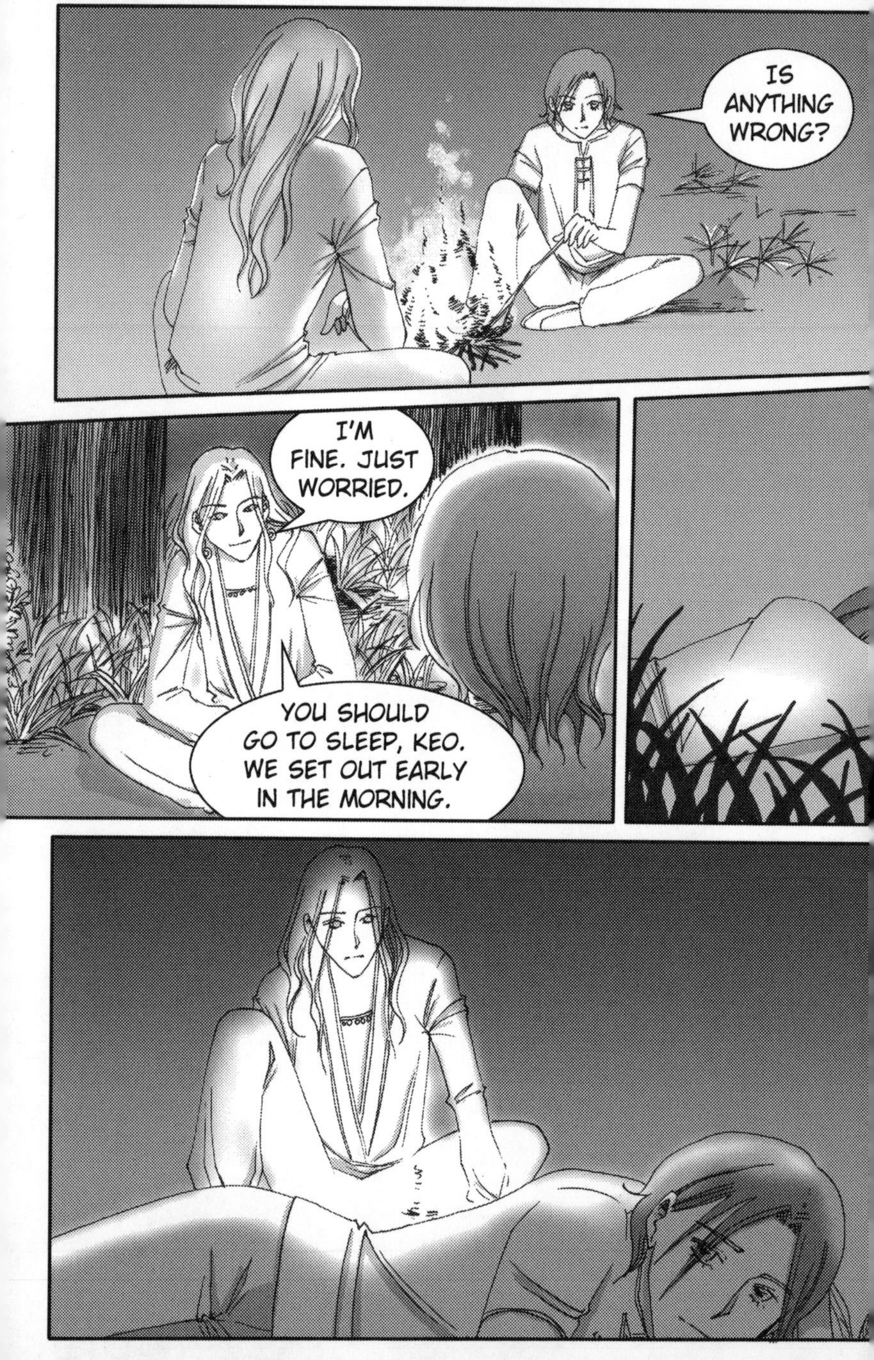
IS ANYTHING WRONG?
I'M FINE. JUST WORRIED.
YOU SHOULD GO TO SLEEP, KEO. WE SET OUT EARLY IN THE MORNING.

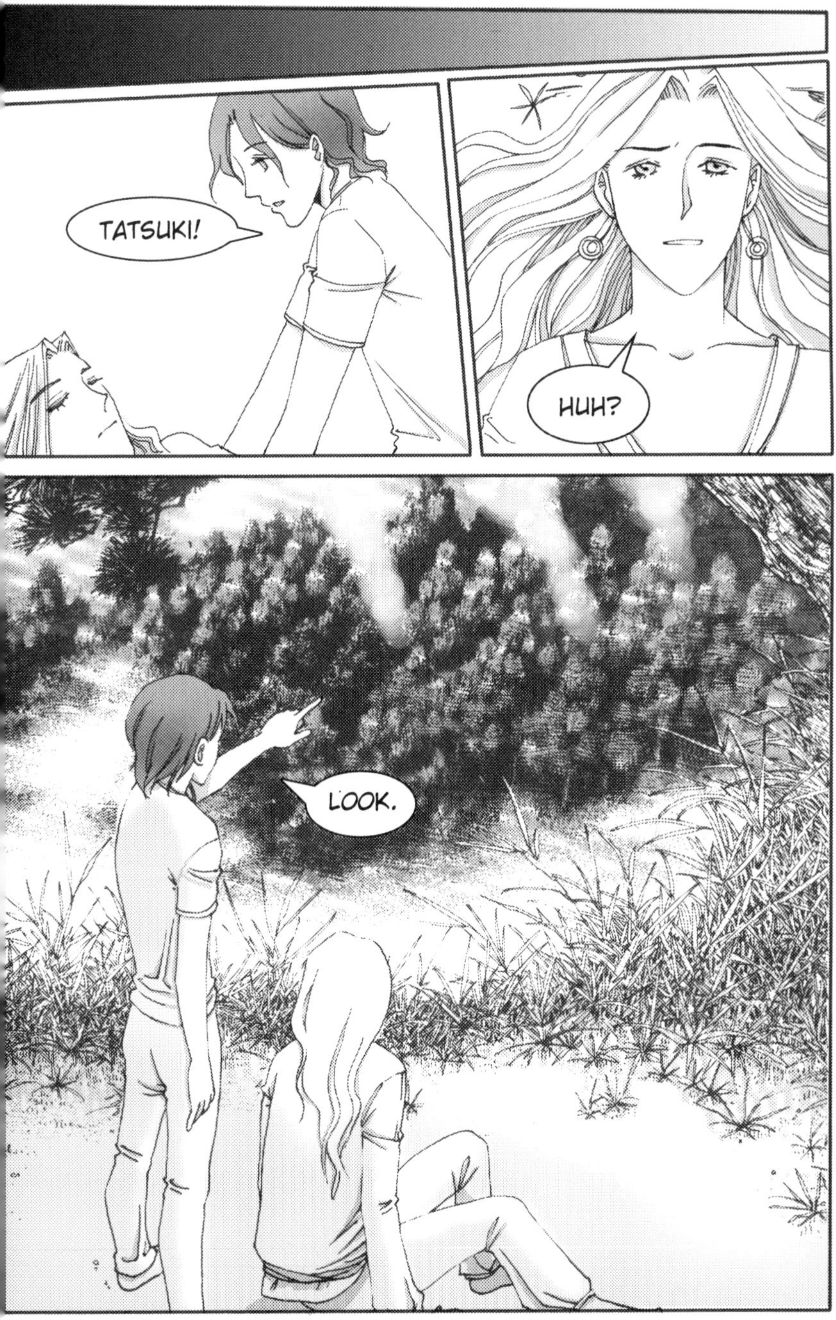
TATSUKI!
HUH?
LOOK.

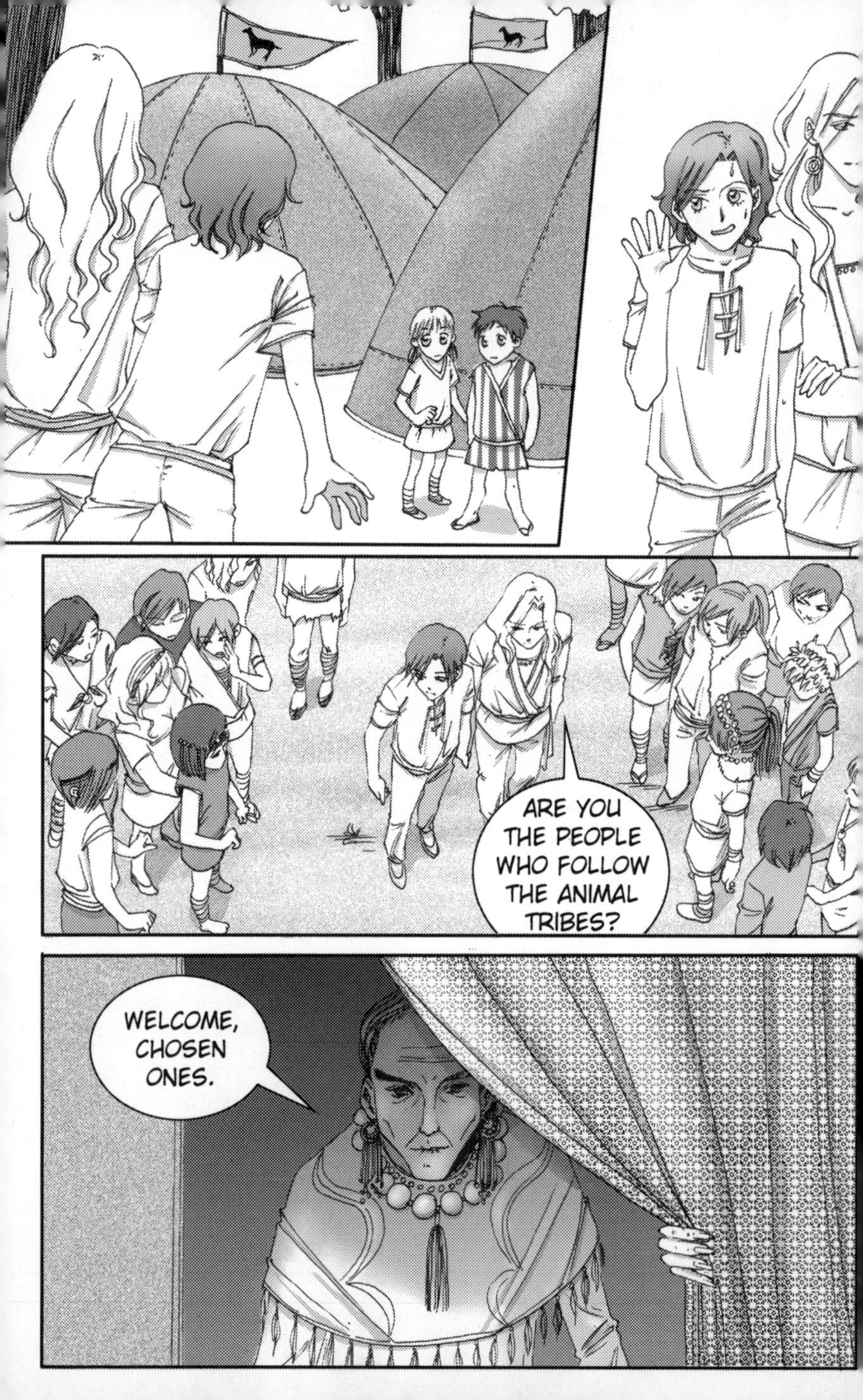
ARE YOU THE PEOPLE WHO FOLLOW THE ANIMAL TRIBES?
WELCOME, CHOSEN ONES.

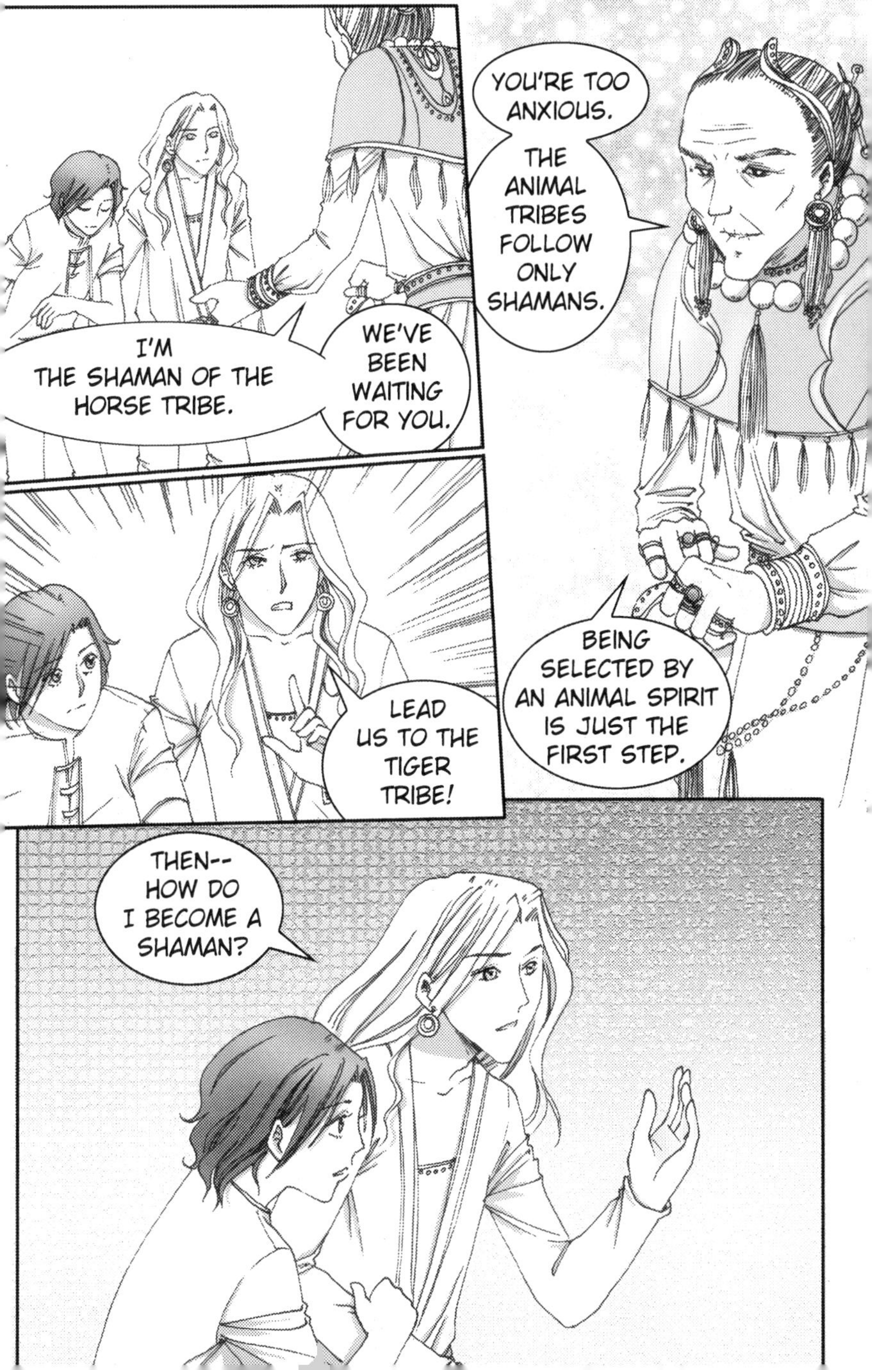
WE'VE BEEN WAITING FOR YOU.
I'M THE SHAMAN OF THE HORSE TRIBE.
YOU'RE TOO ANXIOUS.
THE ANIMAL TRIBES FOLLOW ONLY SHAMANS.
LEAD US TO THE TIGER TRIBE!
BEING SELECTED BY AN ANIMAL SPIRIT IS JUST THE FIRST STEP.
THEN-- HOW DO I BECOME A SHAMAN?

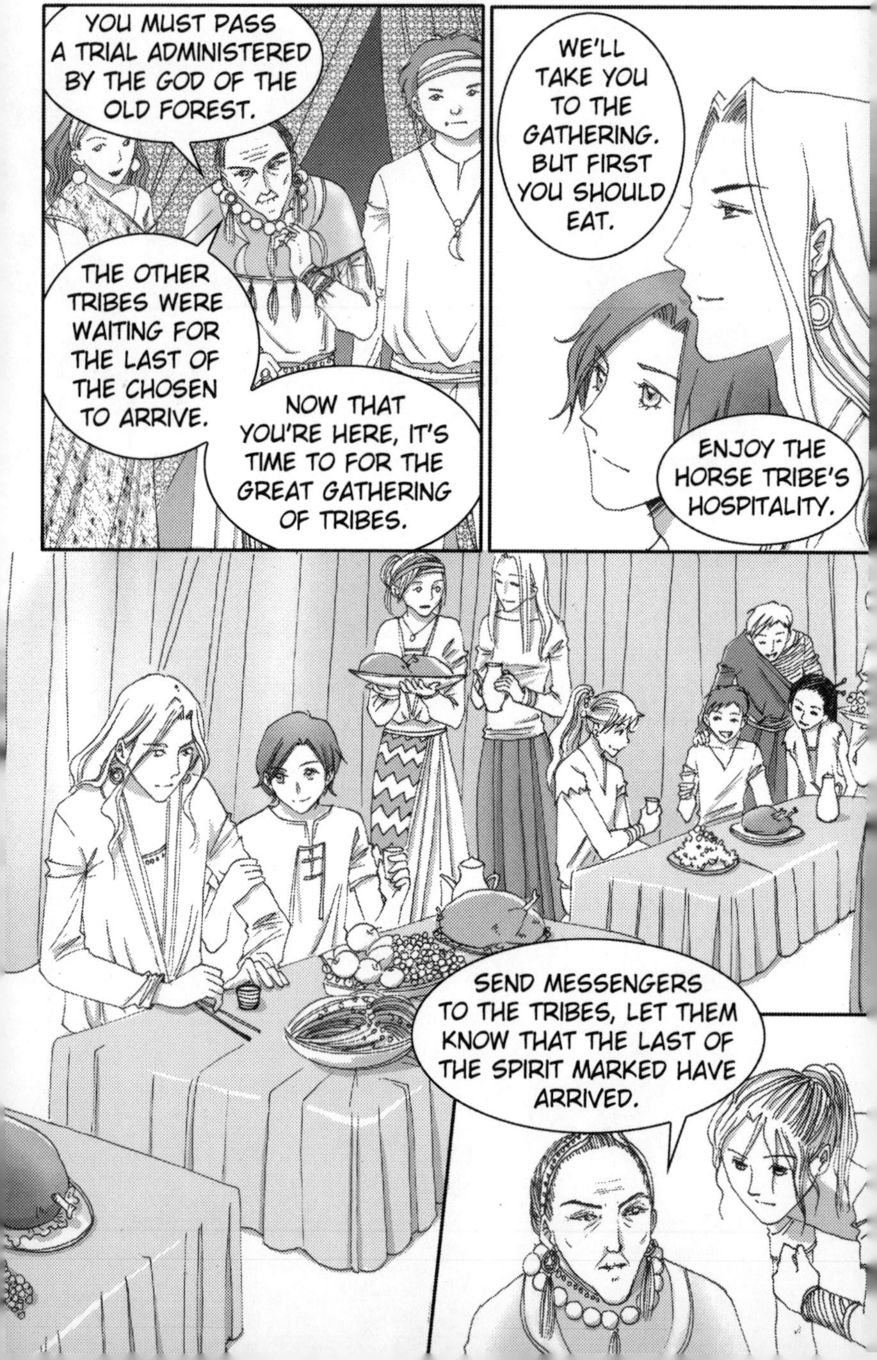
YOU MUST PASS A TRIAL ADMINISTERED BY THE GOD OF THE OLD FOREST.
THE OTHER TRIBES WERE WAITING FOR THE LAST OF THE CHOSEN TO ARRIVE.
NOW THAT YOU'RE HERE, IT'S TIME TO FOR THE GREAT GATHERING OF TRIBES.
WE'LL TAKE YOU TO THE GATHERING. BUT FIRST YOU SHOULD EAT.
ENJOY THE HORSE TRIBE'S HOSPITALITY.
SEND MESSENGERS TO THE TRIBES, LET THEM KNOW THAT THE LAST OF THE SPIRIT MARKED HAVE ARRIVED.

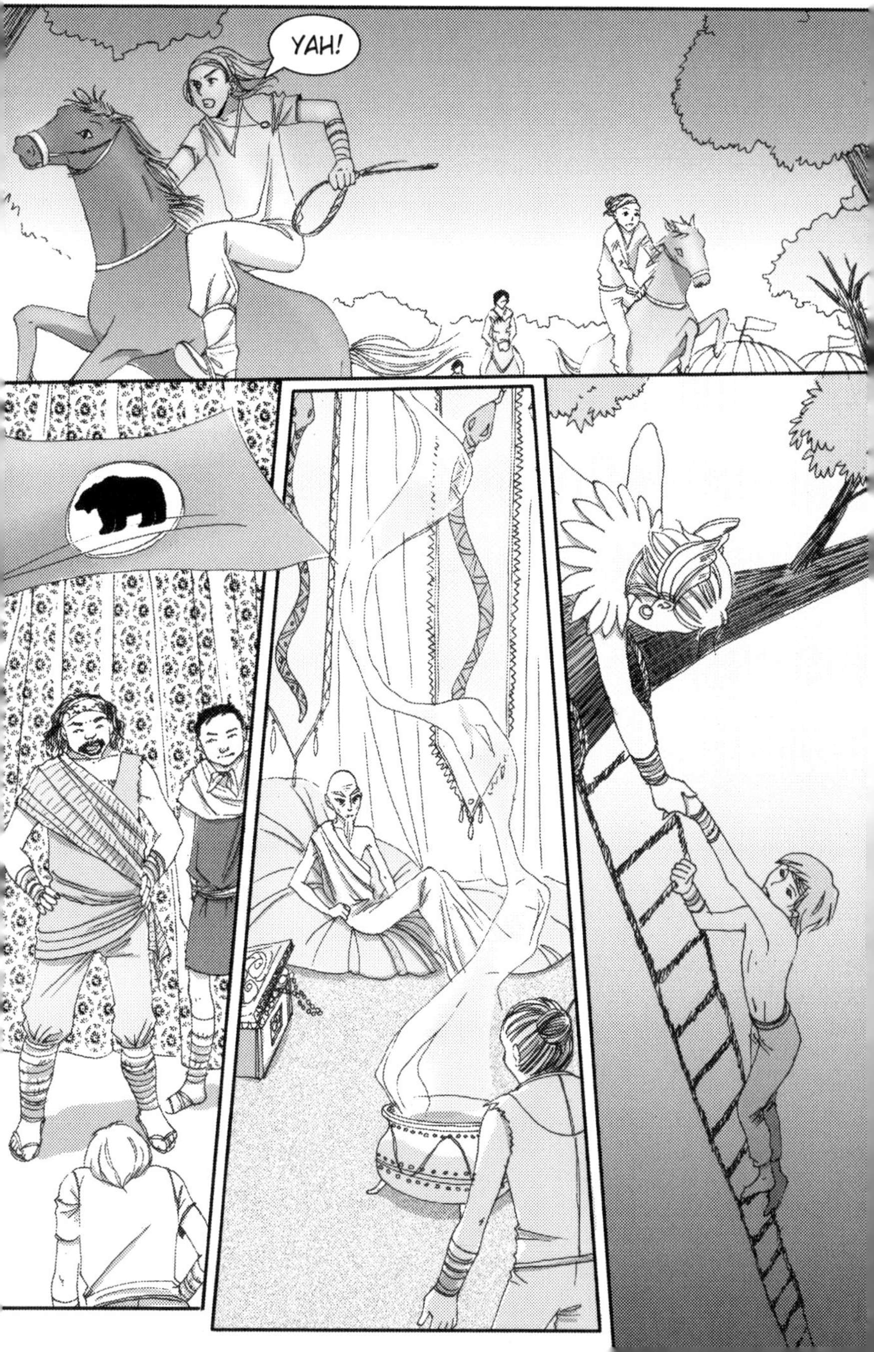
YAH!

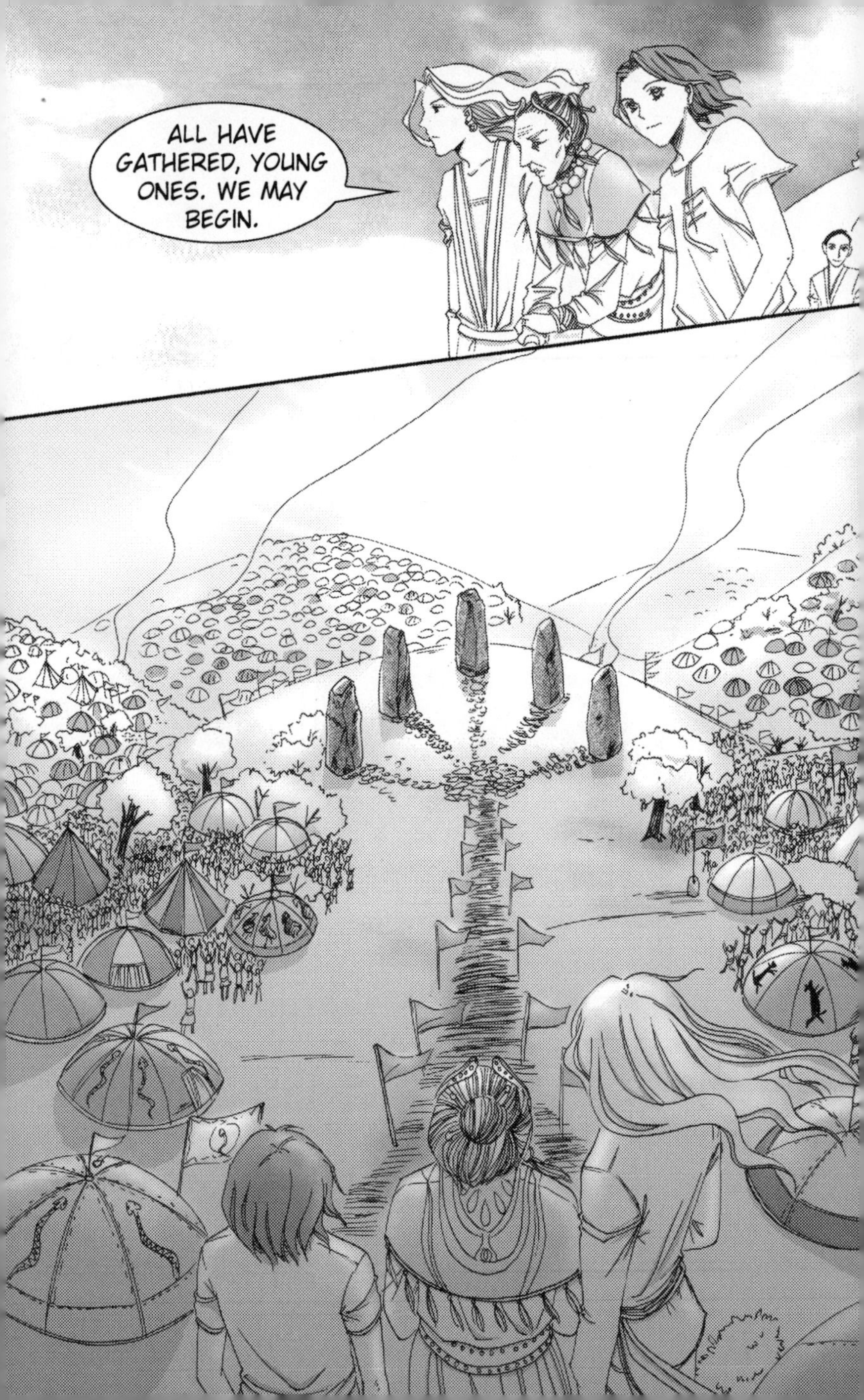
ALL HAVE GATHERED, YOUNG ONES. WE MAY BEGIN.

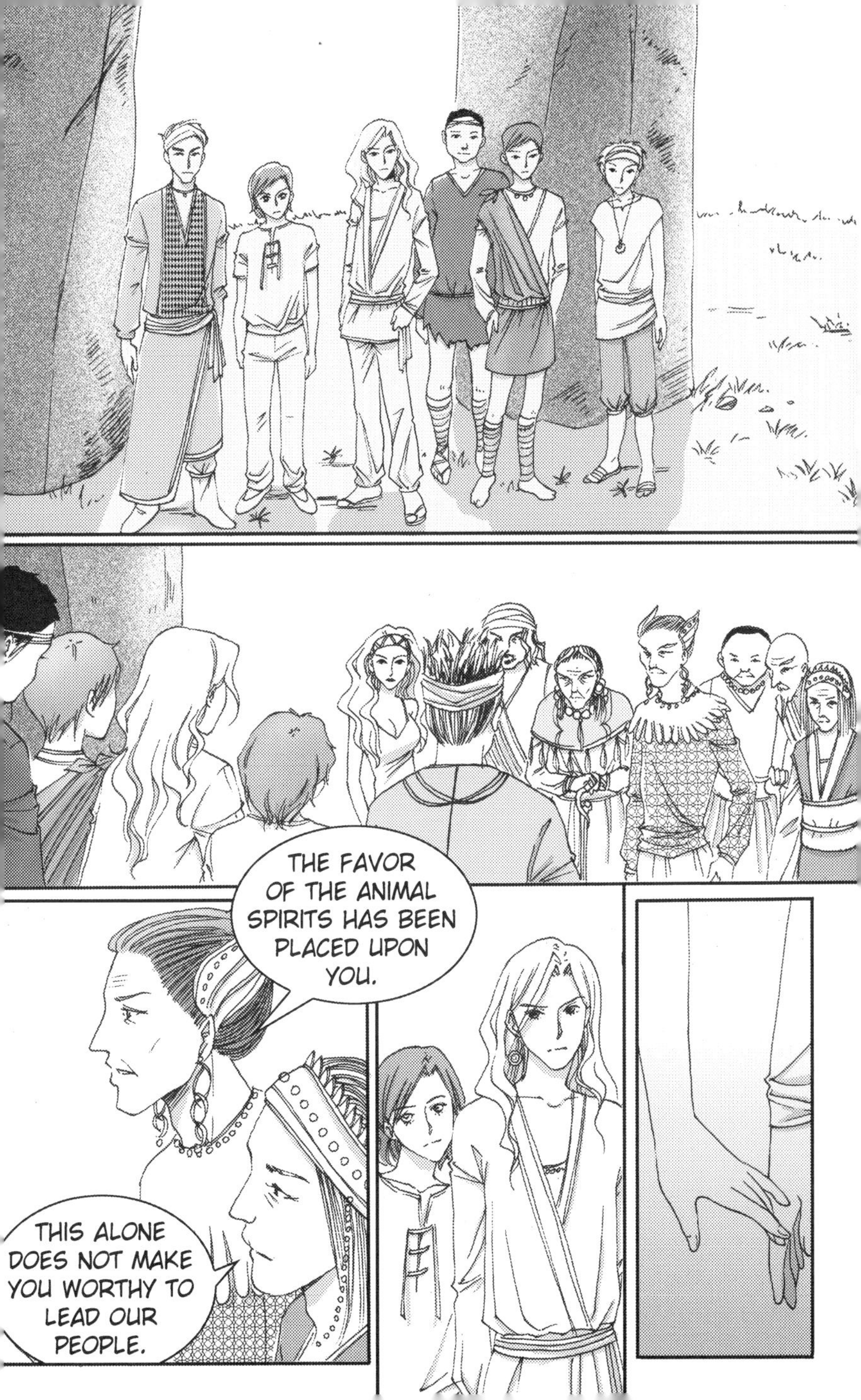
THE FAVOR OF THE ANIMAL SPIRITS HAS BEEN PLACED UPON YOU.
THIS ALONE DOES NOT MAKE YOU WORTHY TO LEAD OUR PEOPLE.

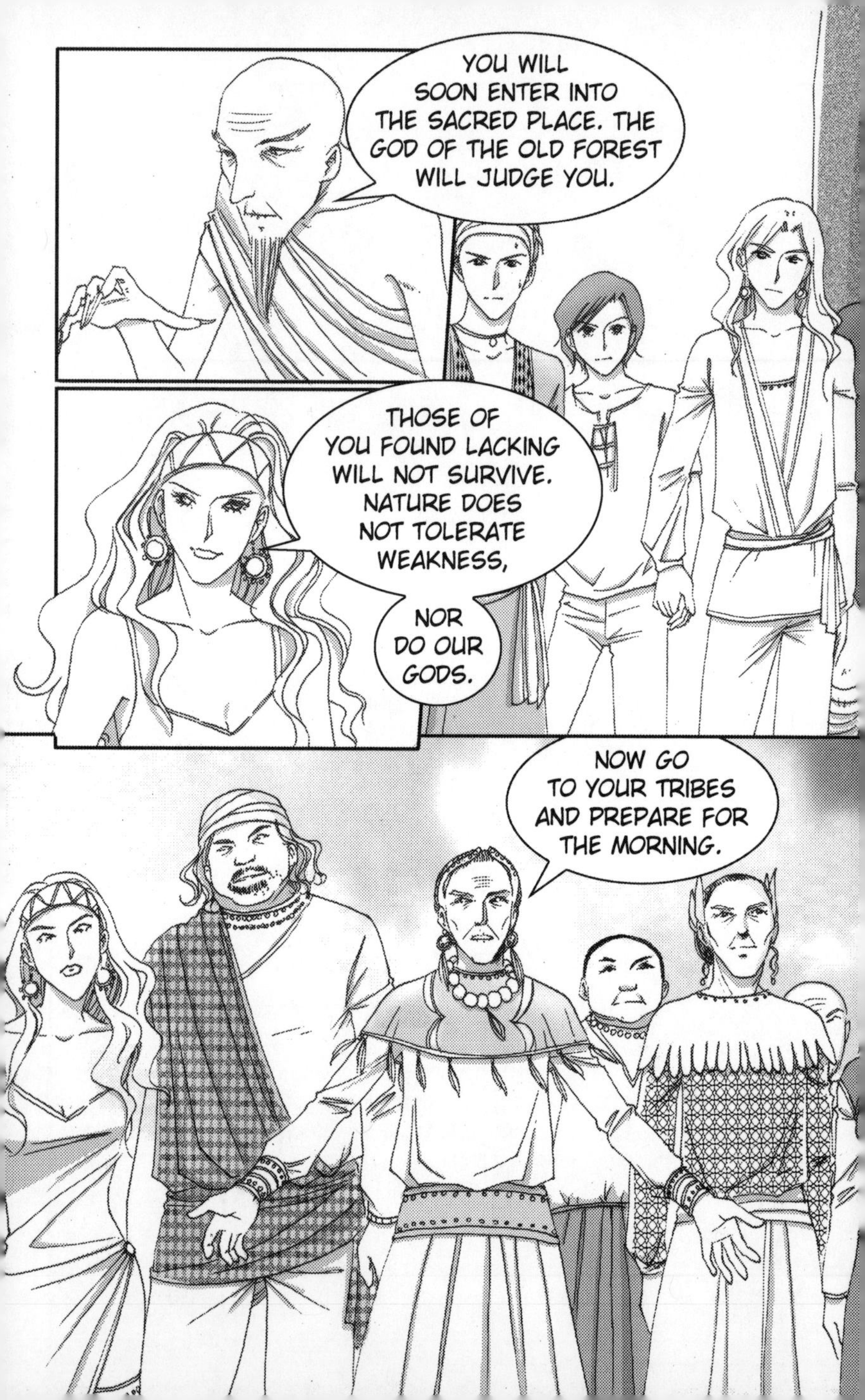
YOU WILL SOON ENTER INTO THE SACRED PLACE. THE GOD OF THE OLD FOREST WILL JUDGE YOU.
THOSE OF YOU FOUND LACKING WILL NOT SURVIVE. NATURE DOES NOT TOLERATE WEAKNESS,
NOR DO OUR GODS.
NOW GO TO YOUR TRIBES AND PREPARE FOR THE MORNING.

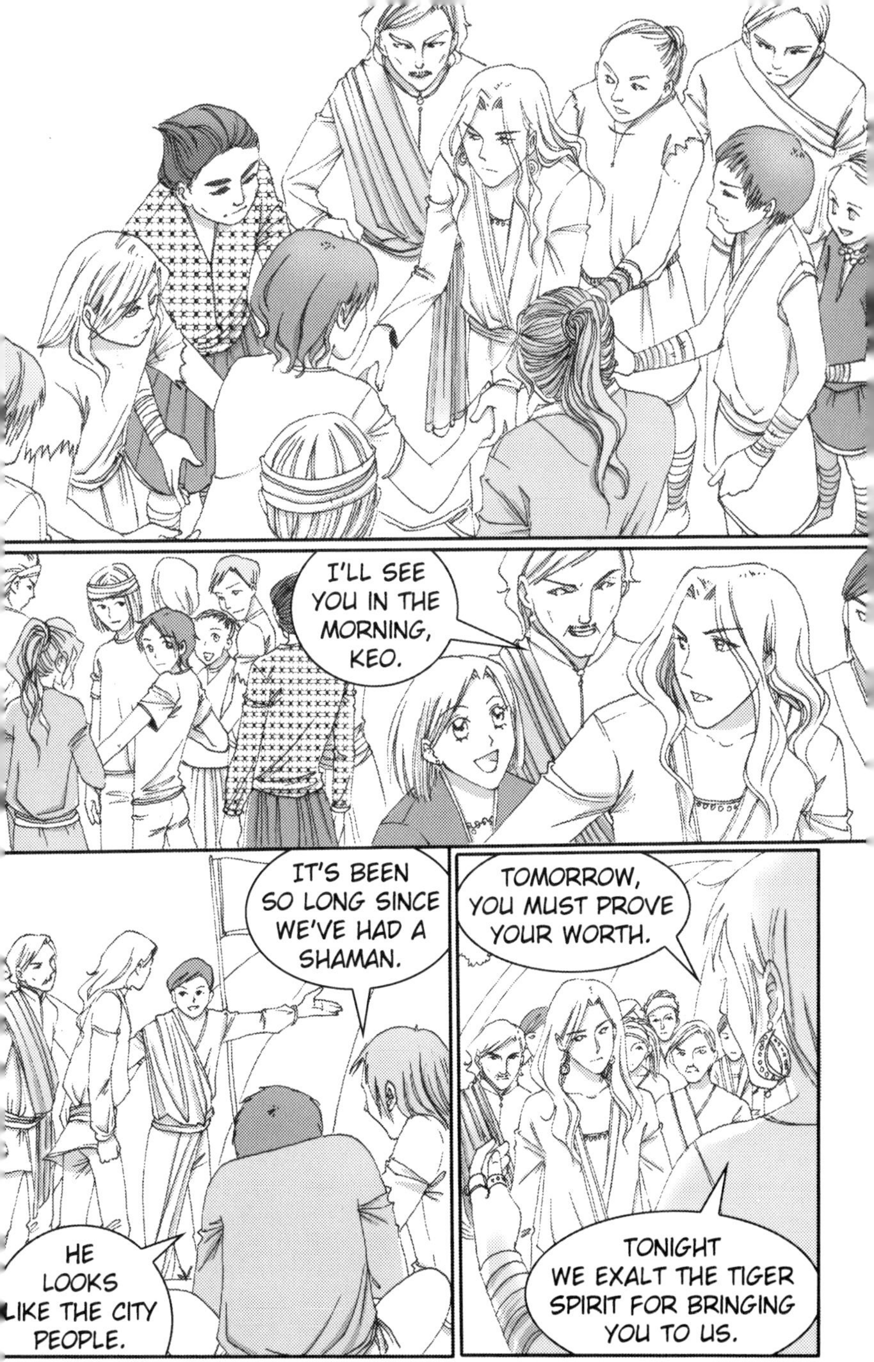
I'LL SEE YOU IN THE MORNING, KEO.
IT'S BEEN SO LONG SINCE WE'VE HAD A SHAMAN.
HE LOOKS LIKE THE CITY PEOPLE.
TOMORROW, YOU MUST PROVE YOUR WORTH.
TONIGHT WE EXALT THE TIGER SPIRIT FOR BRINGING YOU TO US.

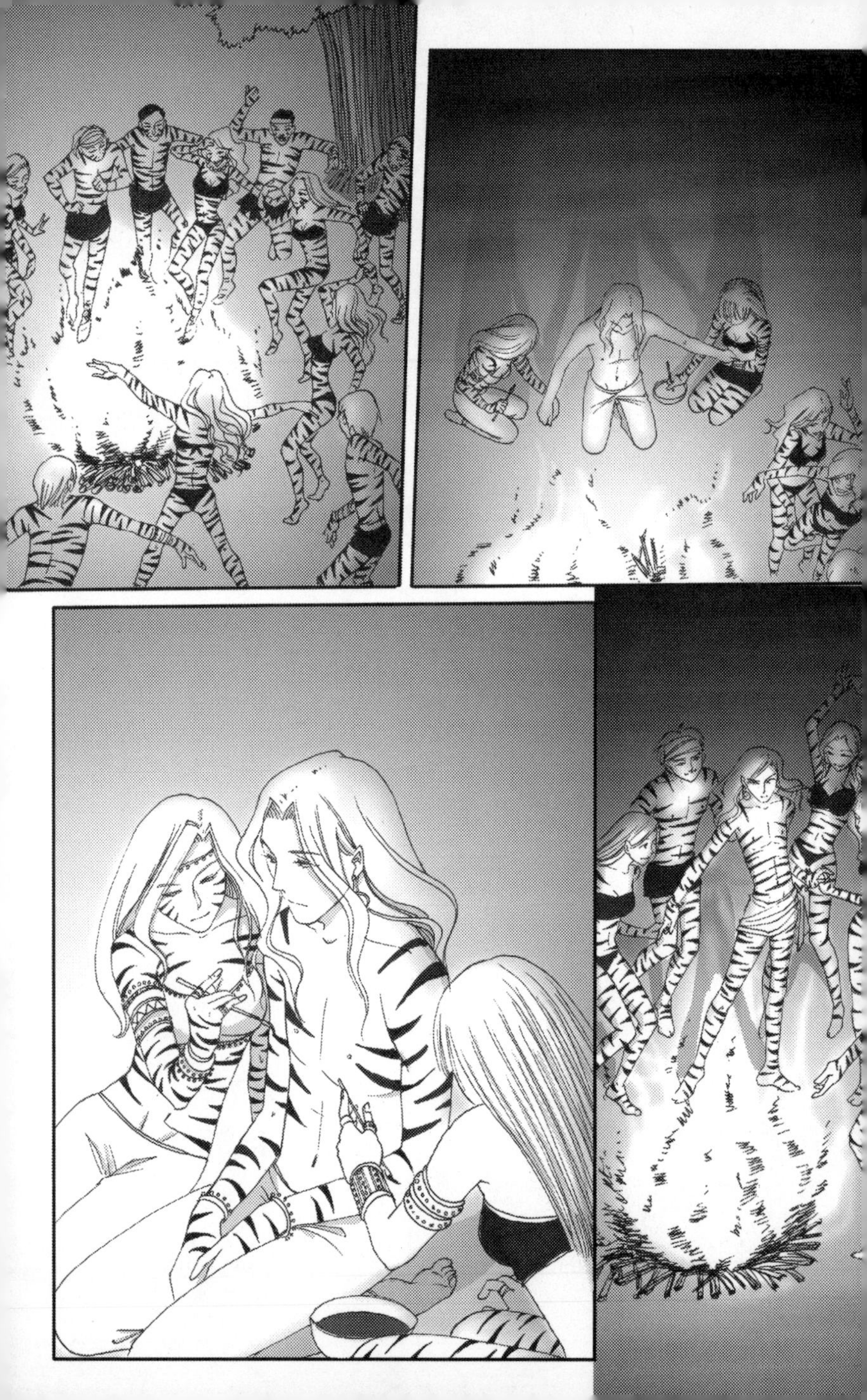

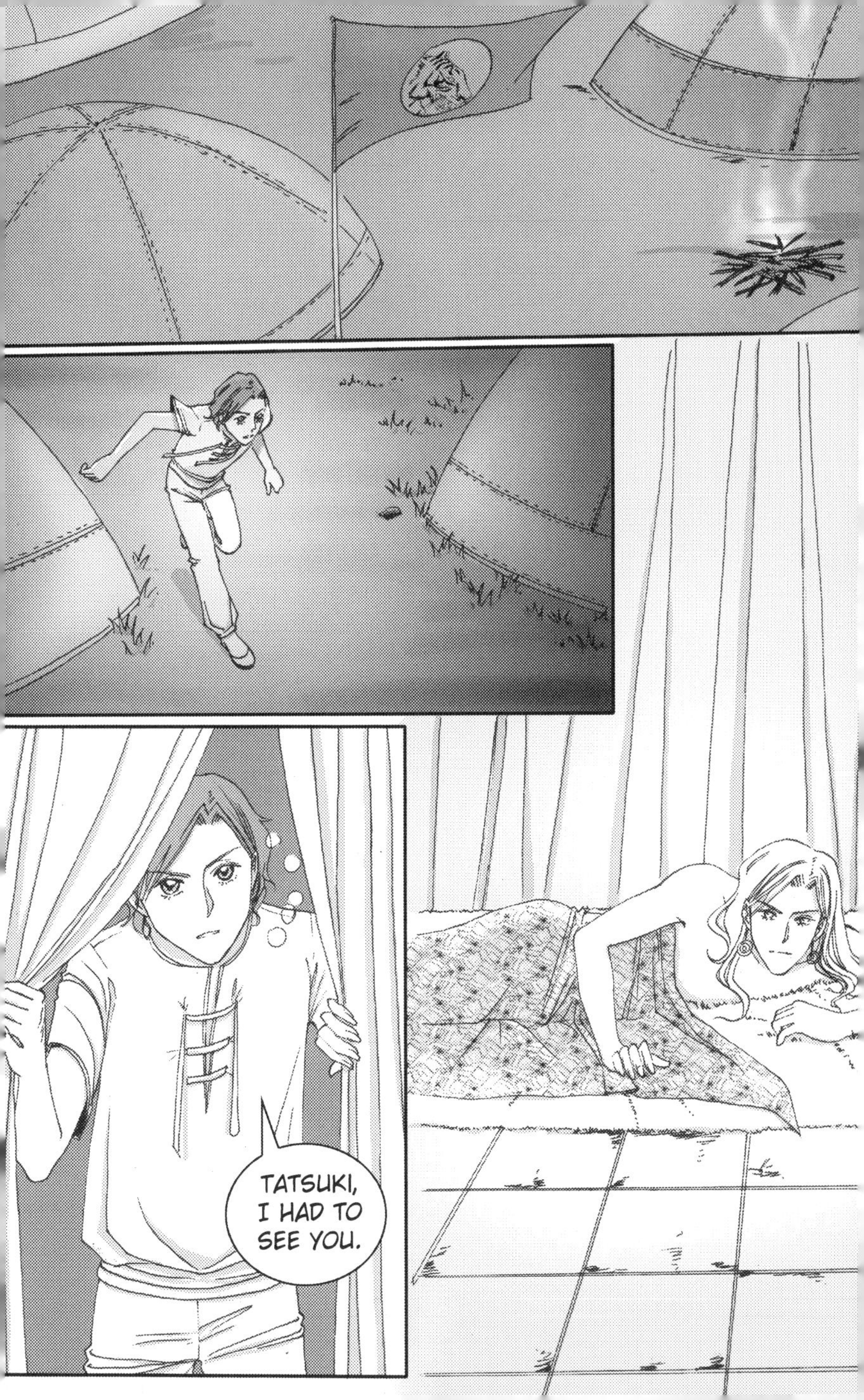
TATSUKI, I HAD TO SEE YOU.

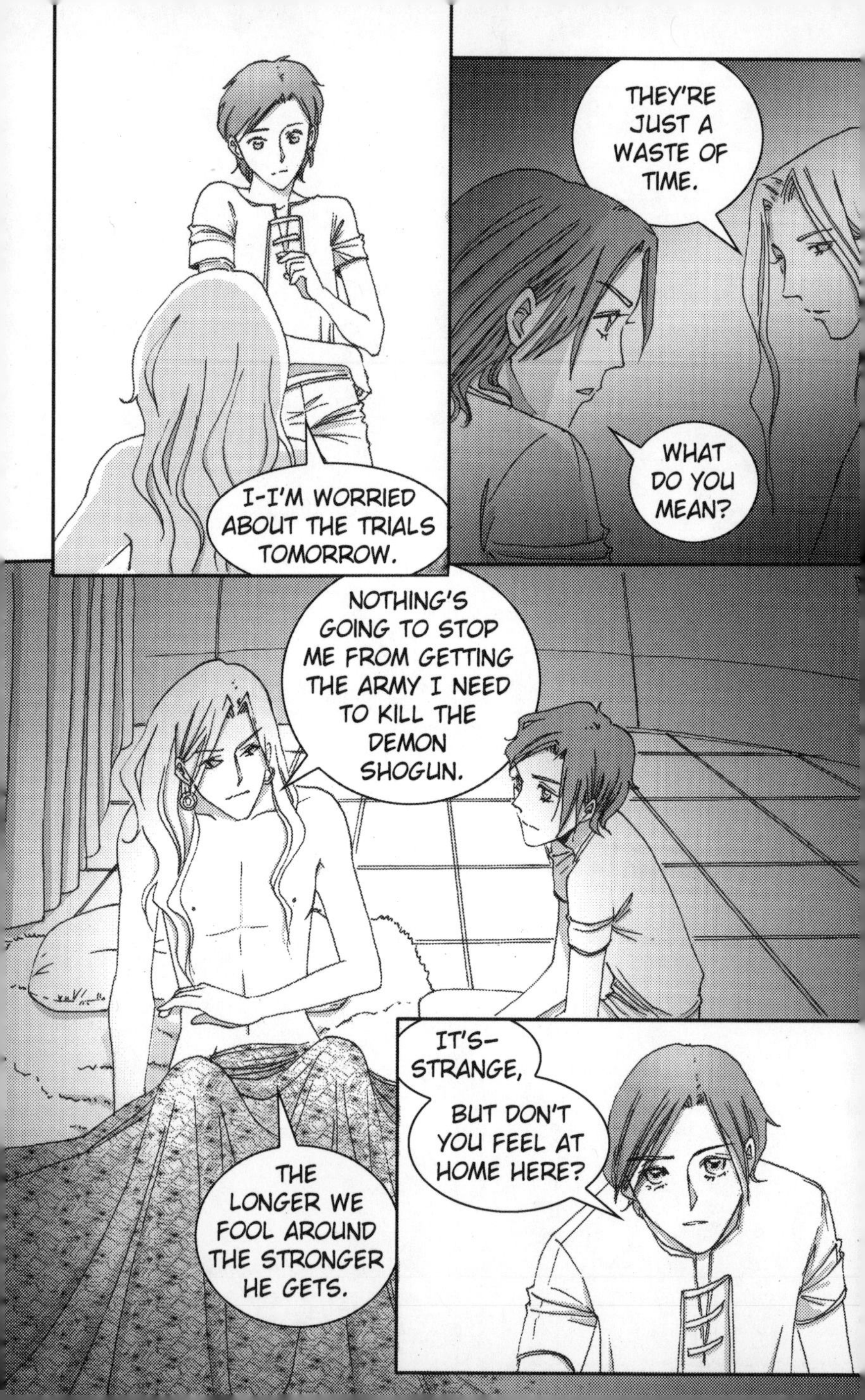
I-I'M WORRIED ABOUT THE TRIALS TOMORROW.
THEY'RE JUST A WASTE OF TIME.
WHAT DO YOU MEAN?
NOTHING'S GOING TO STOP ME FROM GETTING THE ARMY I NEED TO KILL THE DEMON SHOGUN.
THE LONGER WE FOOL AROUND THE STRONGER HE GETS.
IT'S- STRANGE,
BUT DON'T YOU FEEL AT HOME HERE?

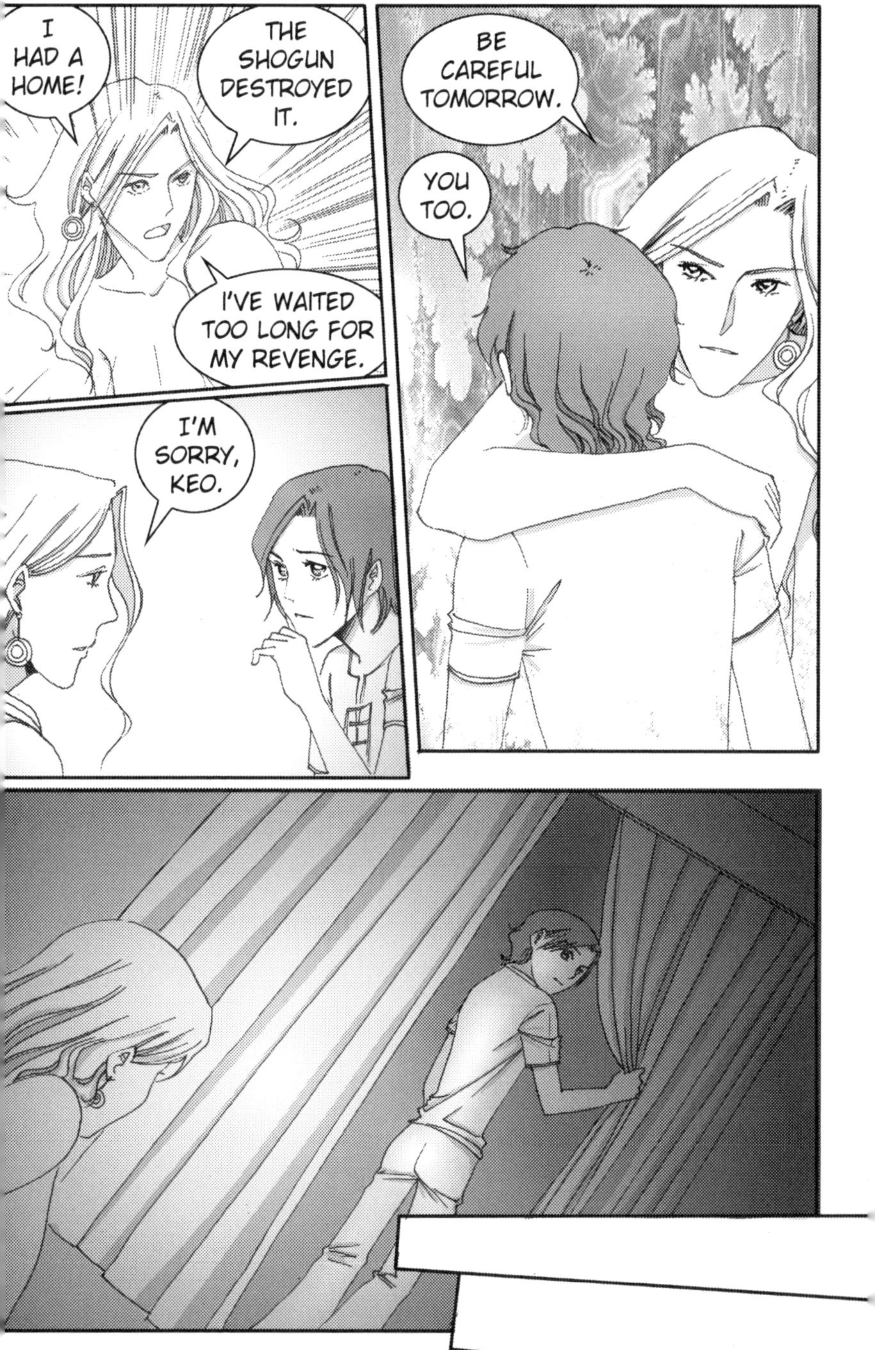
I HAD A HOME!
THE SHOGUN DESTROYED IT.
I'VE WAITED TOO LONG FOR MY REVENGE.
I'M SORRY, KEO.
BE CAREFUL TOMORROW.
YOU TOO.

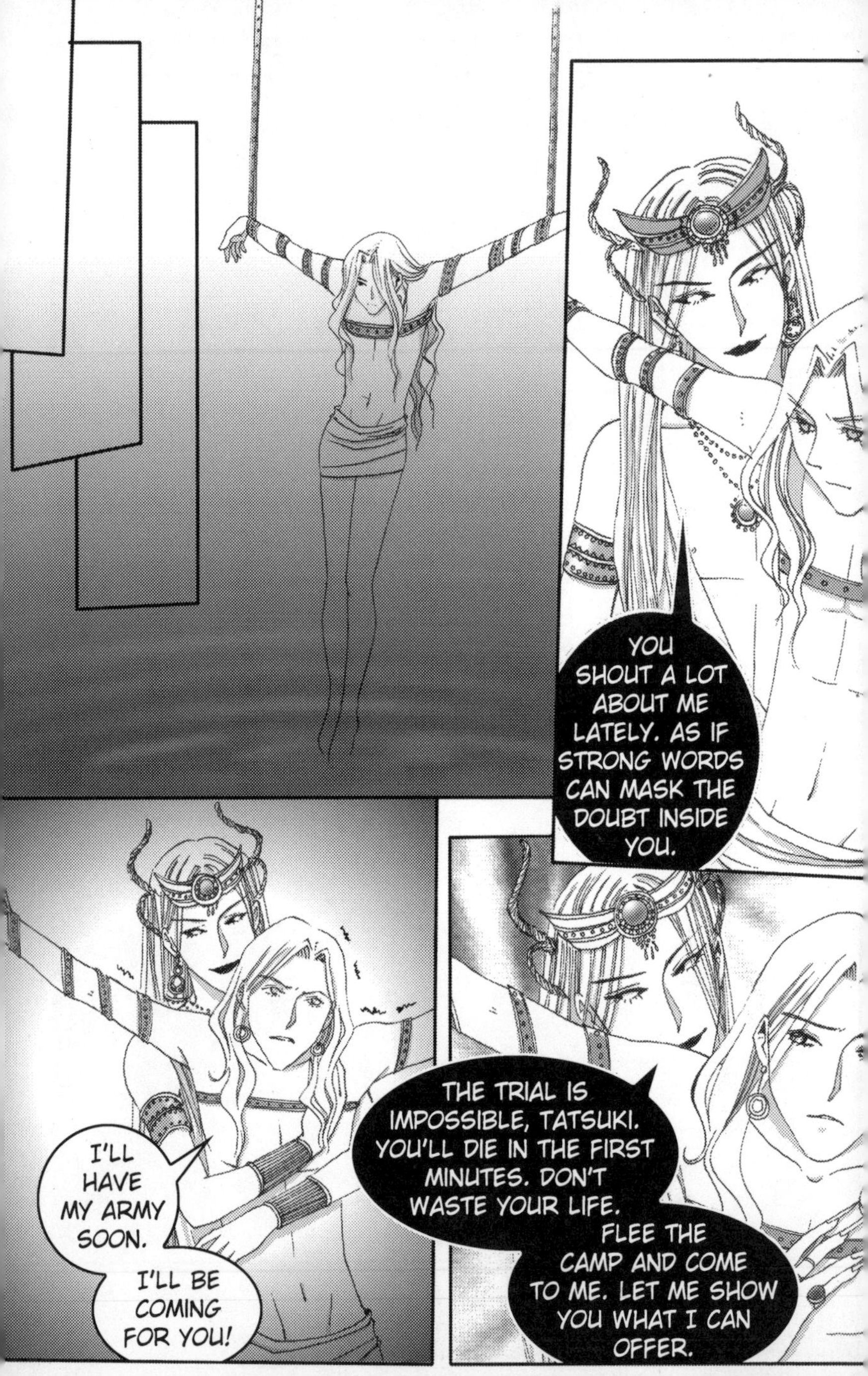
YOU SHOUT A LOT ABOUT ME LATELY. AS IF STRONG WORDS CAN MASK THE DOUBT INSIDE YOU.
THE TRIAL IS IMPOSSIBLE, TATSUKI. YOU'LL DIE IN THE FIRST MINUTES. DON'T WASTE YOUR LIFE.
FLEE THE CAMP AND COME TO ME. LET ME SHOW YOU WHAT I CAN OFFER.
I'LL HAVE MY ARMY SOON.
I'LL BE COMING FOR YOU!

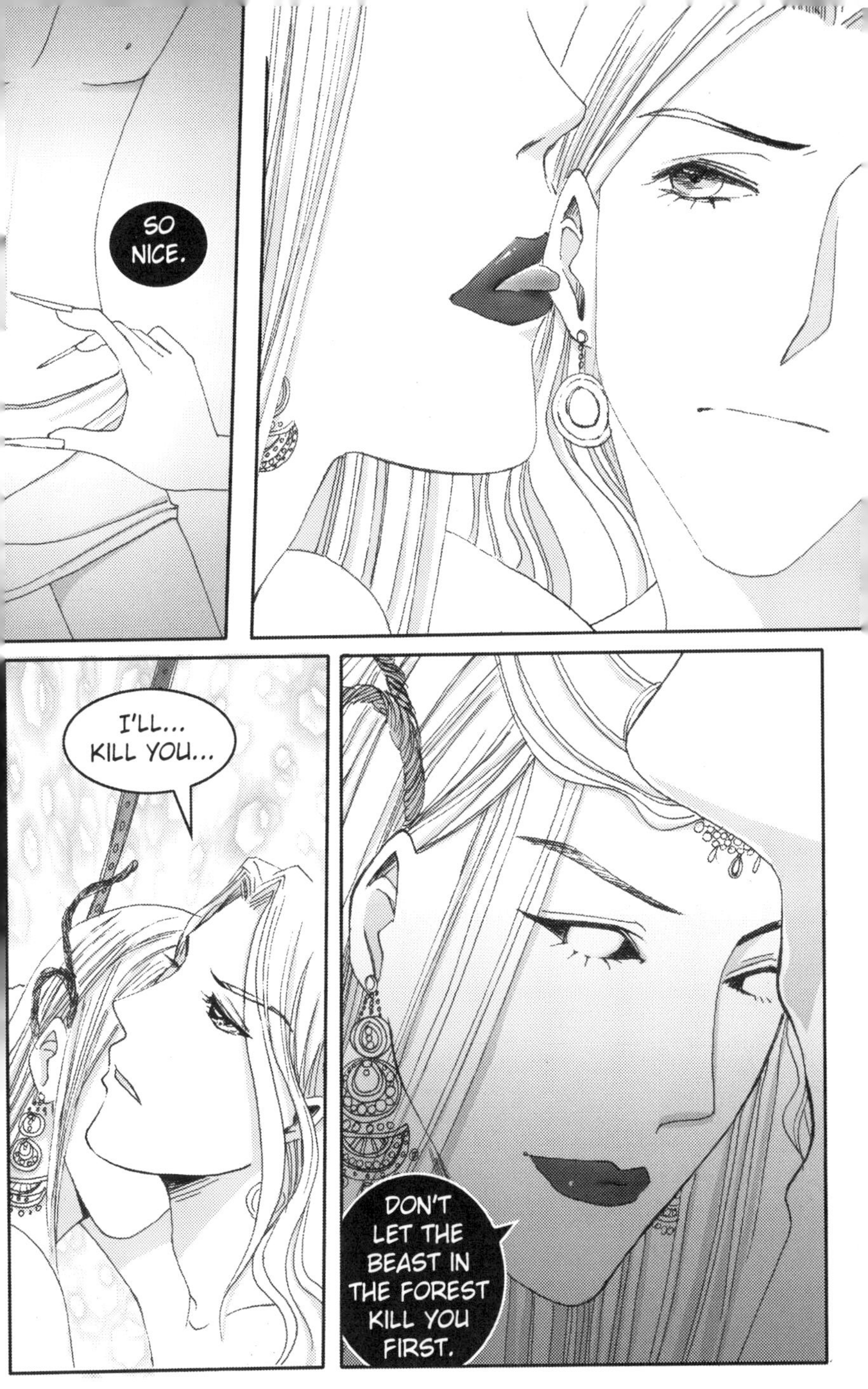
SO NICE.
I'LL... KILL YOU...
DON'T LET THE BEAST IN THE FOREST KILL YOU FIRST.

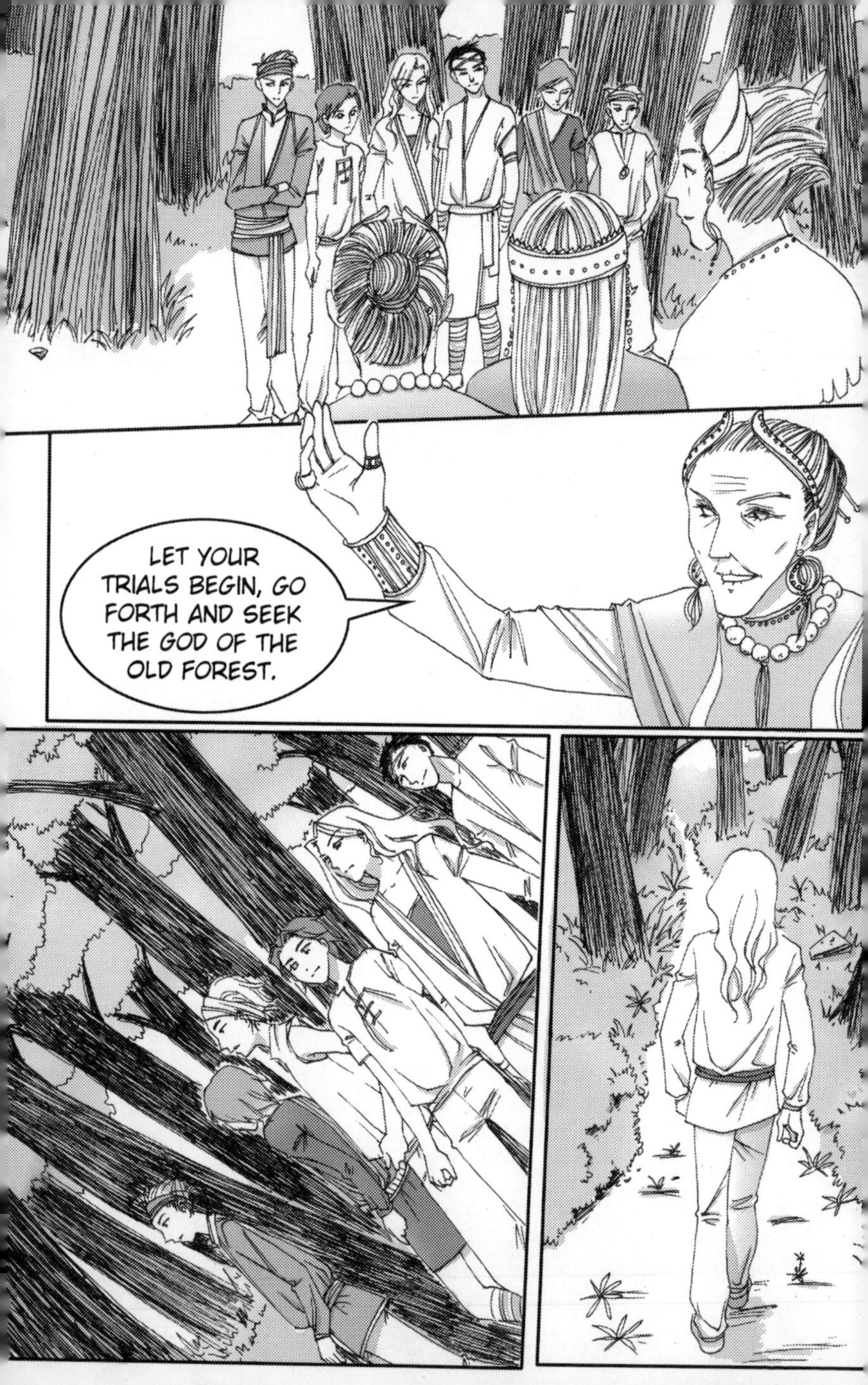
LET YOUR TRIALS BEGIN, GO FORTH AND SEEK THE GOD OF THE OLD FOREST.

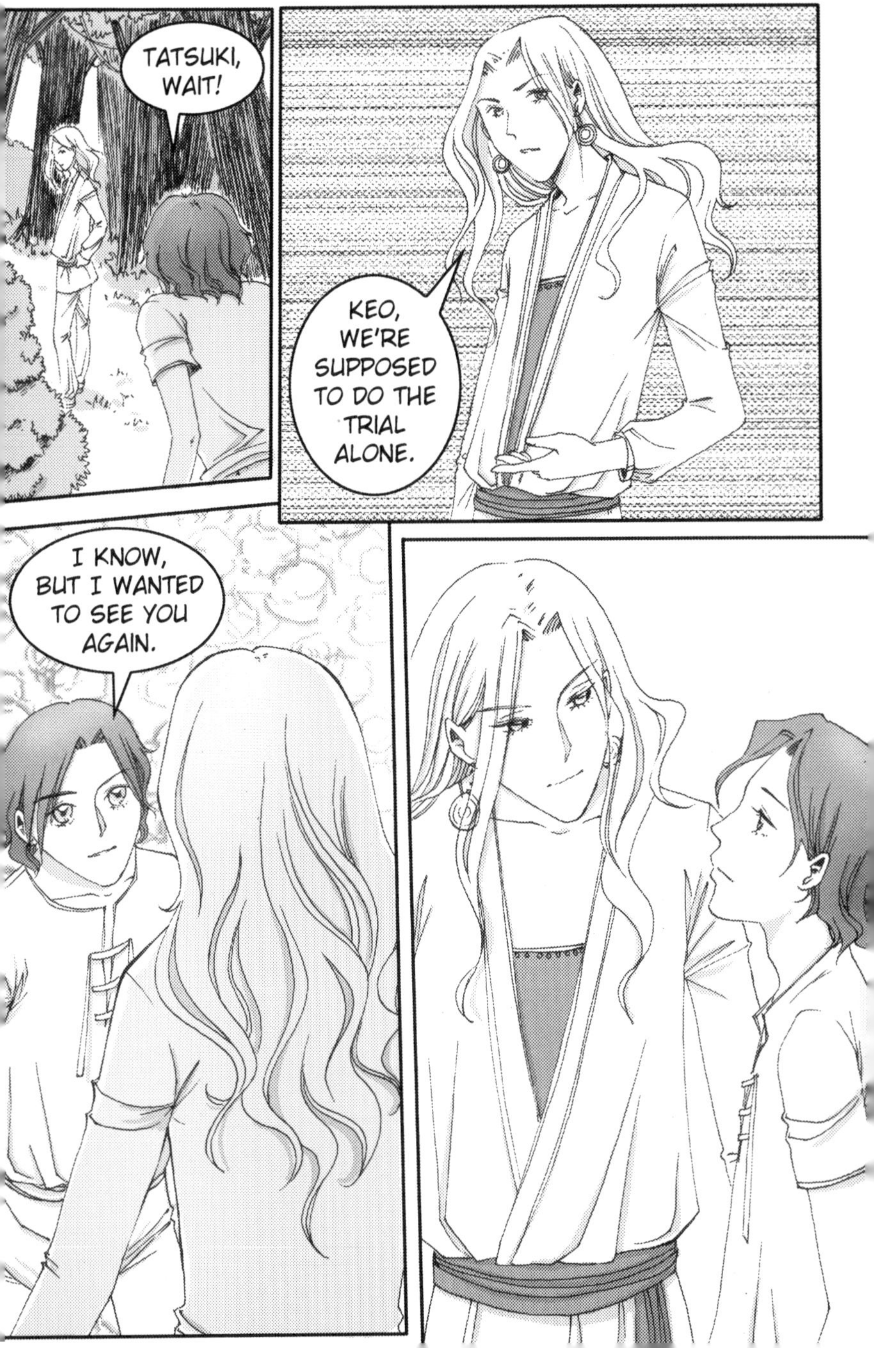
TATSUKI, WAIT!
KEO, WE'RE SUPPOSED TO DO THE TRIAL ALONE.
I KNOW, BUT I WANTED TO SEE YOU AGAIN.

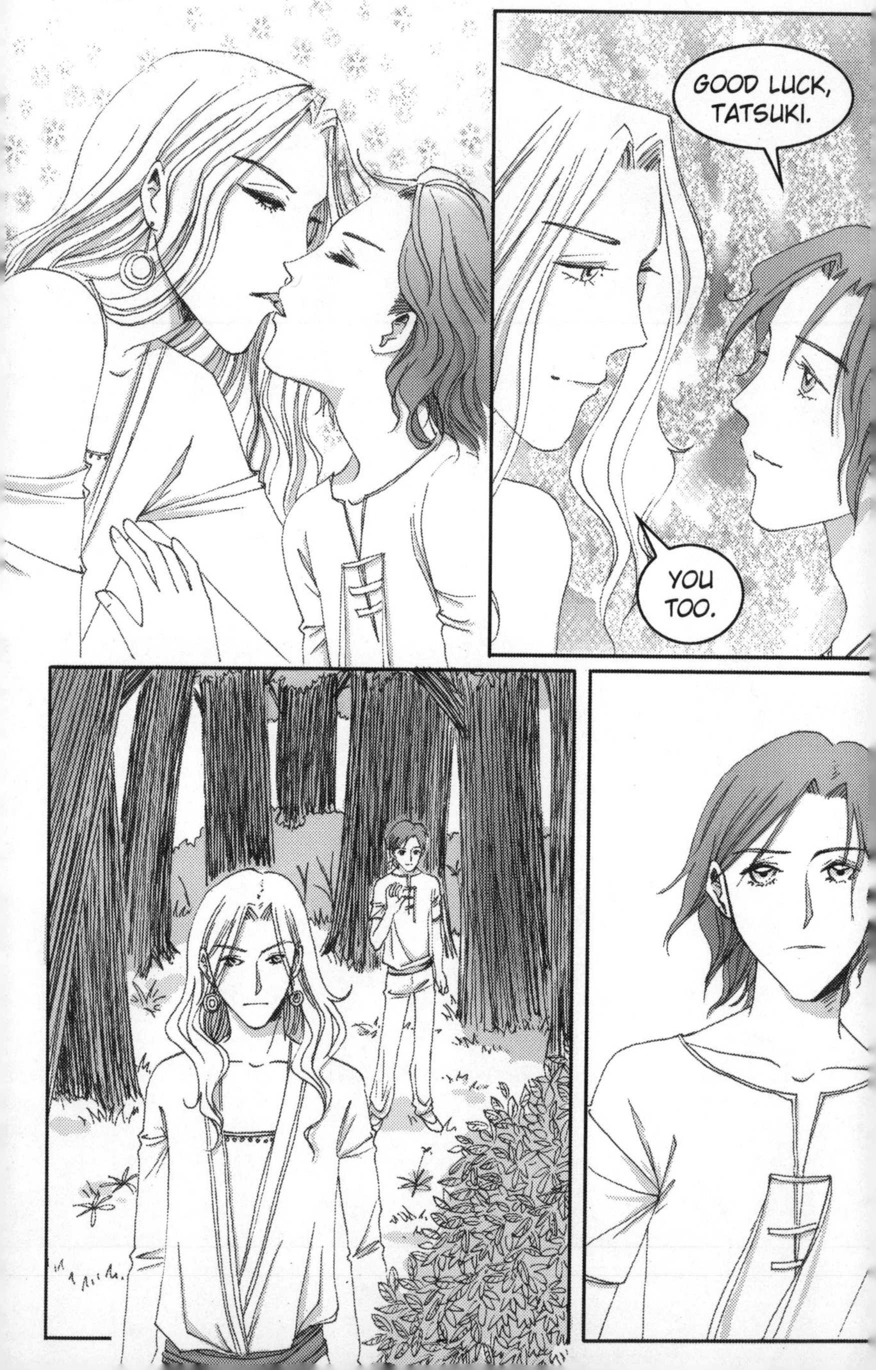

GOOD LUCK, TATSUKI.
YOU TOO.

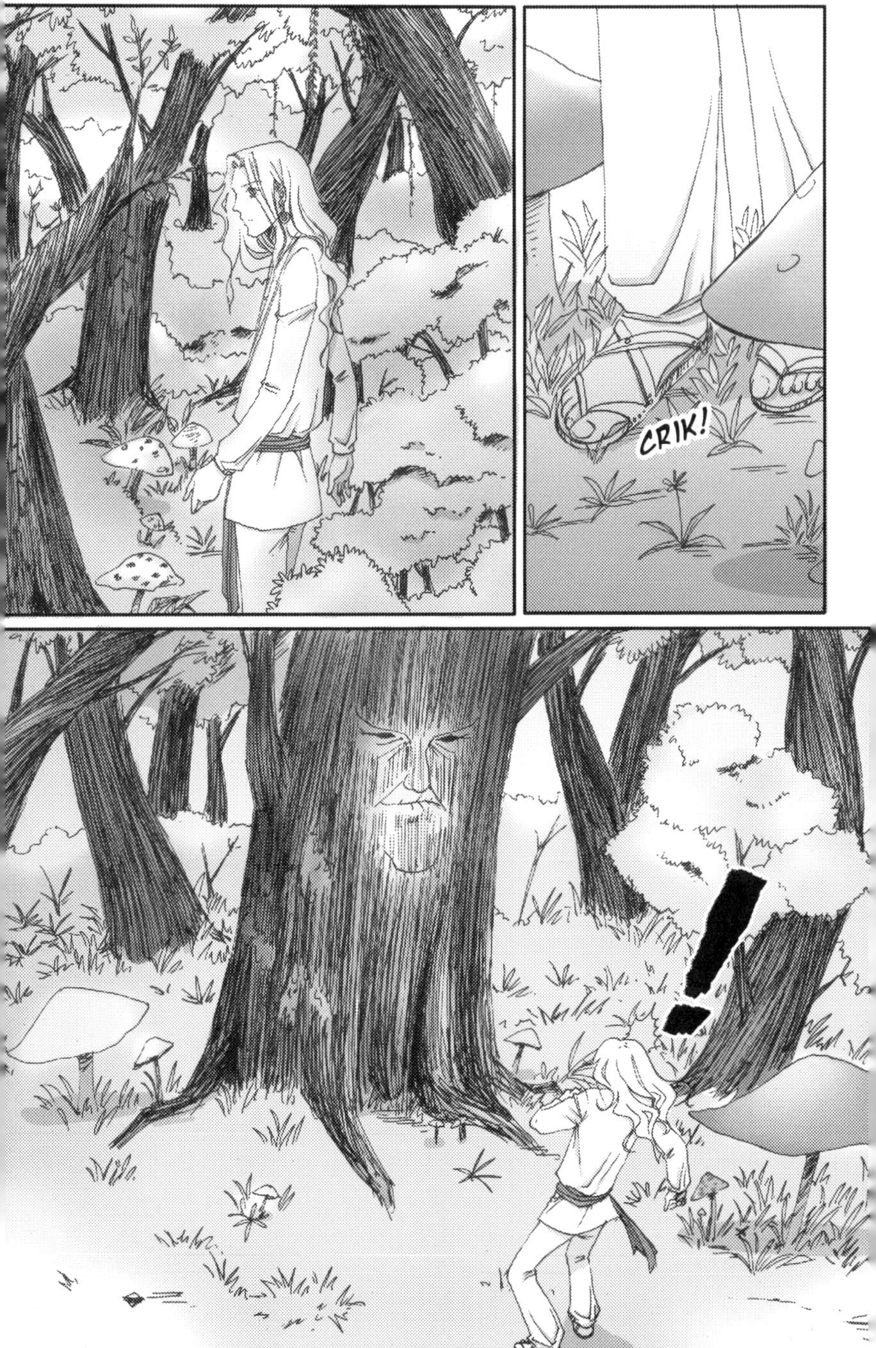
CRIK!
!

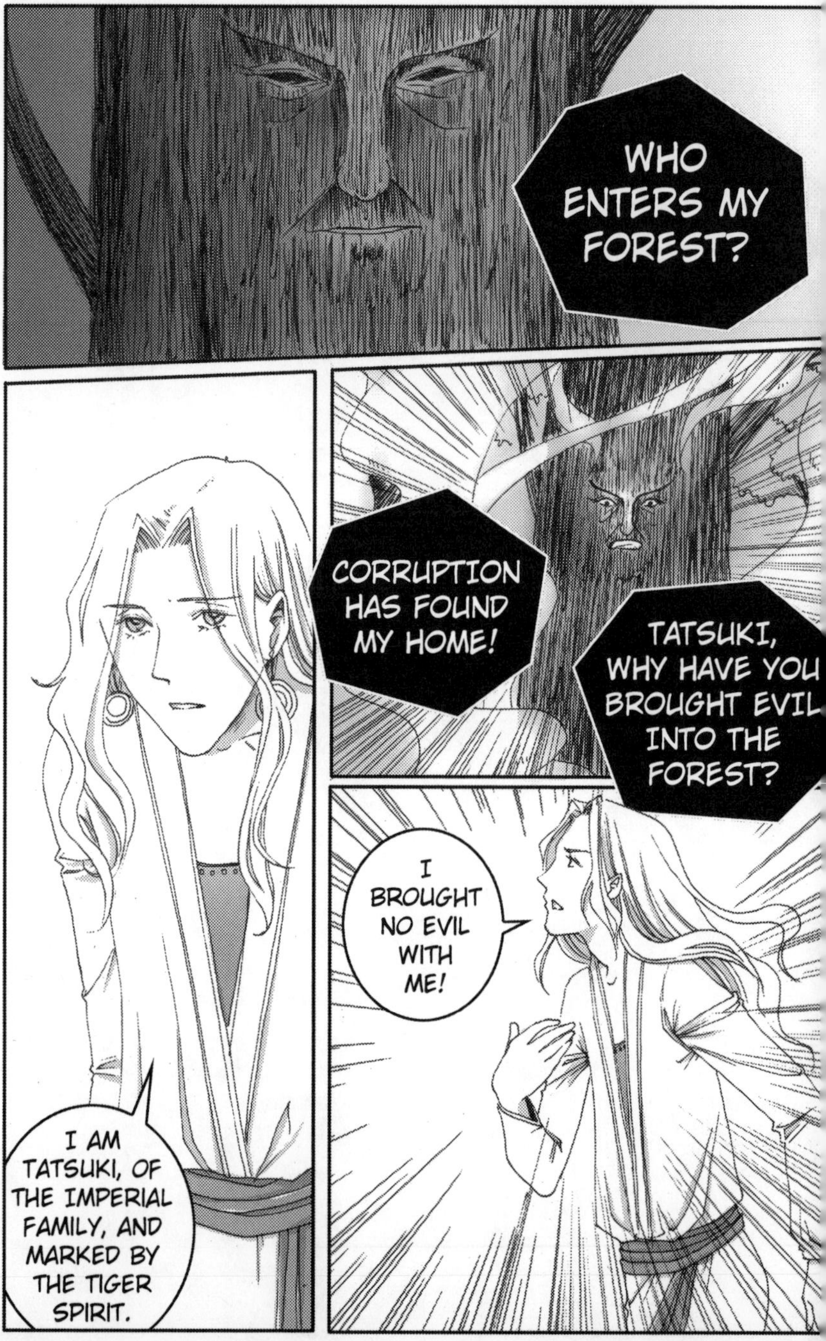
WHO ENTERS MY FOREST?
CORRUPTION HAS FOUND MY HOME!
TATSUKI, WHY HAVE YOU BROUGHT EVIL INTO THE FOREST?
I AM TATSUKI, OF THE IMPERIAL FAMILY, AND MARKED BY THE TIGER SPIRIT.
I BROUGHT NO EVIL WITH ME!

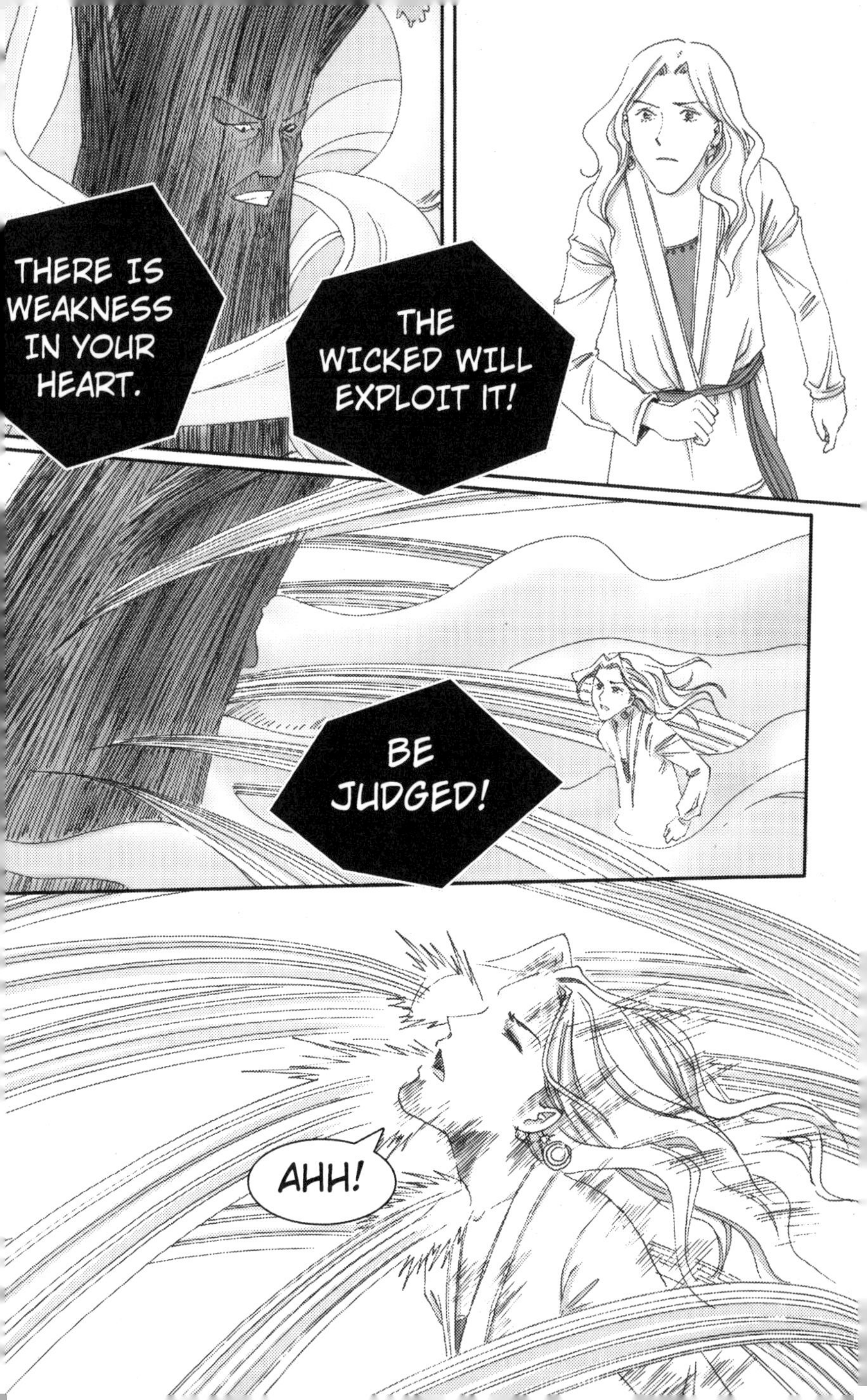
THERE IS WEAKNESS IN YOUR HEART.
THE WICKED WILL EXPLOIT IT!
BE JUDGED!
AHH!

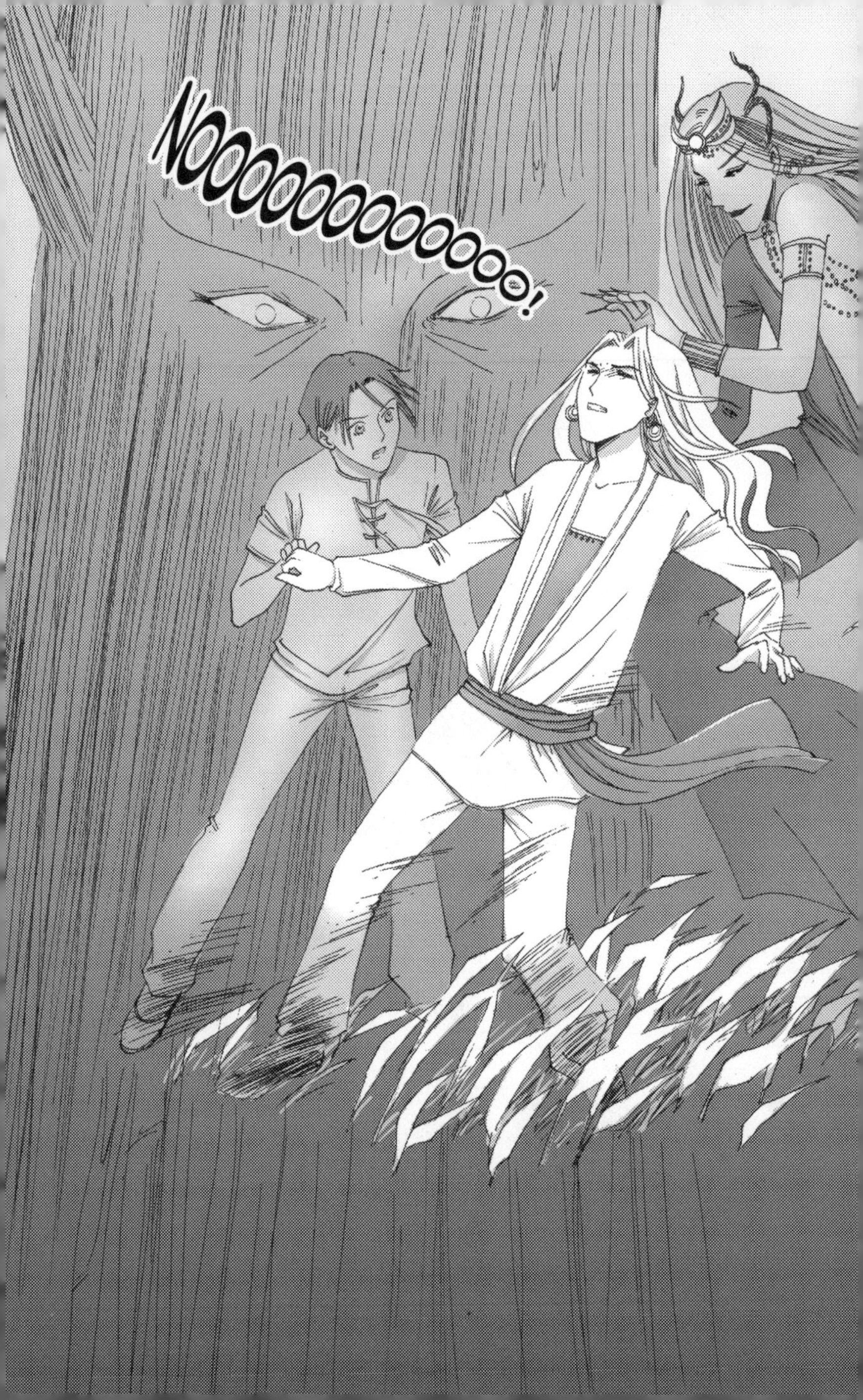
NOOOOOOOOOOOOOO!

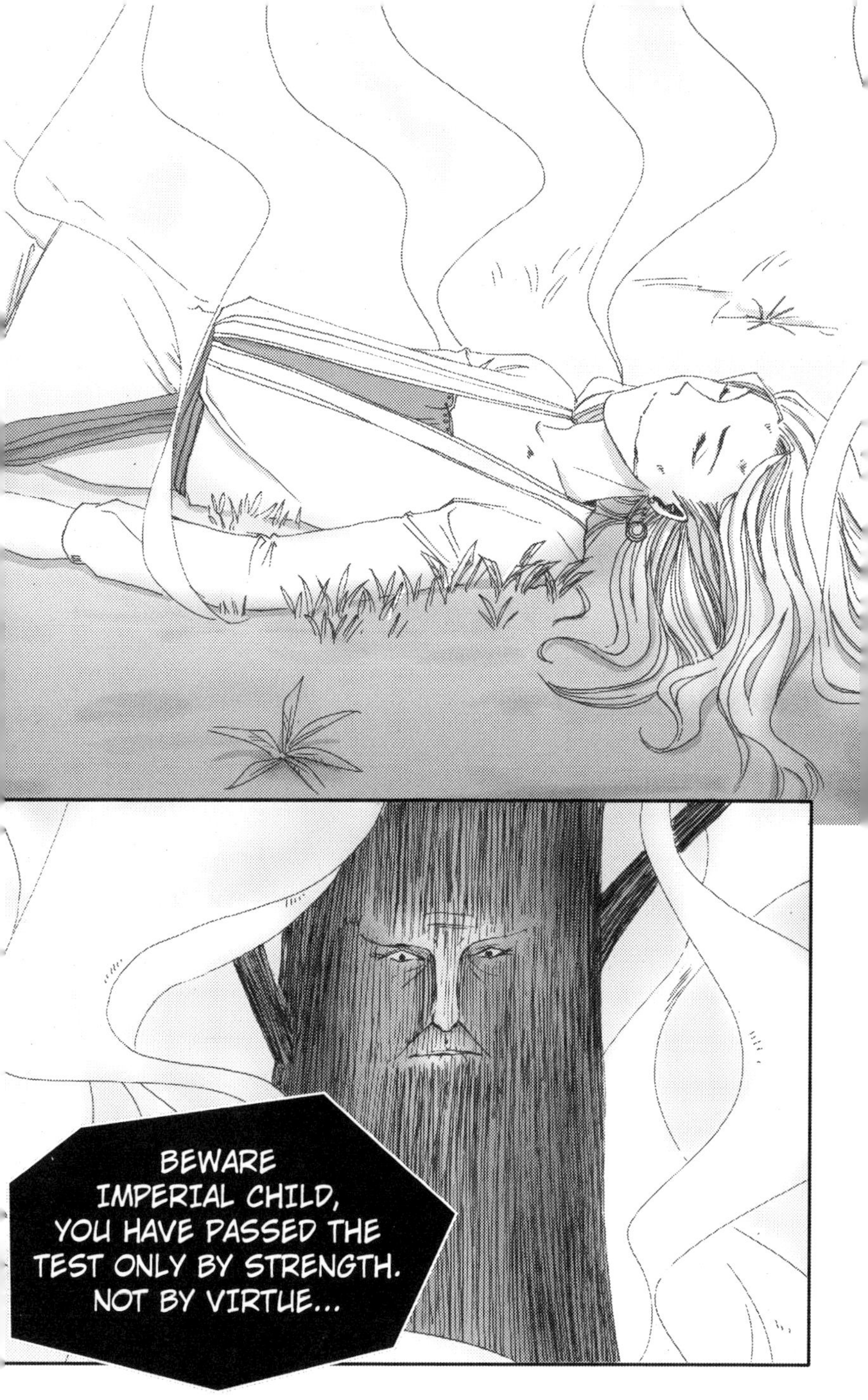
BEWARE IMPERIAL CHILD, YOU HAVE PASSED THE TEST ONLY BY STRENGTH. NOT BY VIRTUE...

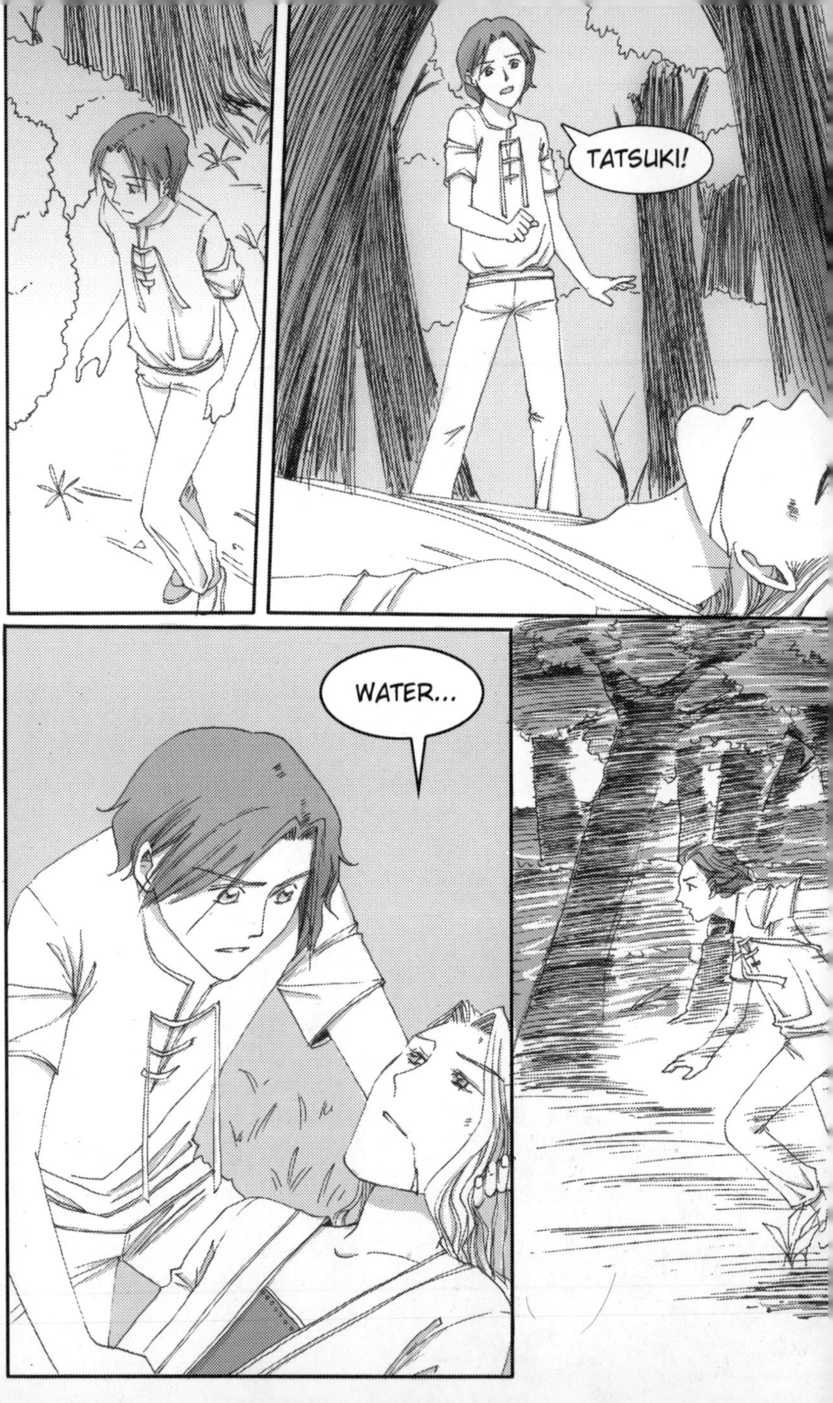
TATSUKI!
WATER...

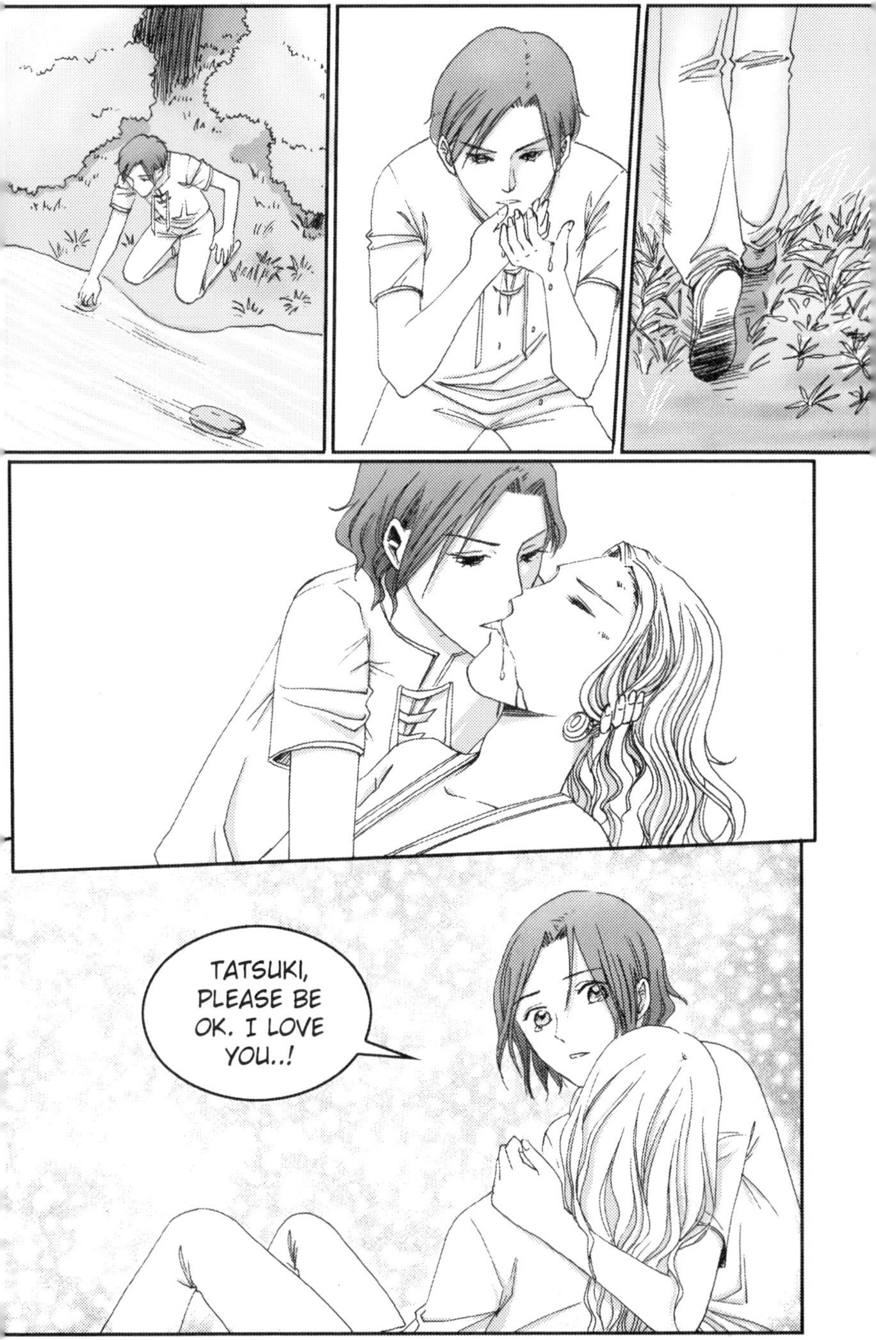
TATSUKI, PLEASE BE OK. I LOVE YOU..!

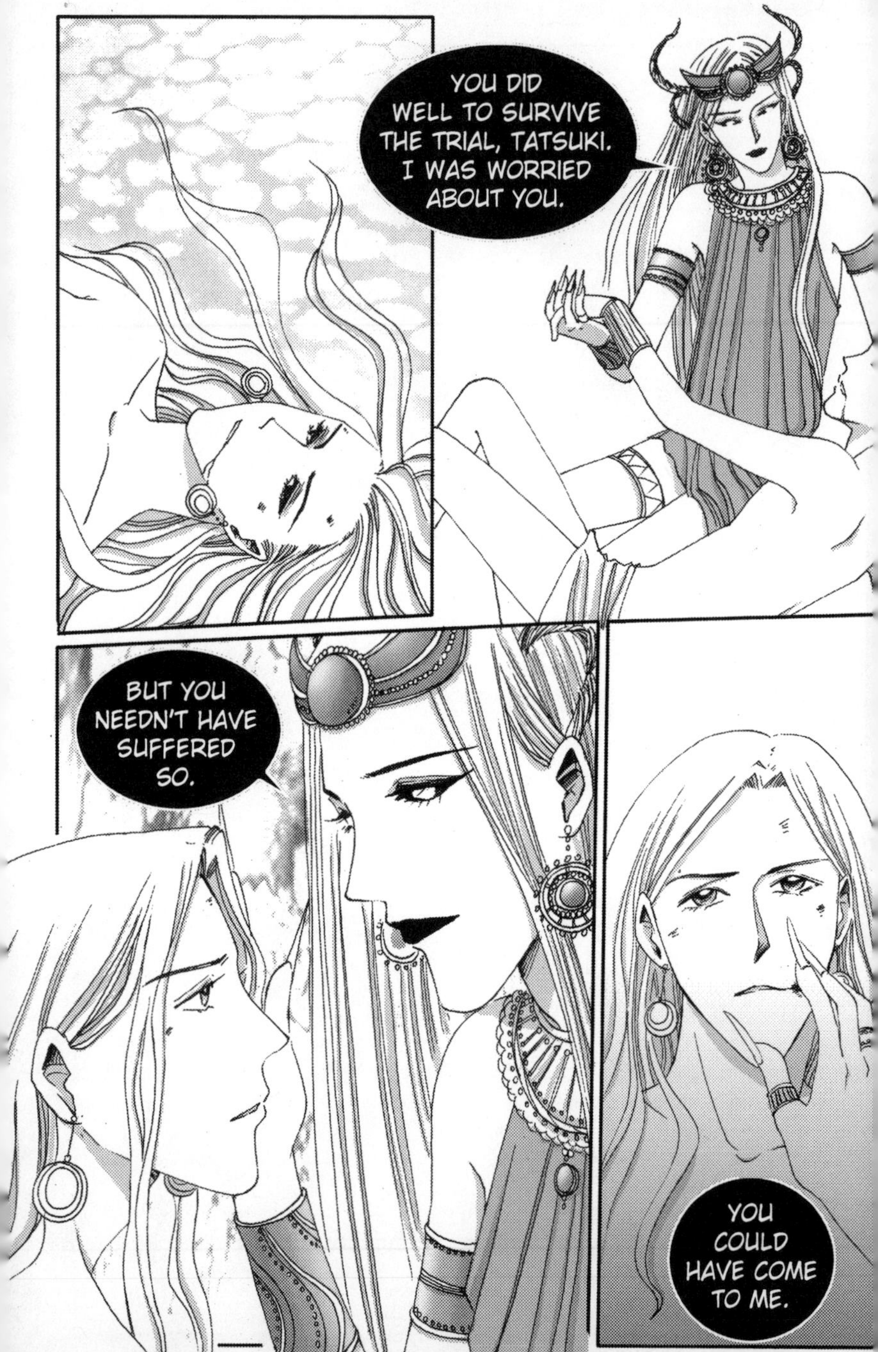
YOU DID WELL TO SURVIVE THE TRIAL, TATSUKI. I WAS WORRIED ABOUT YOU.
BUT YOU NEEDN'T HAVE SUFFERED SO.
YOU COULD HAVE COME TO ME.

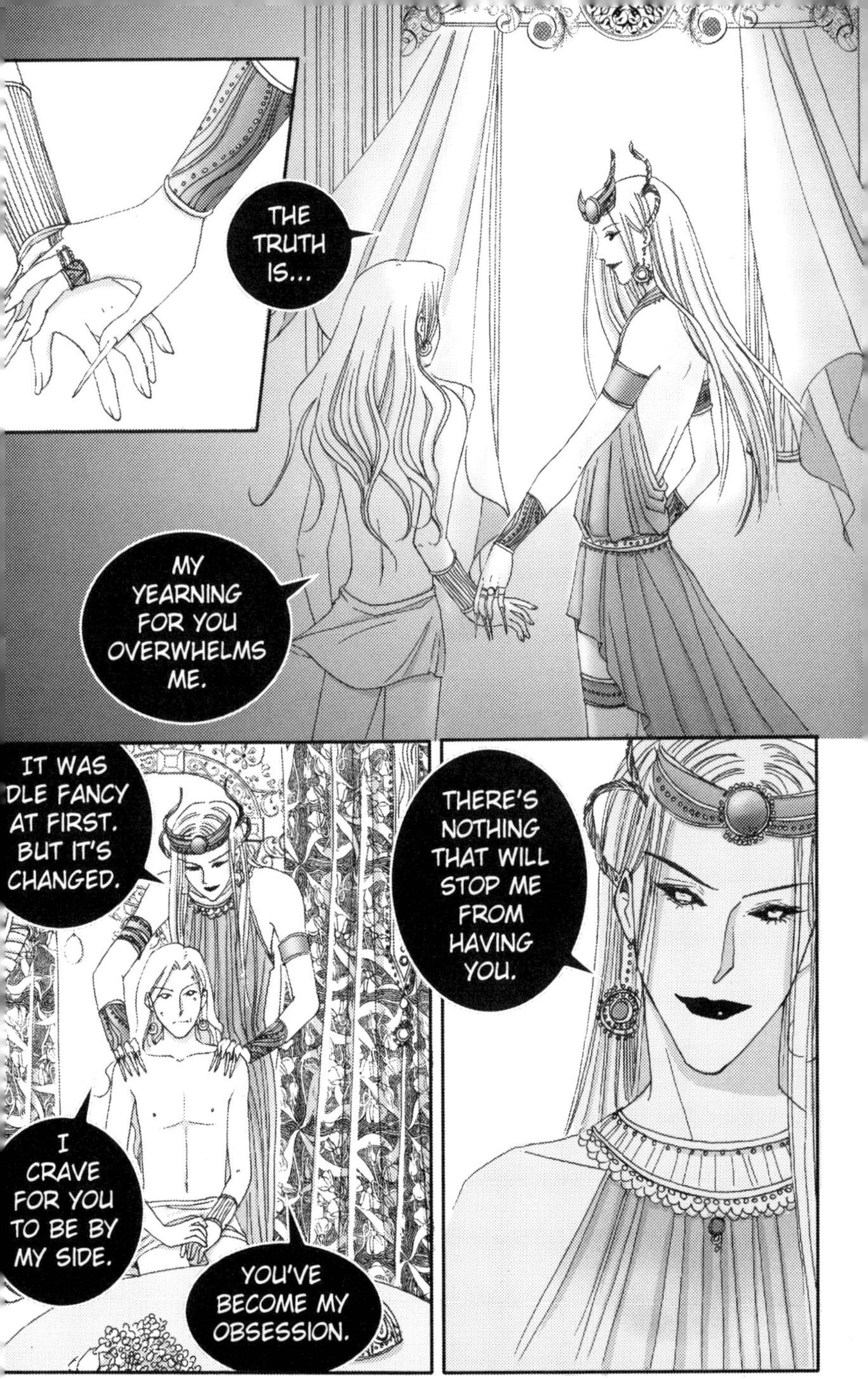
THE TRUTH IS...
MY YEARNING FOR YOU OVERWHELMS ME.
IT WAS DLE FANCY AT FIRST. BUT IT'S CHANGED.
I CRAVE FOR YOU TO BE BY MY SIDE.
YOU'VE BECOME MY OBSESSION.
THERE'S NOTHING THAT WILL STOP ME FROM HAVING YOU.

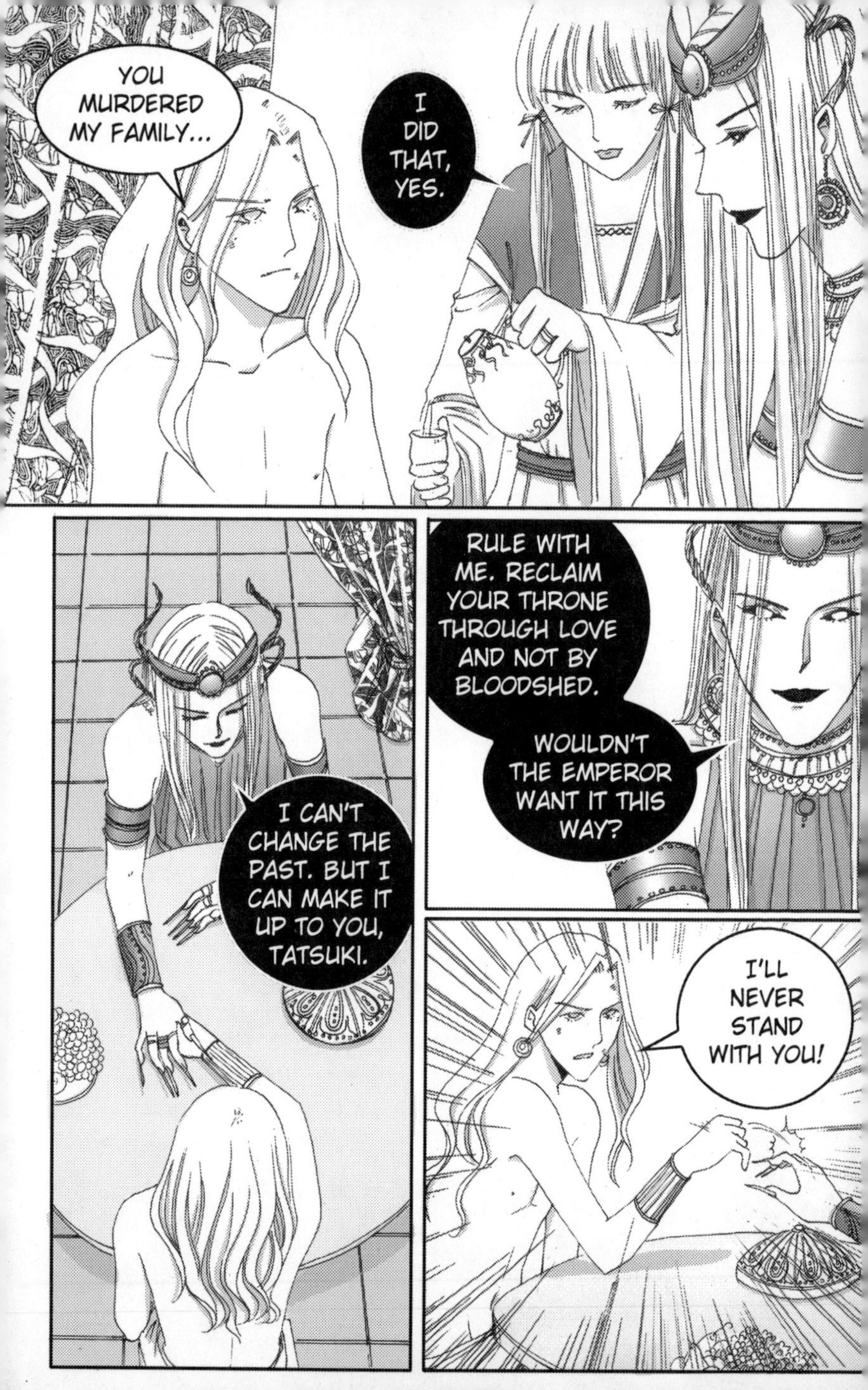
YOU MURDERED MY FAMILY...
I DID THAT, YES.
I CAN'T CHANGE THE PAST. BUT I CAN MAKE IT UP TO YOU, TATSUKI.
RULE WITH ME. RECLAIM YOUR THRONE THROUGH LOVE AND NOT BY BLOODSHED.
WOULDN'T THE EMPEROR WANT IT THIS WAY?
I'LL NEVER STAND WITH YOU!

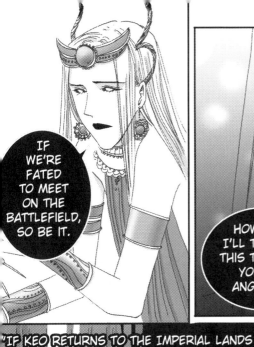

IF WE'RE FATED TO MEET ON THE BATTLEFIELD, SO BE IT.

HOWEVER, I'LL TELL YOU THIS TO SPARE YOU THE ANGUISH...

"IF KEO RETURNS TO THE IMPERIAL LANDS WITH YOU, HE'LL BE KILLED.

"I SEE HIM AS A RIVAL. I'LL MAKE CERTAIN MY FORCES TARGET HIM ESPECIALLY."

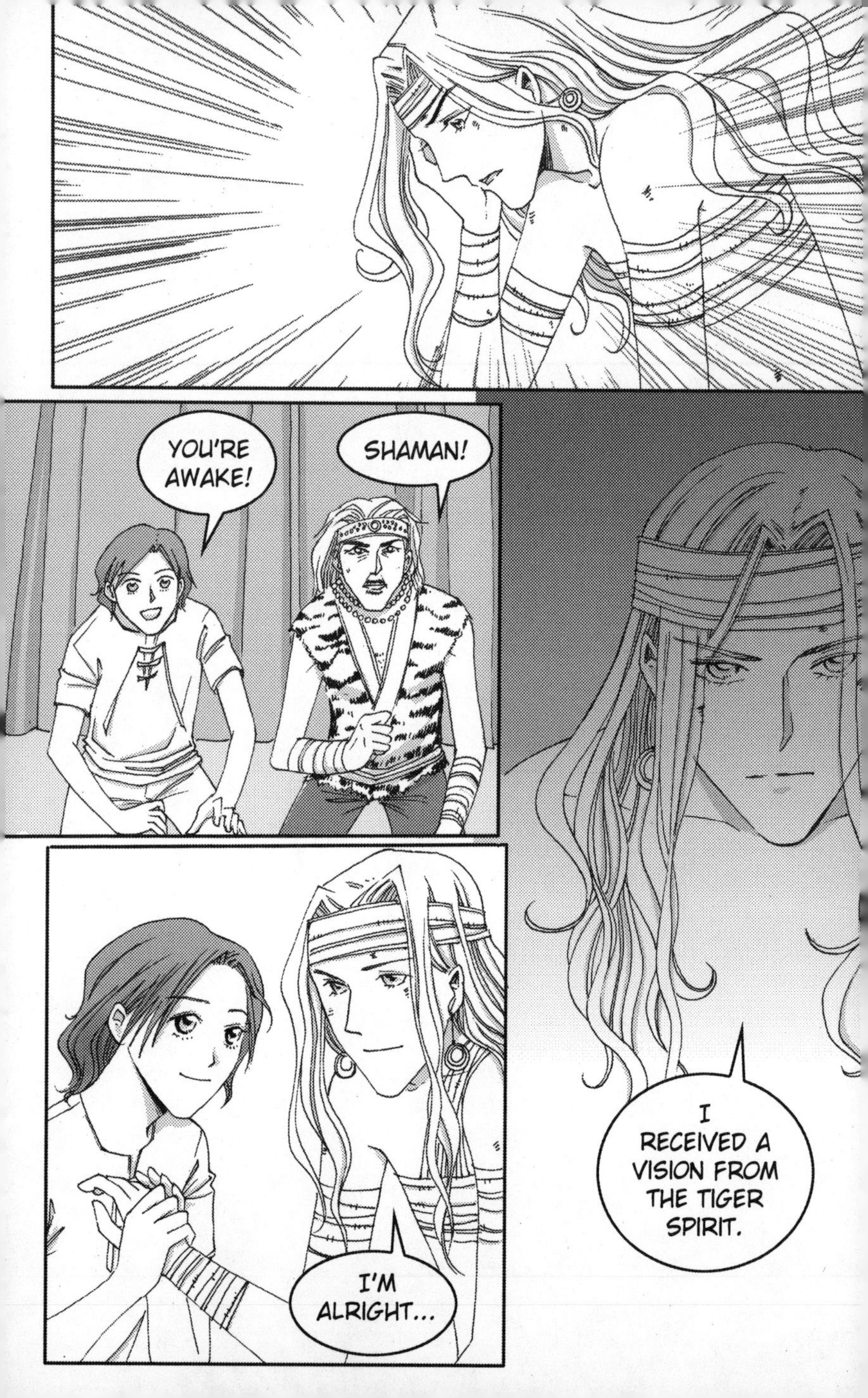
YOU'RE AWAKE!
SHAMAN!
I'M ALRIGHT...
I RECEIVED A VISION FROM THE TIGER SPIRIT.

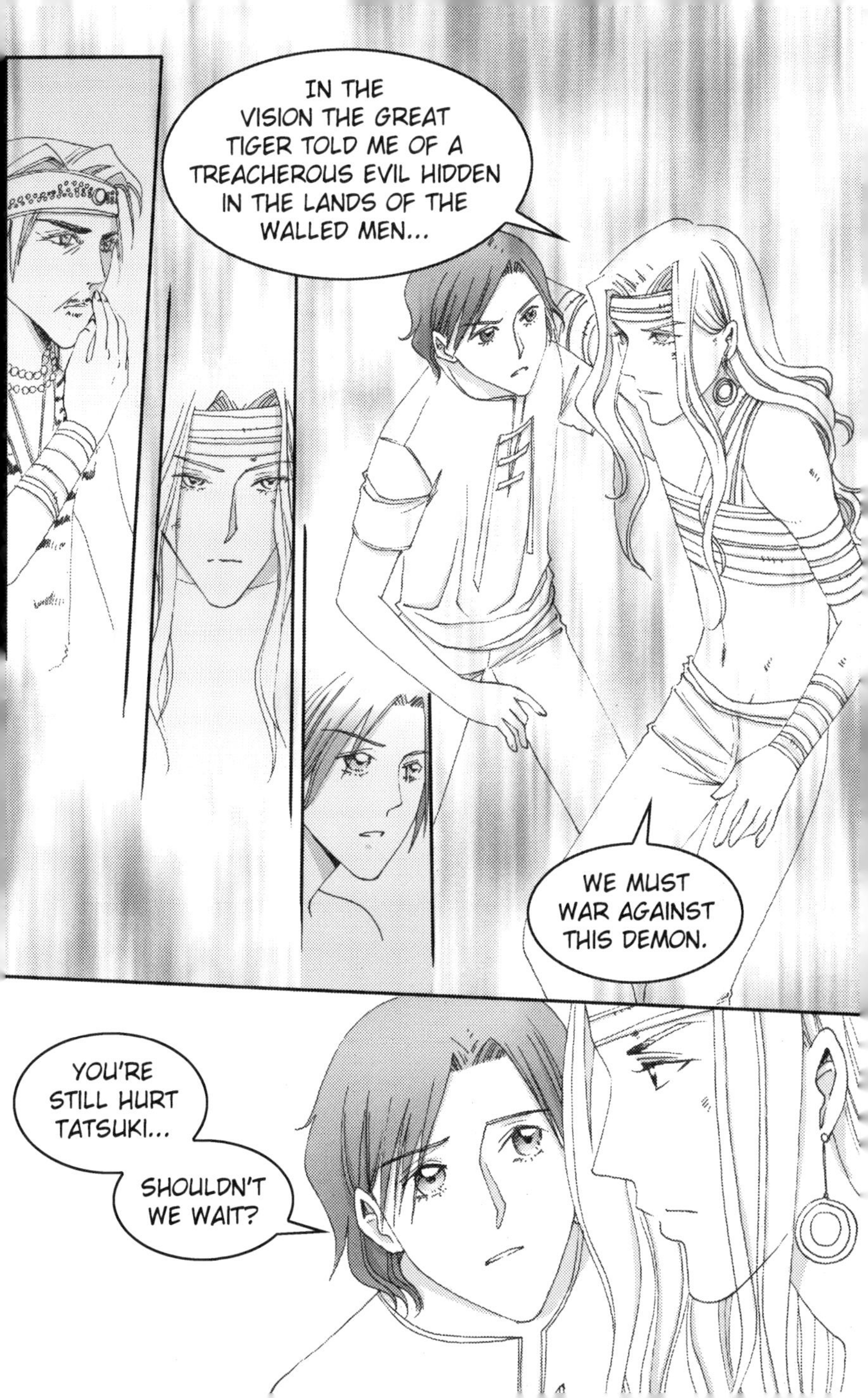
IN THE VISION THE GREAT TIGER TOLD ME OF A TREACHEROUS EVIL HIDDEN IN THE LANDS OF THE WALLED MEN...
WE MUST WAR AGAINST THIS DEMON.
YOU'RE STILL HURT TATSUKI...
SHOULDN'T WE WAIT?

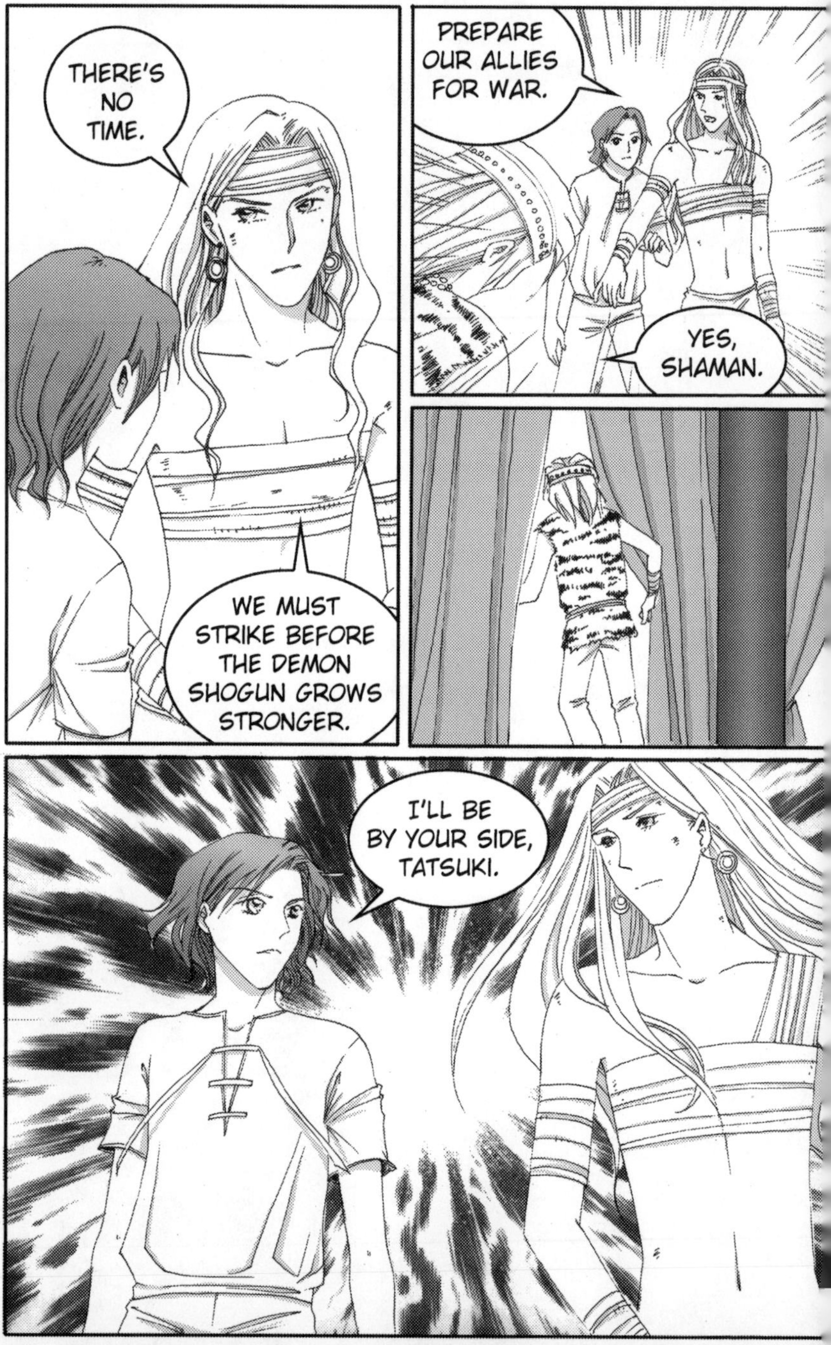
THERE'S NO TIME.
WE MUST STRIKE BEFORE THE DEMON SHOGUN GROWS STRONGER.
PREPARE OUR ALLIES FOR WAR.
YES, SHAMAN.
I'LL BE BY YOUR SIDE, TATSUKI.

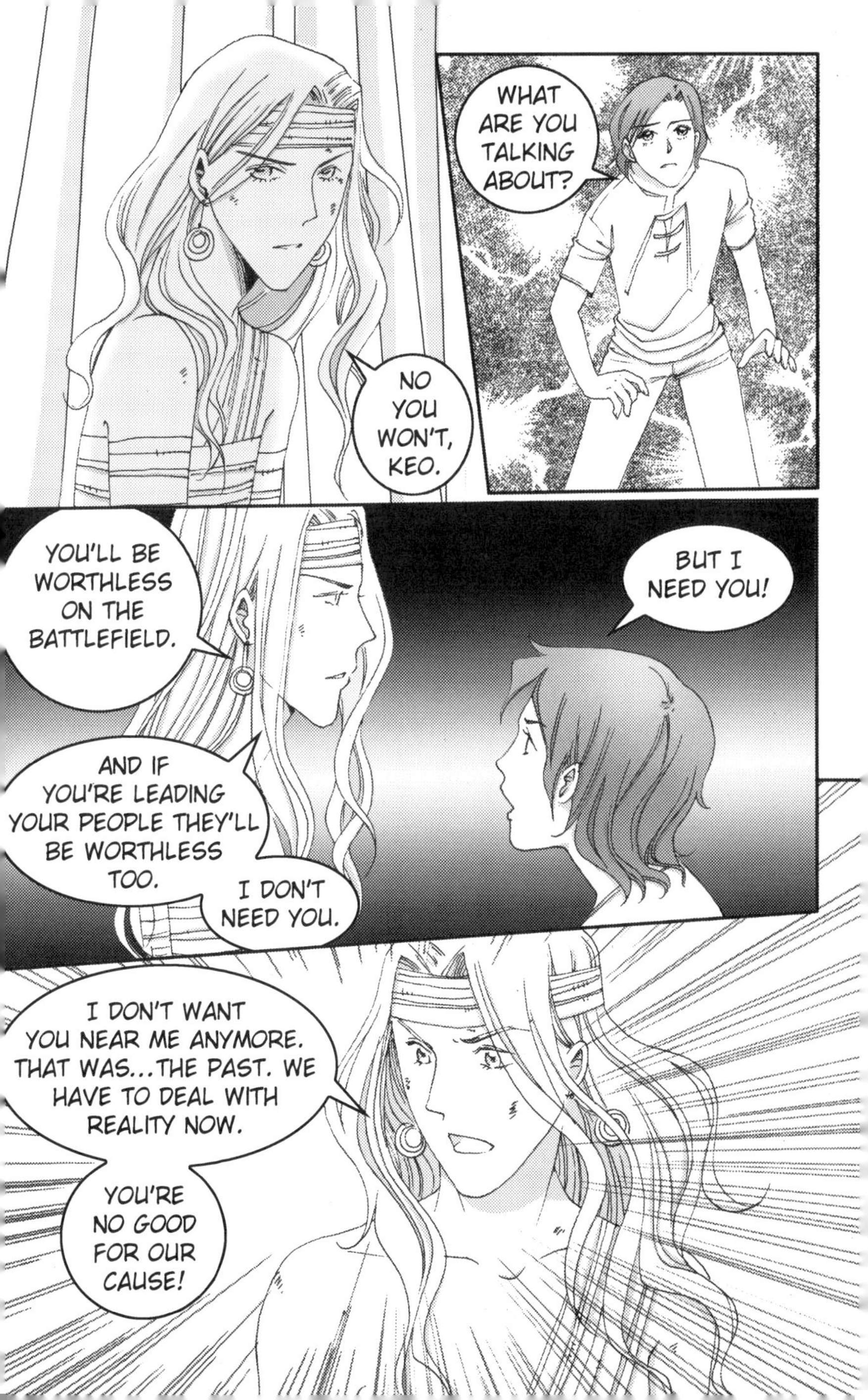
WHAT ARE YOU TALKING ABOUT?
NO YOU WON'T, KEO.
YOU'LL BE WORTHLESS ON THE BATTLEFIELD.
BUT I NEED YOU!
AND IF YOU'RE LEADING YOUR PEOPLE THEY'LL BE WORTHLESS TOO.
I DON'T NEED YOU.
I DON'T WANT YOU NEAR ME ANYMORE. THAT WAS...THE PAST. WE HAVE TO DEAL WITH REALITY NOW.
YOU'RE NO GOOD FOR OUR CAUSE!

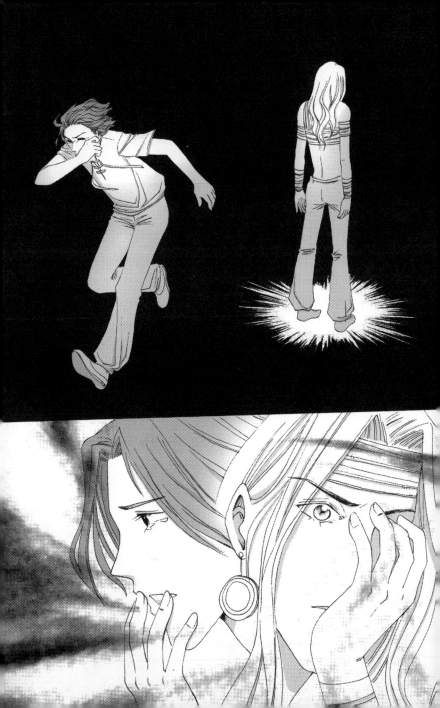

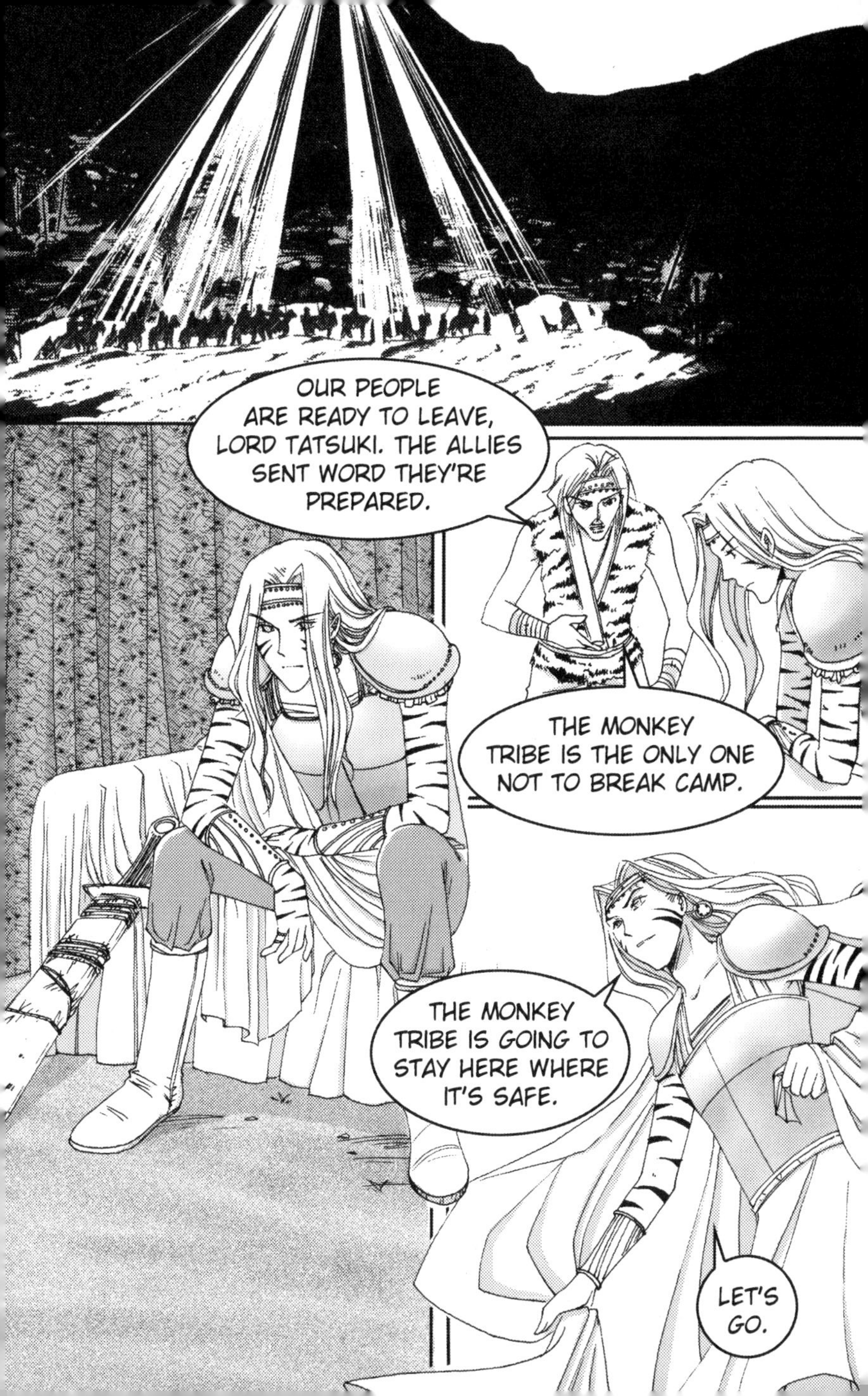
OUR PEOPLE ARE READY TO LEAVE, LORD TATSUKI. THE ALLIES SENT WORD THEY'RE PREPARED.
THE MONKEY TRIBE IS THE ONLY ONE NOT TO BREAK CAMP.
THE MONKEY TRIBE IS GOING TO STAY HERE WHERE IT'S SAFE.
LET'S GO.

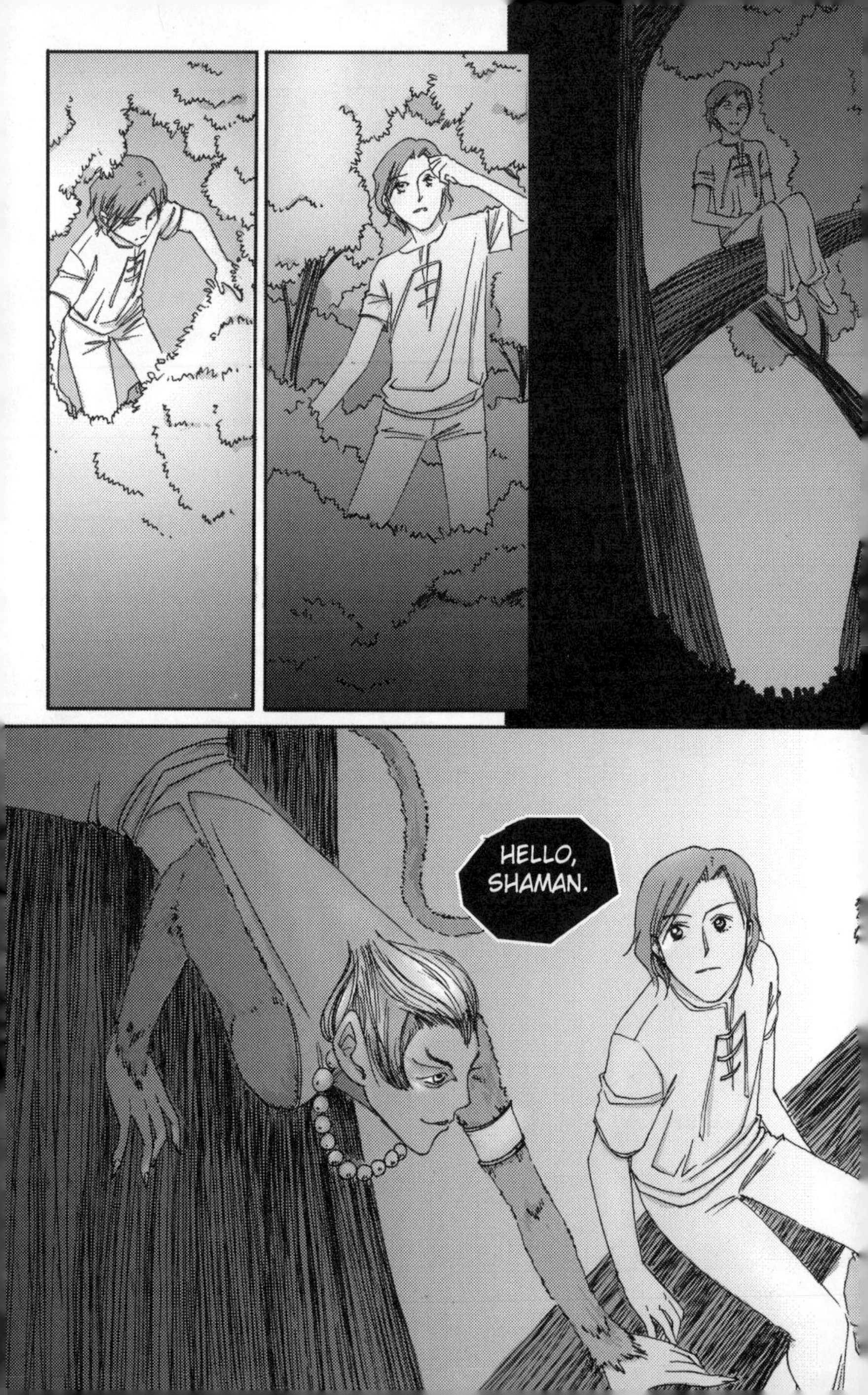
HELLO, SHAMAN.

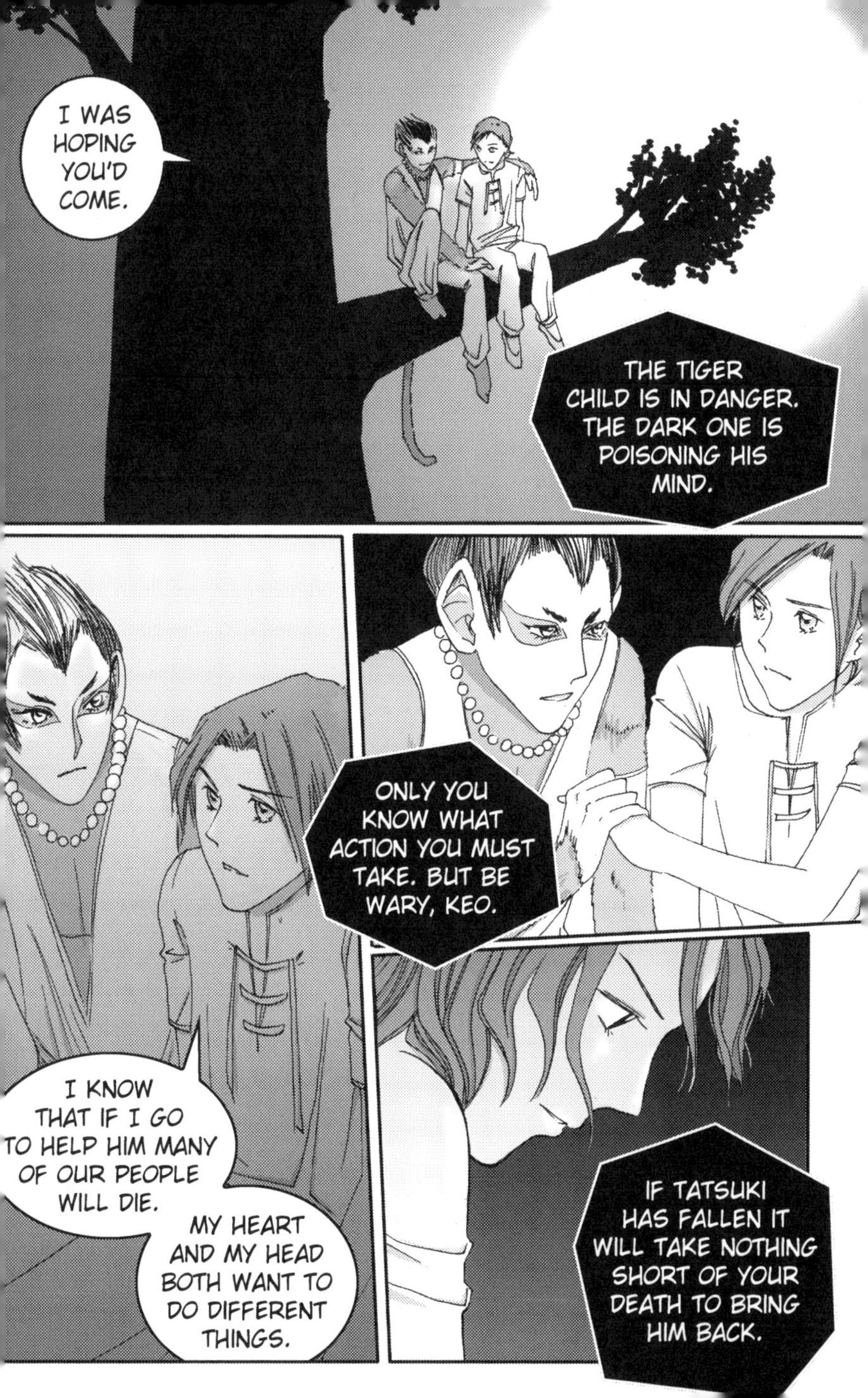
I WAS HOPING YOU'D COME.
THE TIGER CHILD IS IN DANGER. THE DARK ONE IS POISONING HIS MIND.
I KNOW THAT IF I GO TO HELP HIM MANY OF OUR PEOPLE WILL DIE.
MY HEART AND MY HEAD BOTH WANT TO DO DIFFERENT THINGS.
ONLY YOU KNOW WHAT ACTION YOU MUST TAKE. BUT BE WARY, KEO.
IF TATSUKI HAS FALLEN IT WILL TAKE NOTHING SHORT OF YOUR DEATH TO BRING HIM BACK.

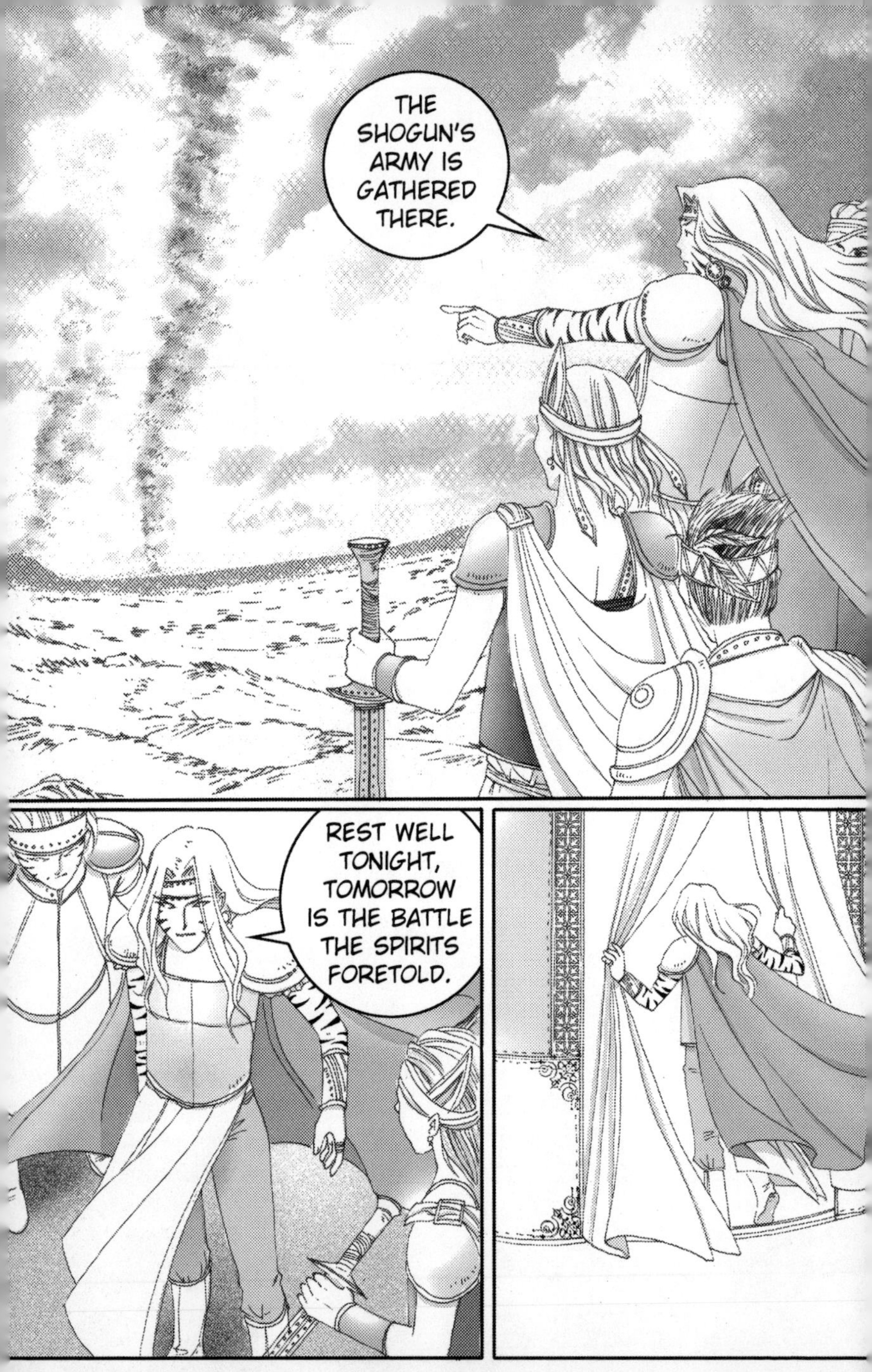
THE SHOGUN'S ARMY IS GATHERED THERE.
REST WELL TONIGHT, TOMORROW IS THE BATTLE THE SPIRITS FORETOLD.

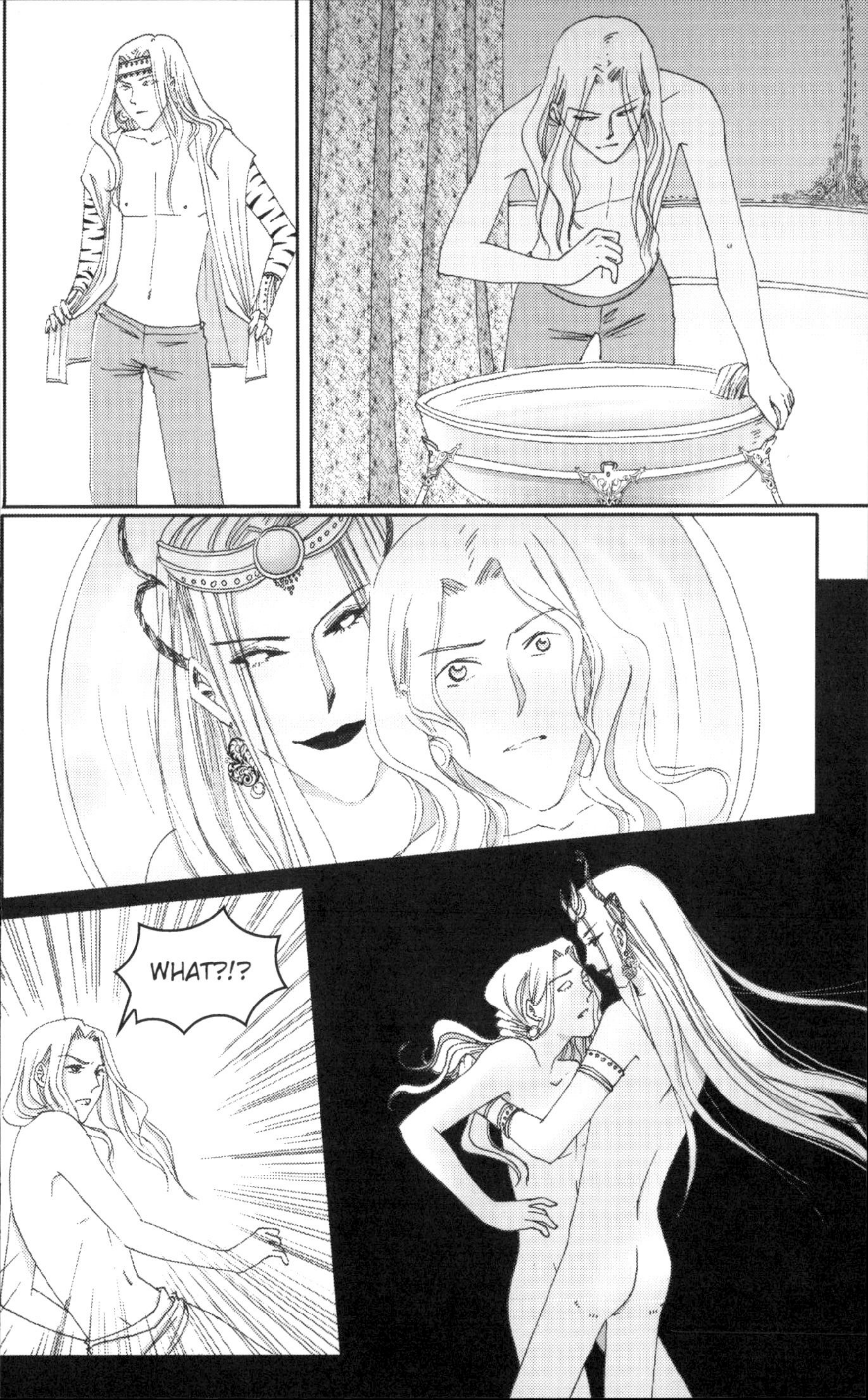
WHAT?!?

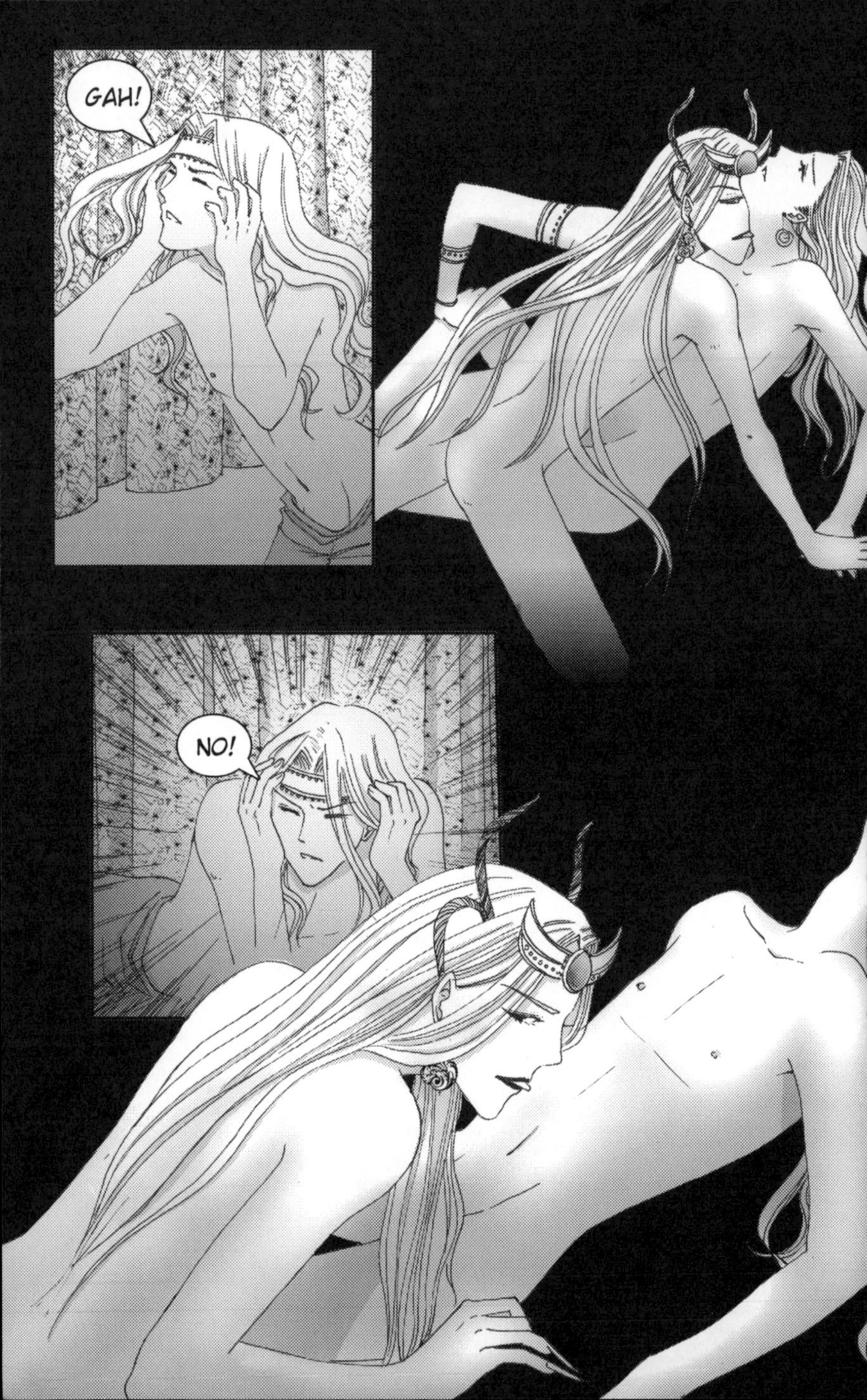
GAH!
NO!

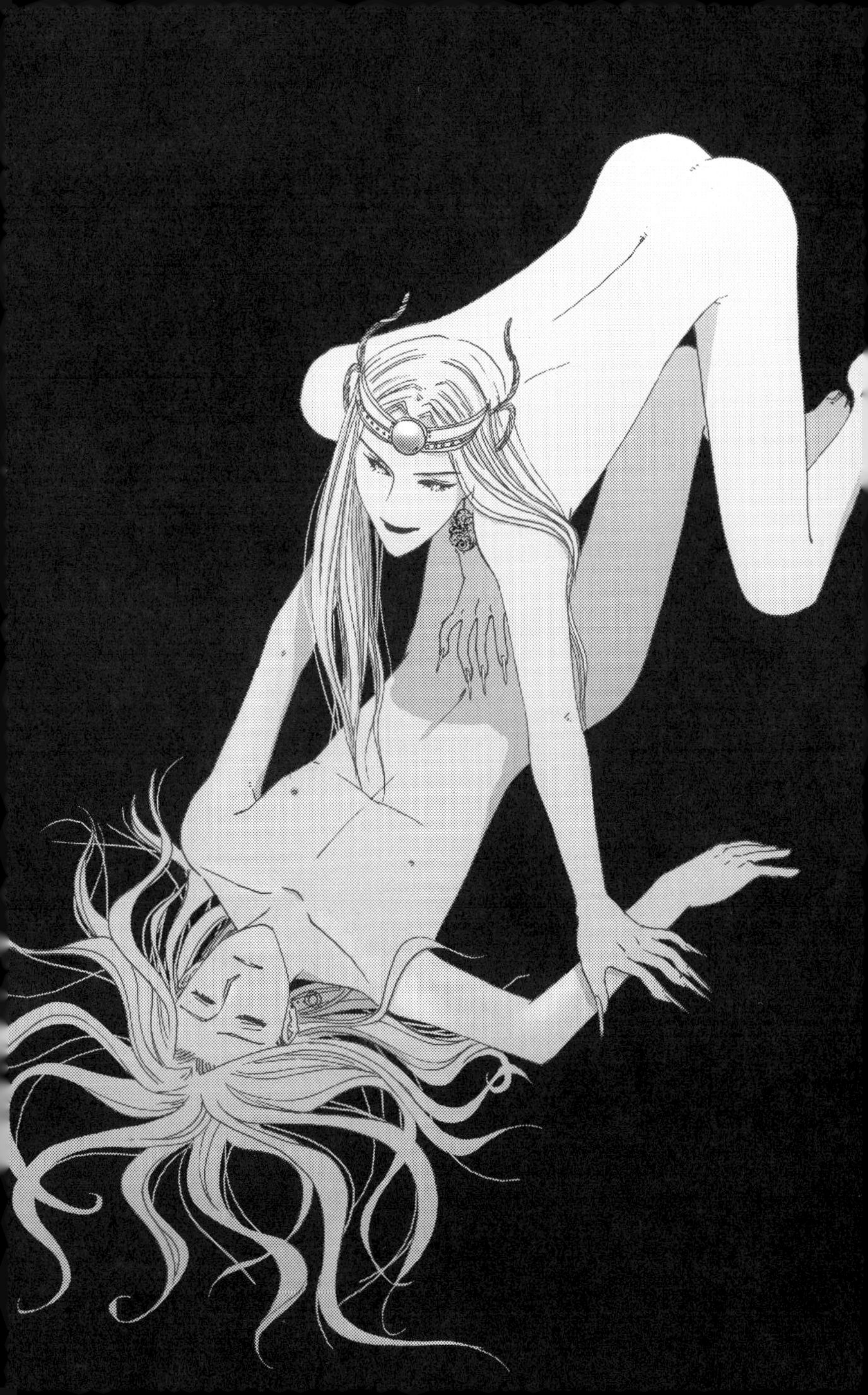

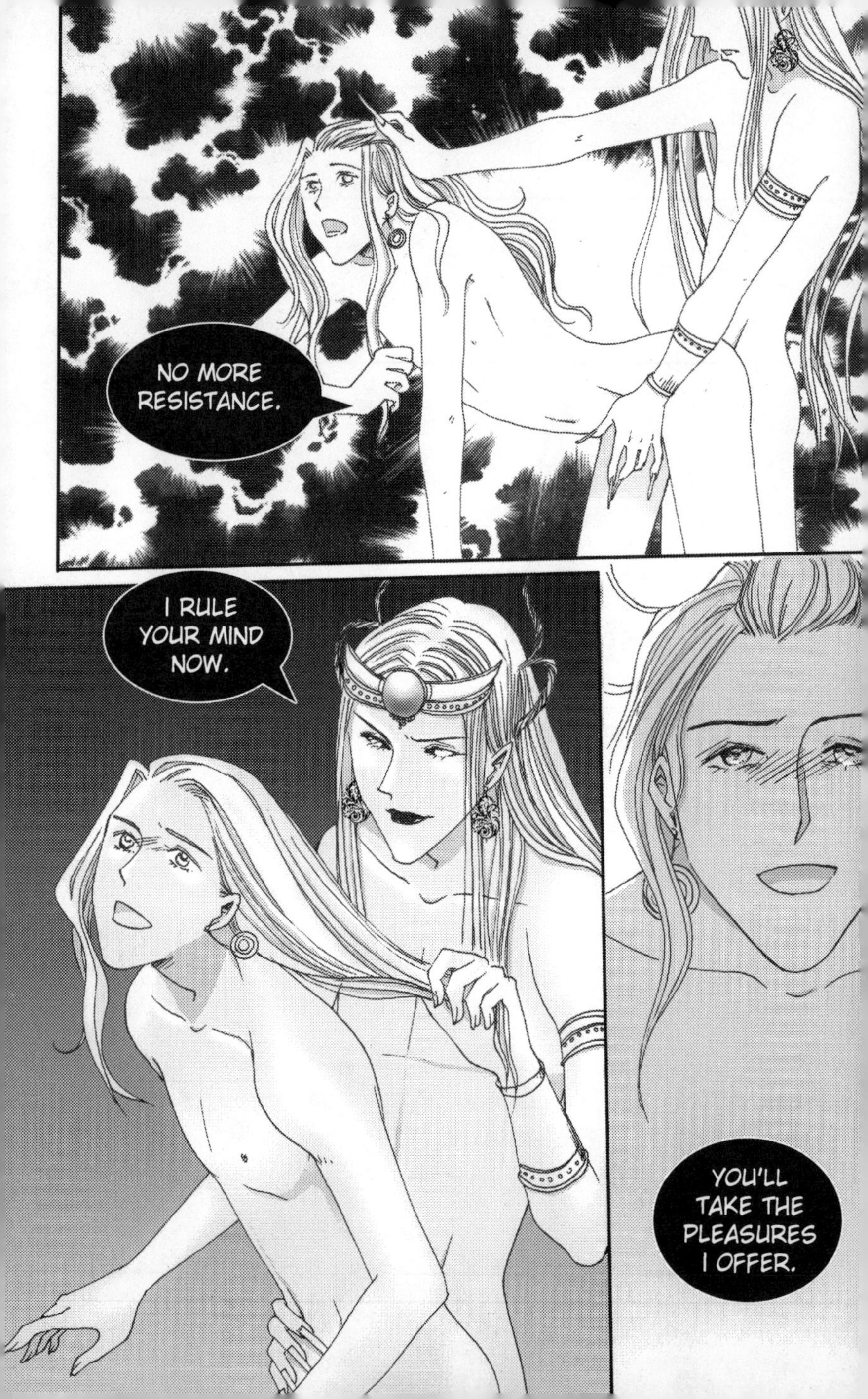
NO MORE RESISTANCE.
I RULE YOUR MIND NOW.
YOU'LL TAKE THE PLEASURES I OFFER.

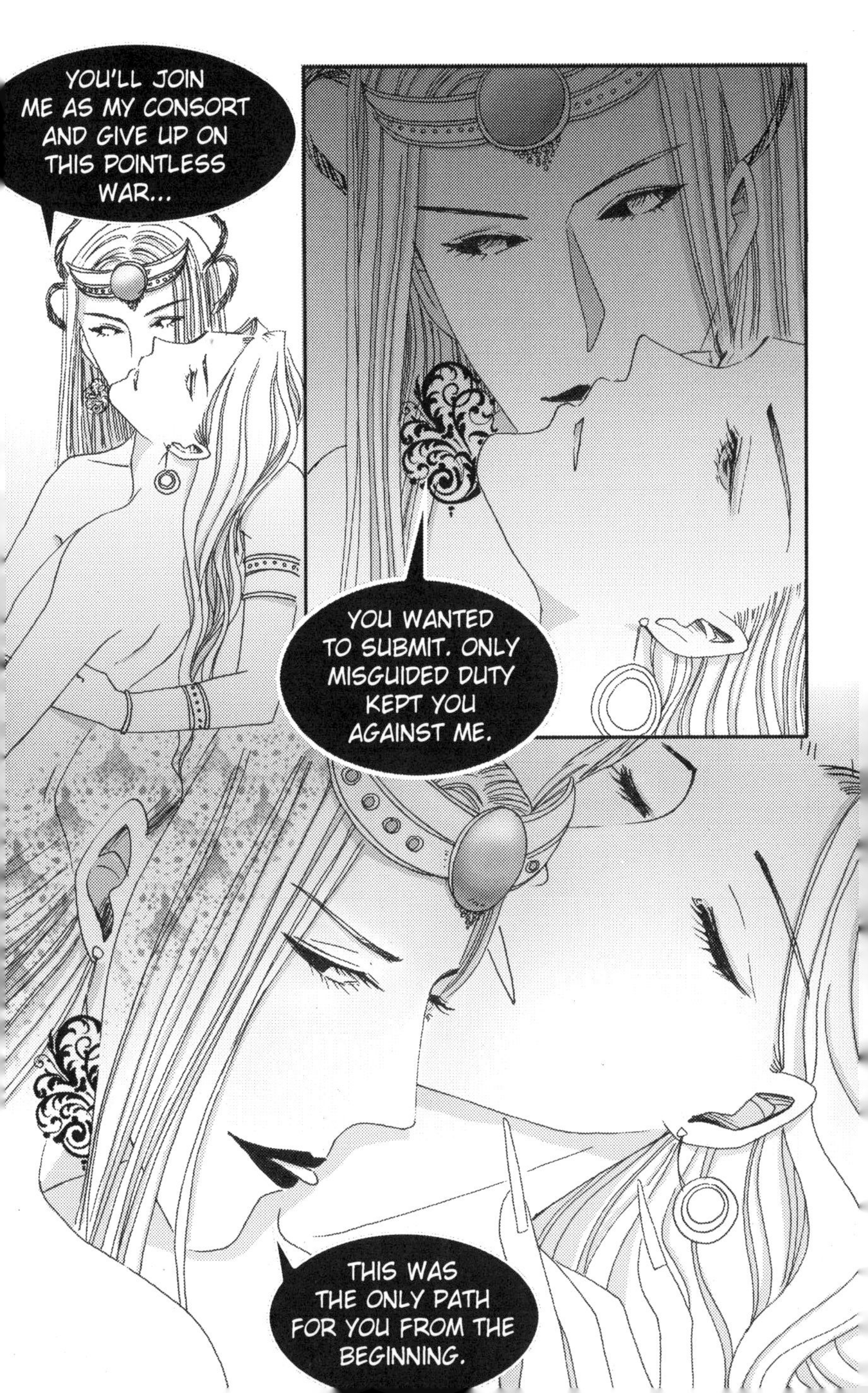
YOU'LL JOIN ME AS MY CONSORT AND GIVE UP ON THIS POINTLESS WAR...
YOU WANTED TO SUBMIT. ONLY MISGUIDED DUTY KEPT YOU AGAINST ME.
THIS WAS THE ONLY PATH FOR YOU FROM THE BEGINNING.

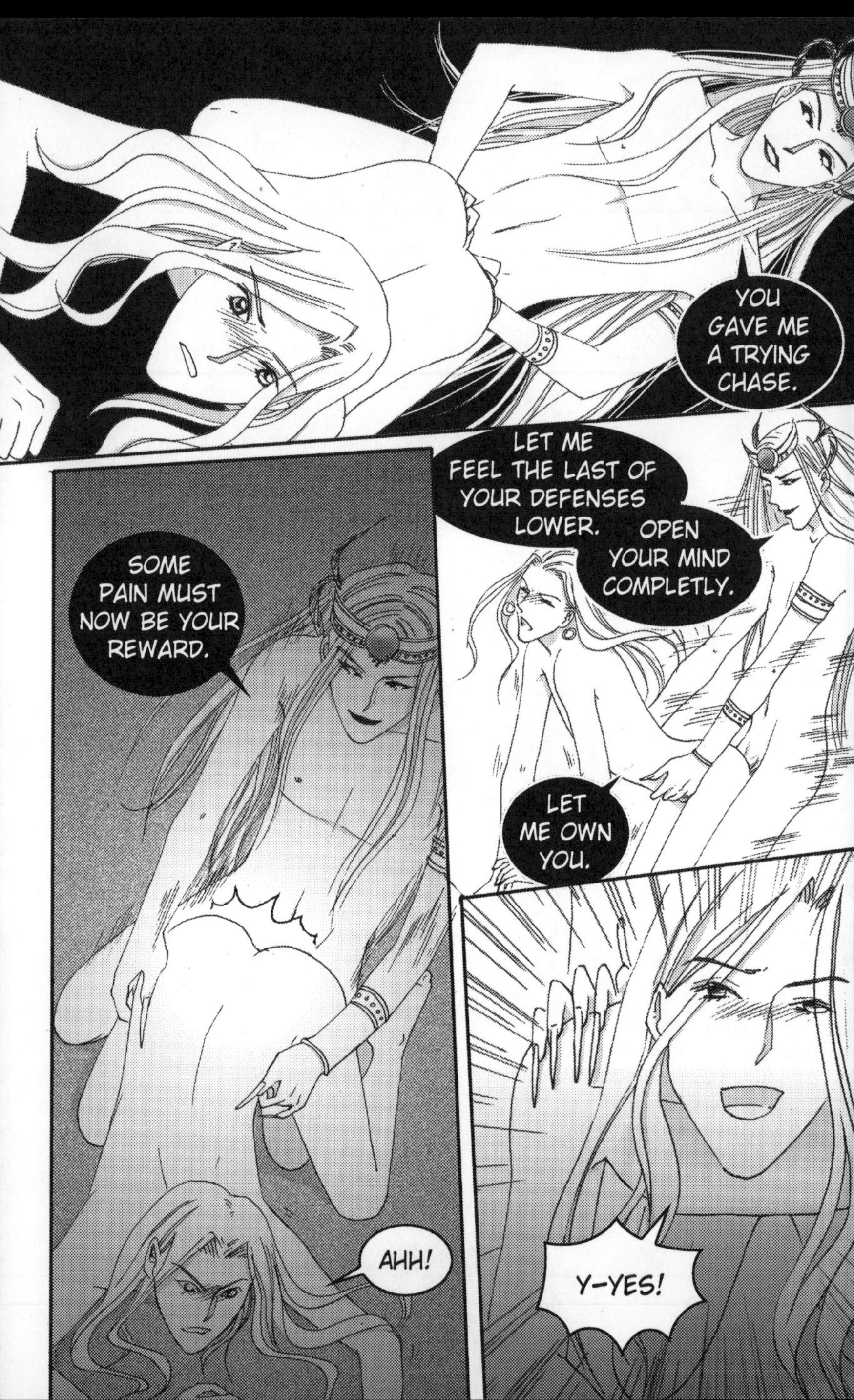

YOU GAVE ME A TRYING CHASE.
LET ME FEEL THE LAST OF YOUR DEFENSES LOWER.
OPEN YOUR MIND COMPLETLY.
LET ME OWN YOU.
SOME PAIN MUST NOW BE YOUR REWARD.
AHH!
Y-YES!

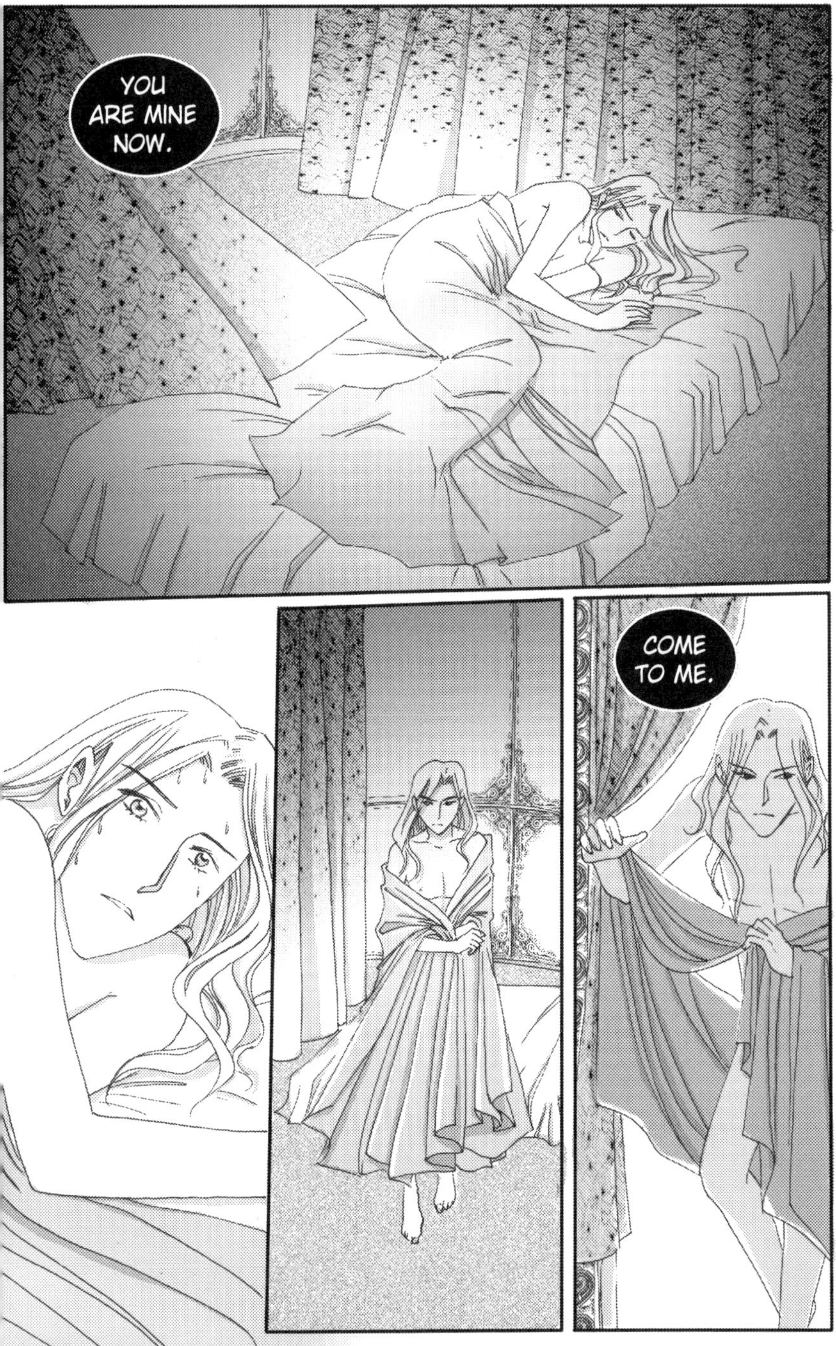
YOU ARE MINE NOW.
COME TO ME.

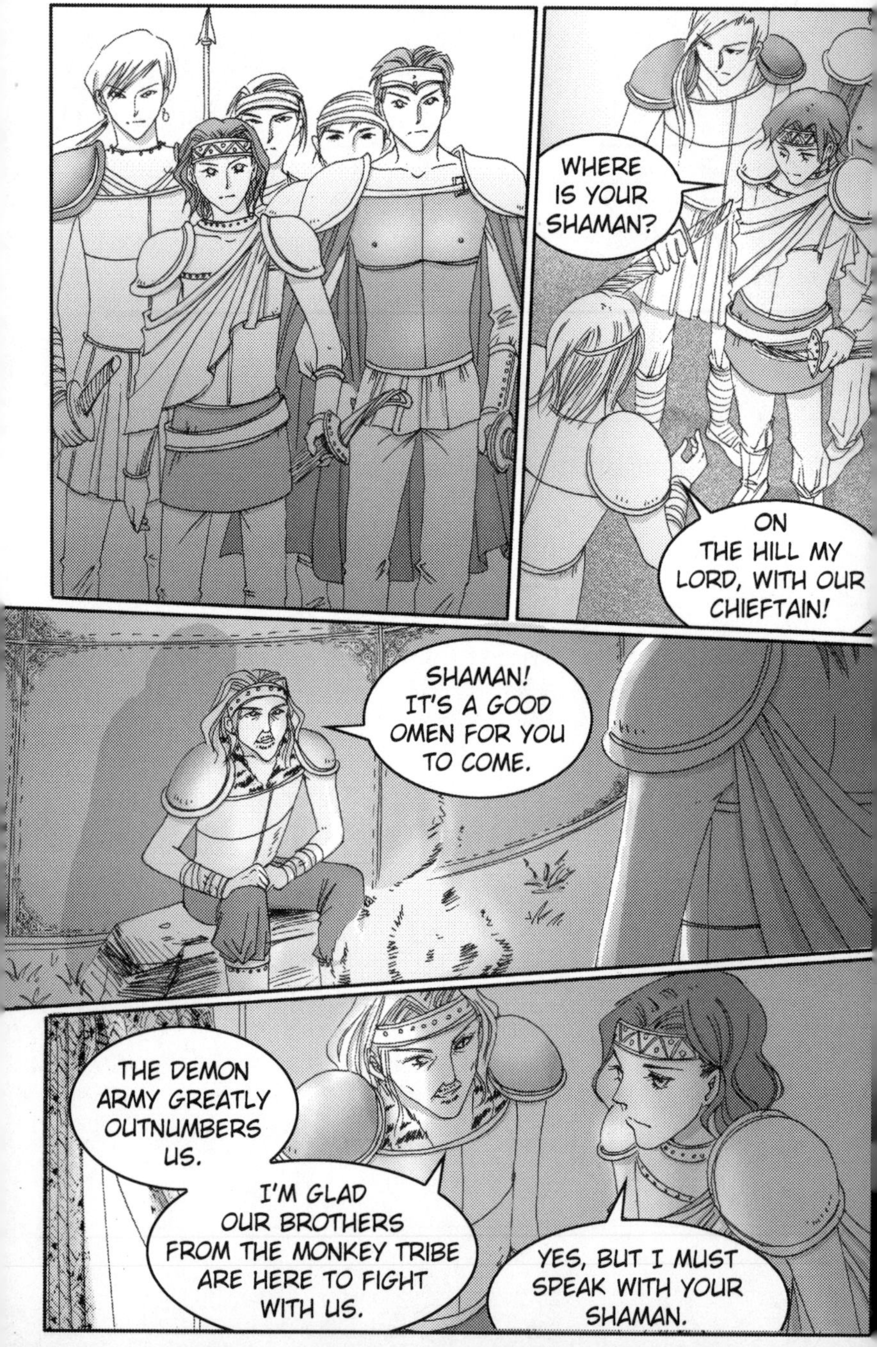
WHERE IS YOUR SHAMAN?
ON THE HILL MY LORD, WITH OUR CHIEFTAIN!
SHAMAN! IT'S A GOOD OMEN FOR YOU TO COME.
THE DEMON ARMY GREATLY OUTNUMBERS US.
I'M GLAD OUR BROTHERS FROM THE MONKEY TRIBE ARE HERE TO FIGHT WITH US.
YES, BUT I MUST SPEAK WITH YOUR SHAMAN.

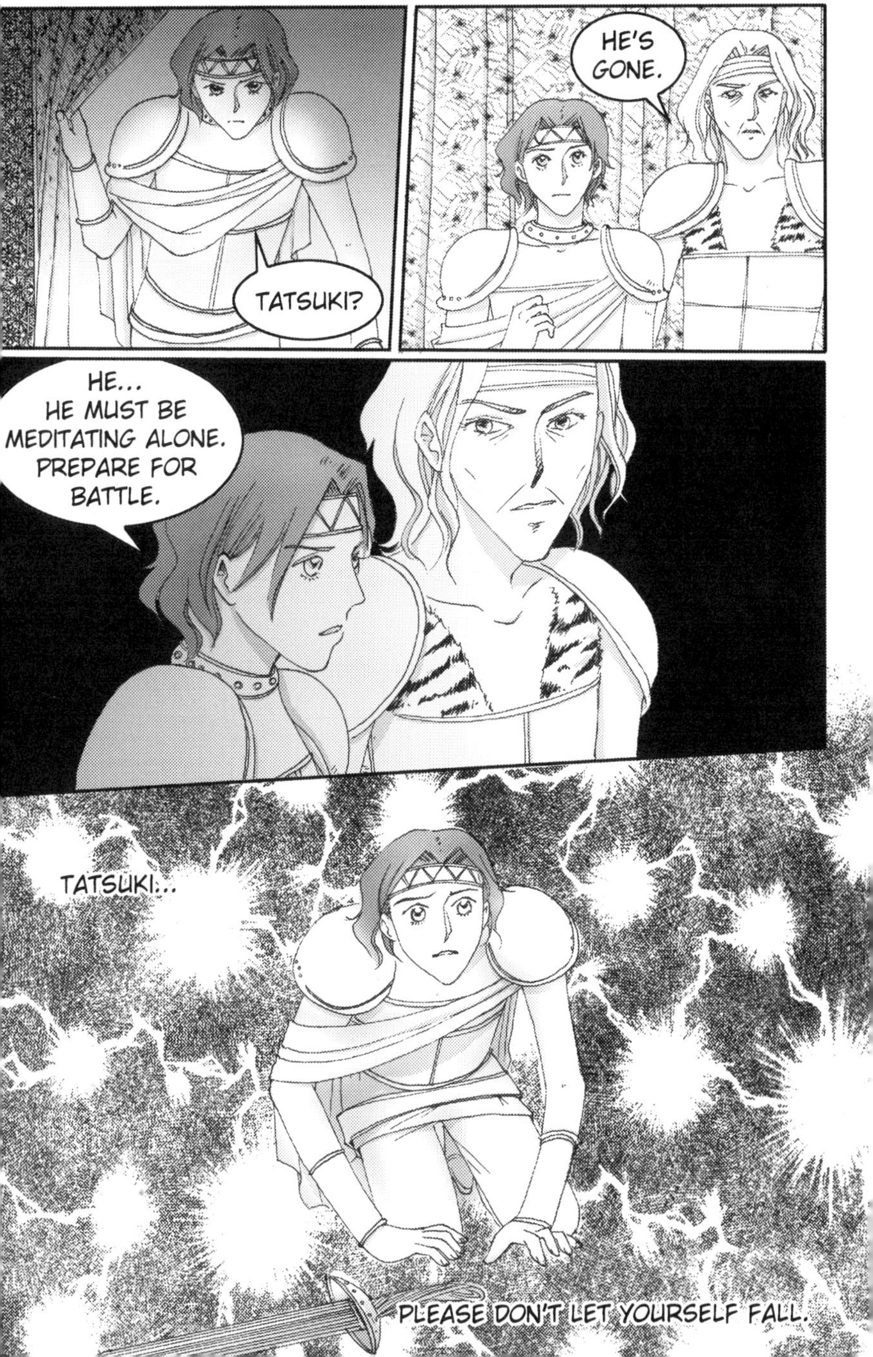
TATSUKI?
HE'S GONE.
HE... HE MUST BE MEDITATING ALONE. PREPARE FOR BATTLE.
TATSUKI...
PLEASE DON'T LET YOURSELF FALL.

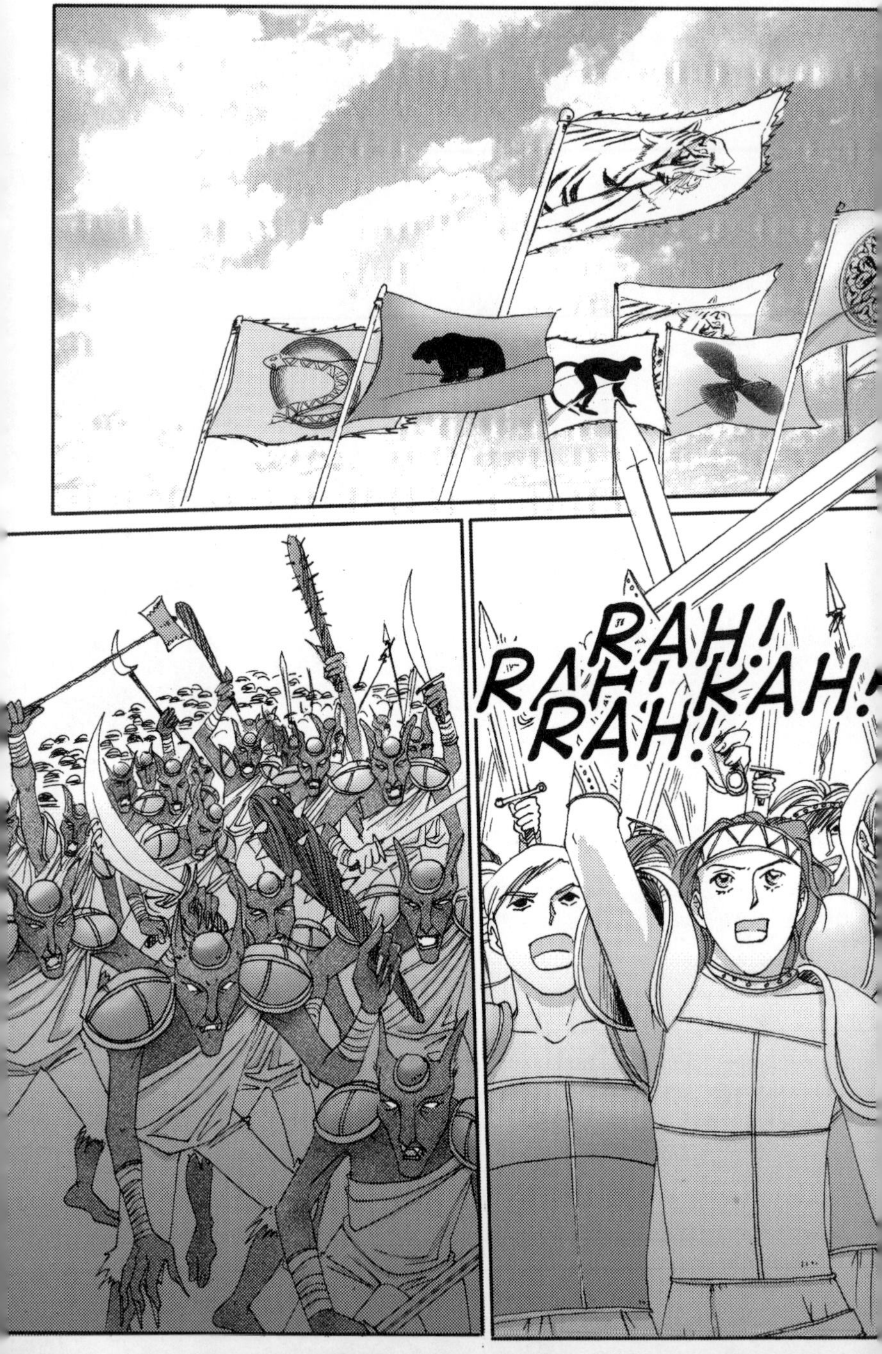
RAH! RAH! RAH! RAH!

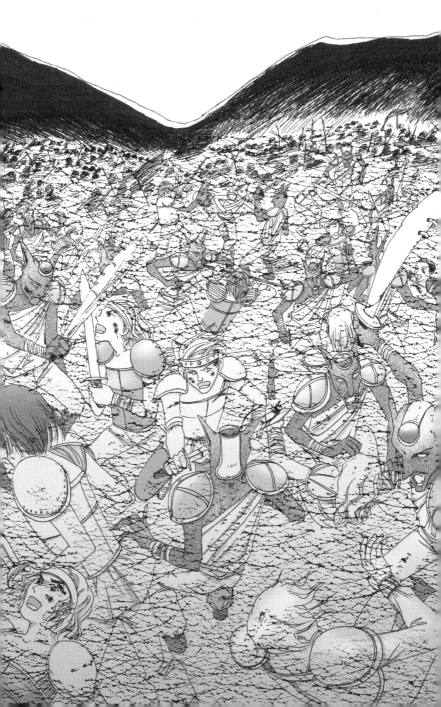

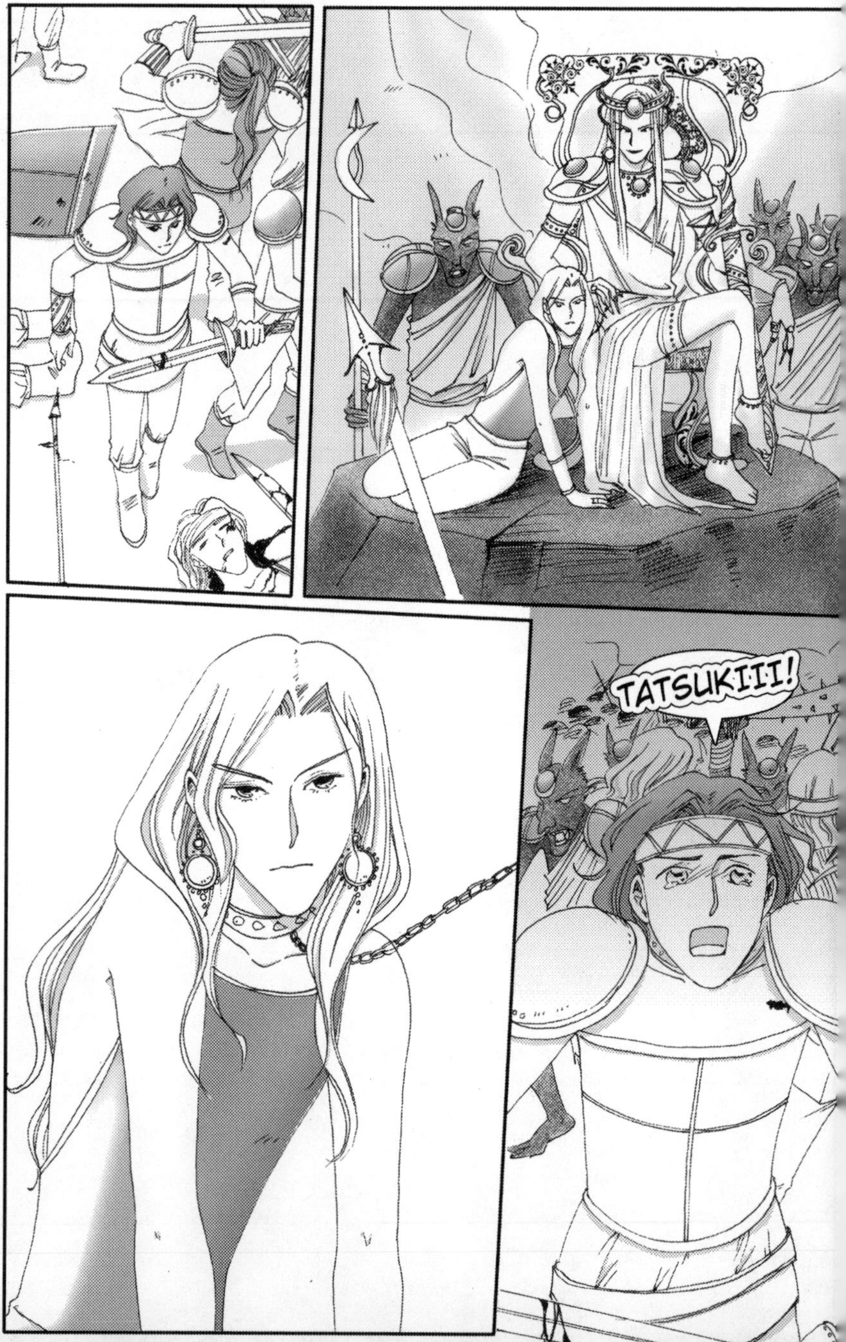
TATSUKIII!

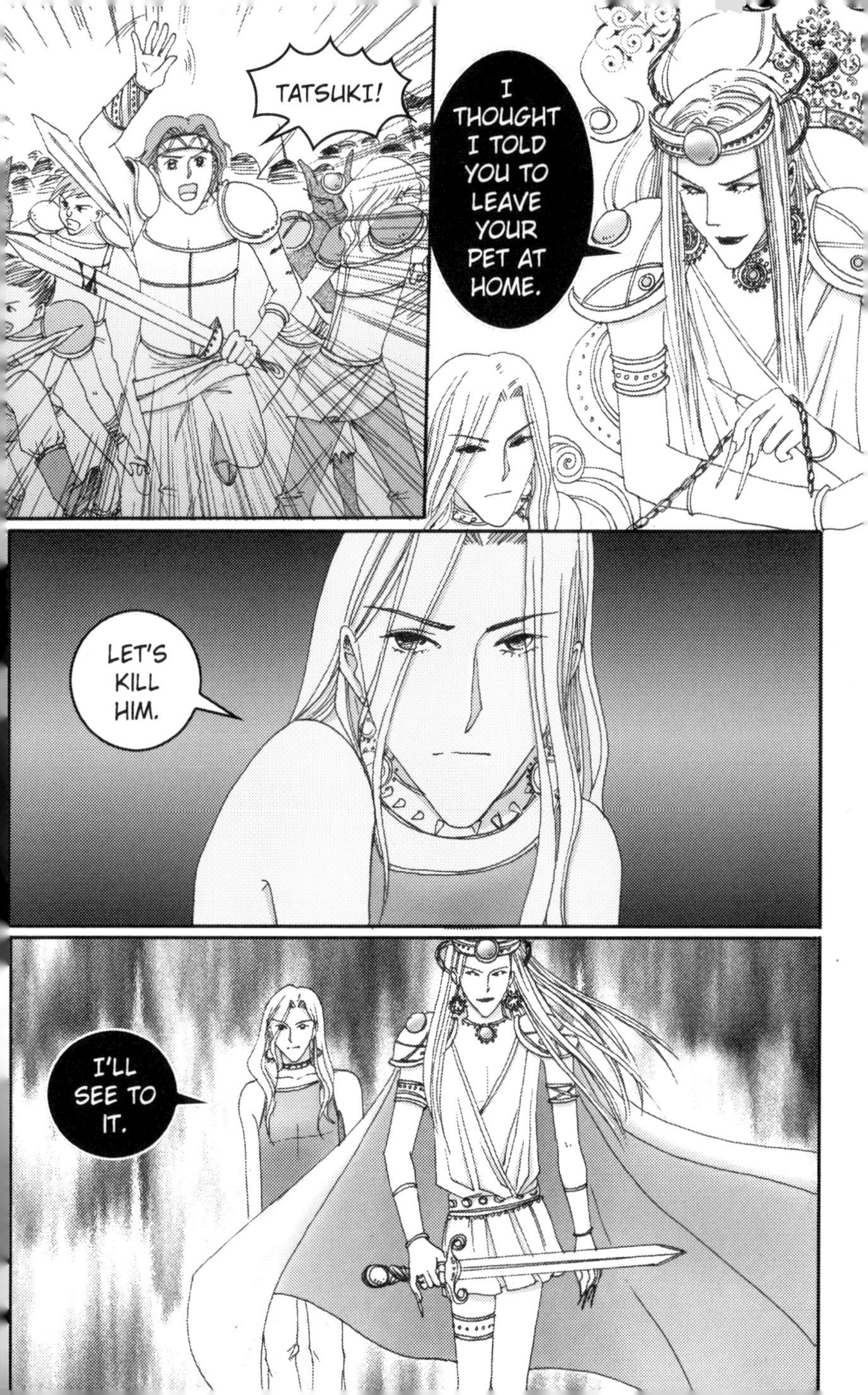
TATSUKI!
I THOUGHT I TOLD YOU TO LEAVE YOUR PET AT HOME.
LET'S KILL HIM.
I'LL SEE TO IT.

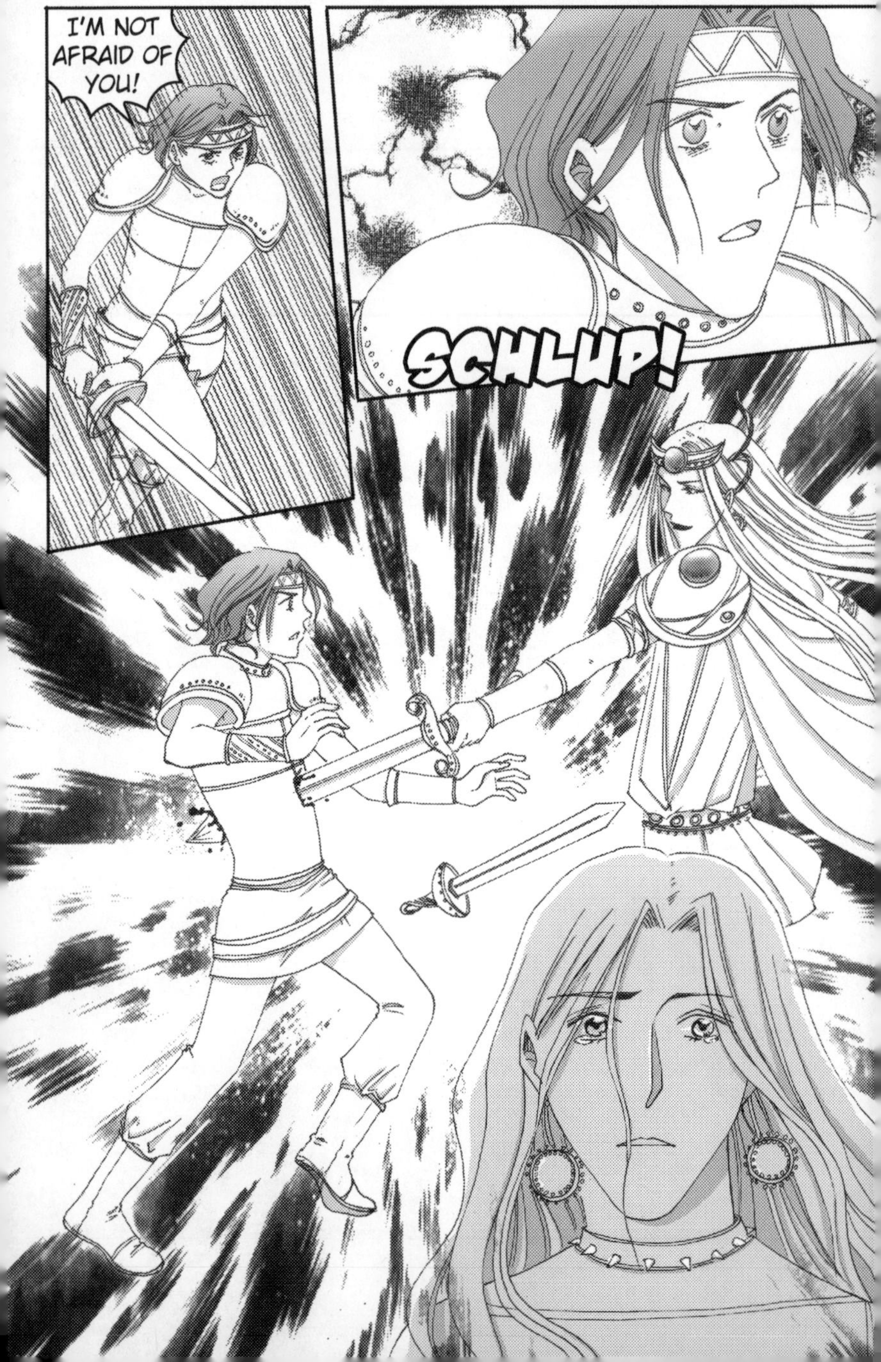
I'M NOT AFRAID OF YOU!
SCHLUP!

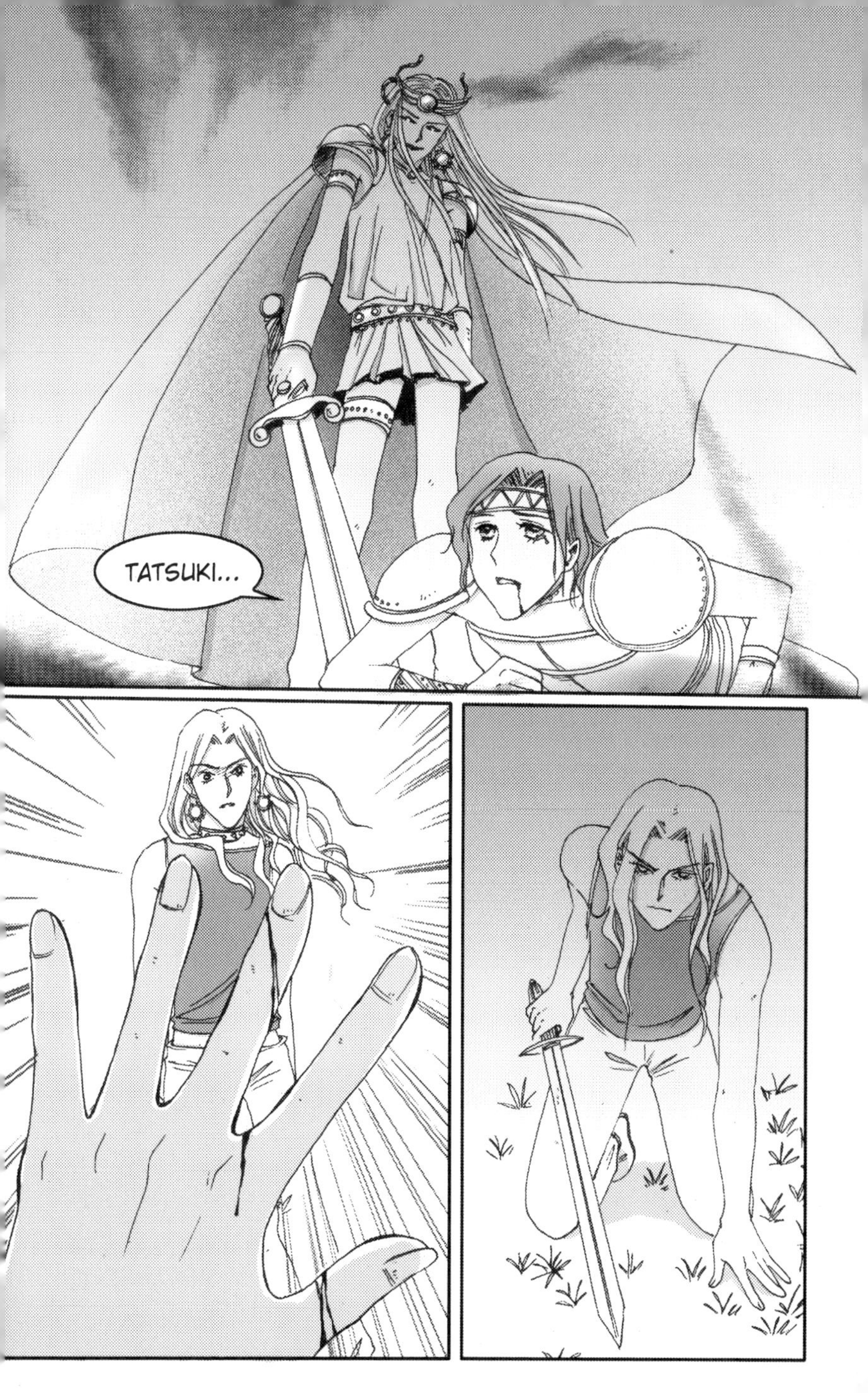
TATSUKI...

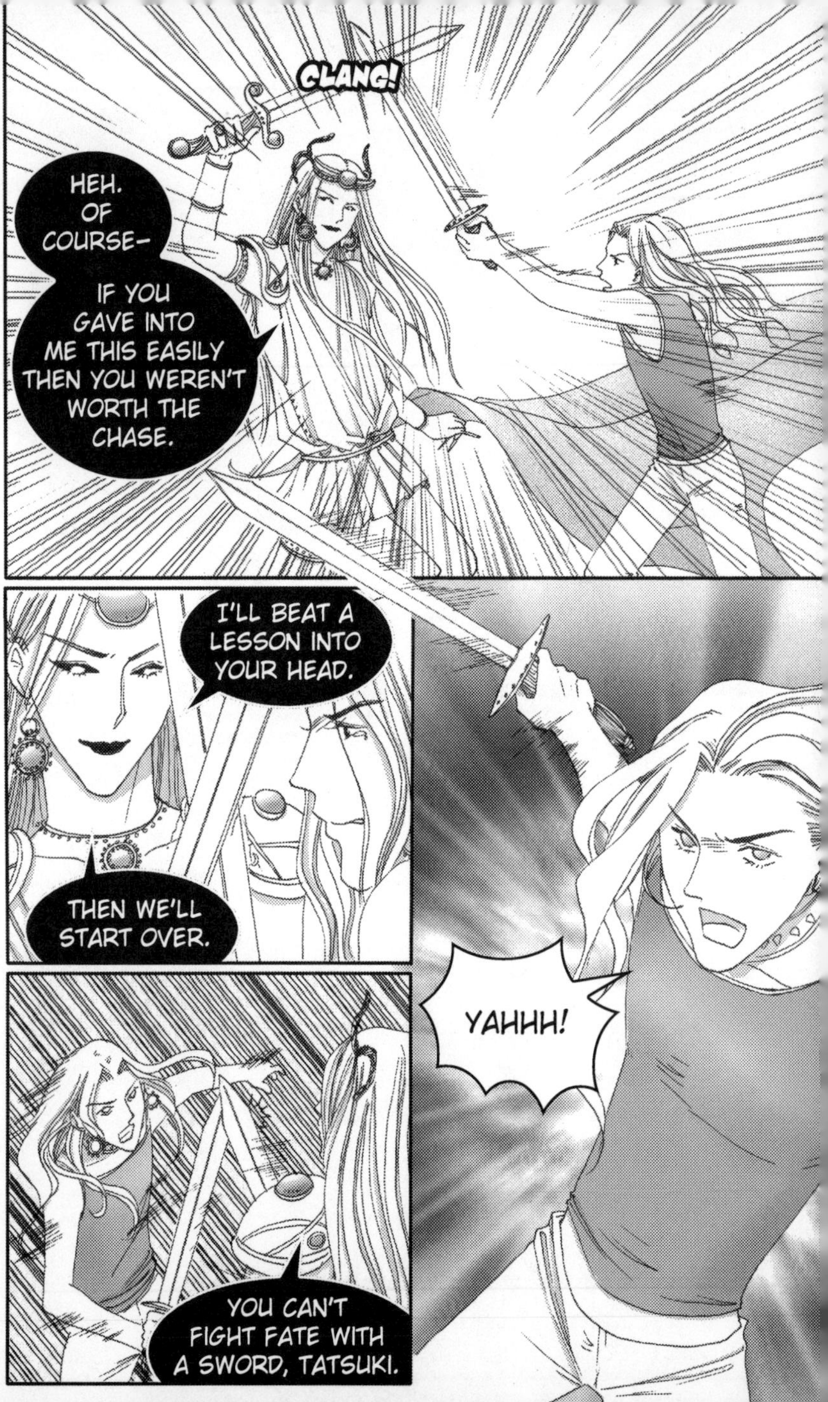
CLANG!
HEH. OF COURSE-
IF YOU GAVE INTO ME THIS EASILY THEN YOU WEREN'T WORTH THE CHASE.
I'LL BEAT A LESSON INTO YOUR HEAD.
THEN WE'LL START OVER.
YAHHH!
YOU CAN'T FIGHT FATE WITH A SWORD, TATSUKI.

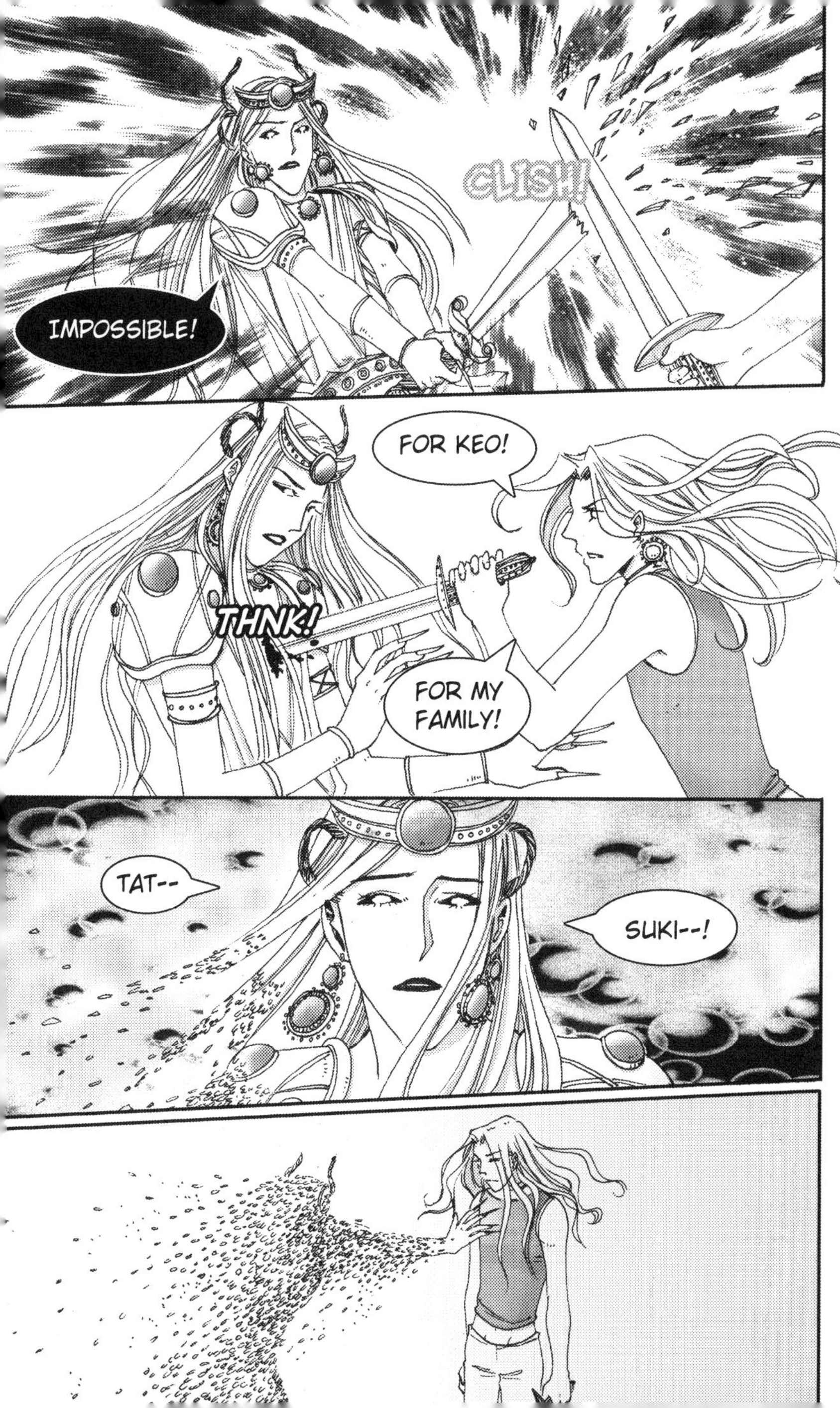
CLISH!
IMPOSSIBLE!
FOR KEO!
THNK!
FOR MY FAMILY!
TAT--
SUKI--!

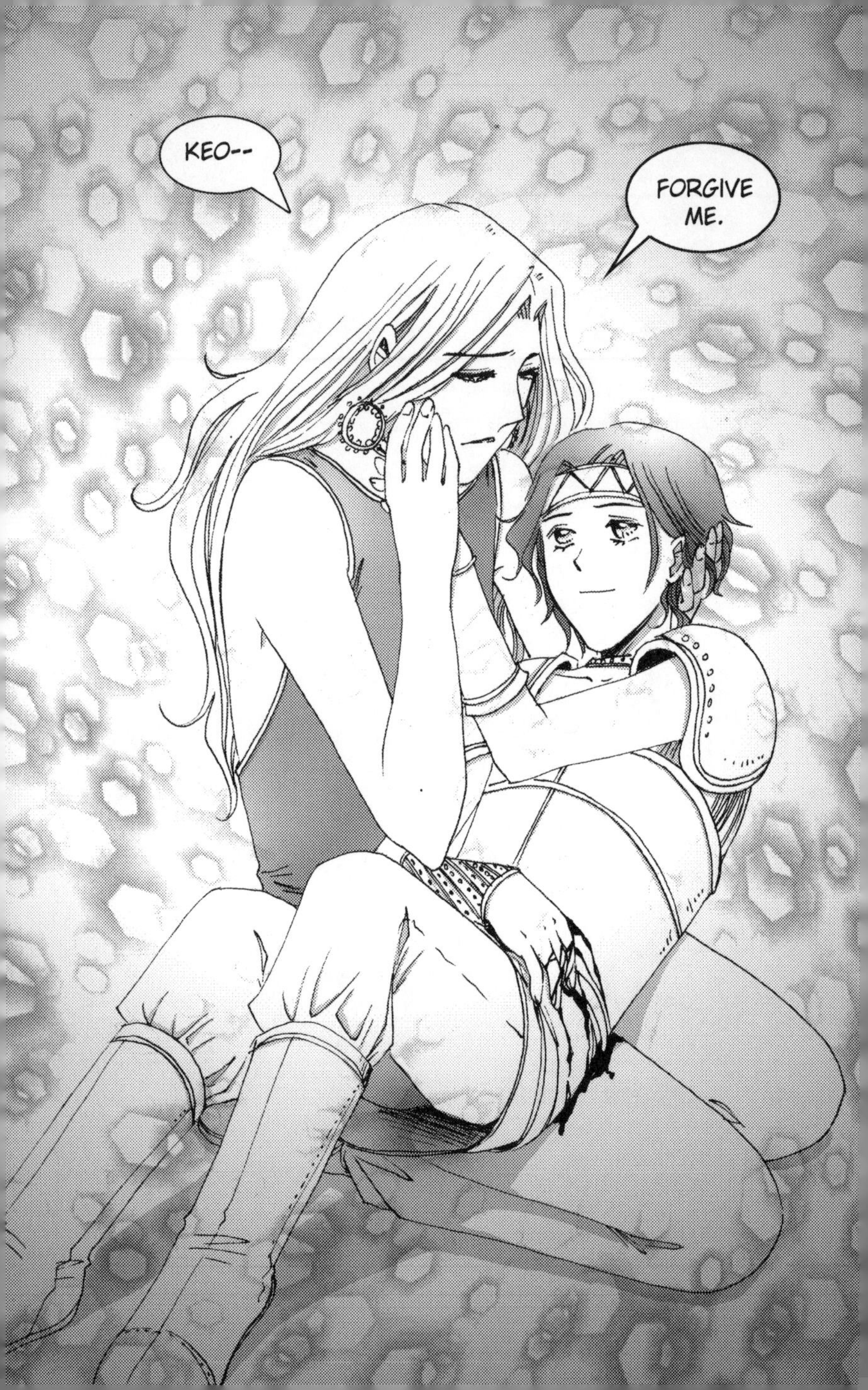
FORGIVE ME.
KEO--

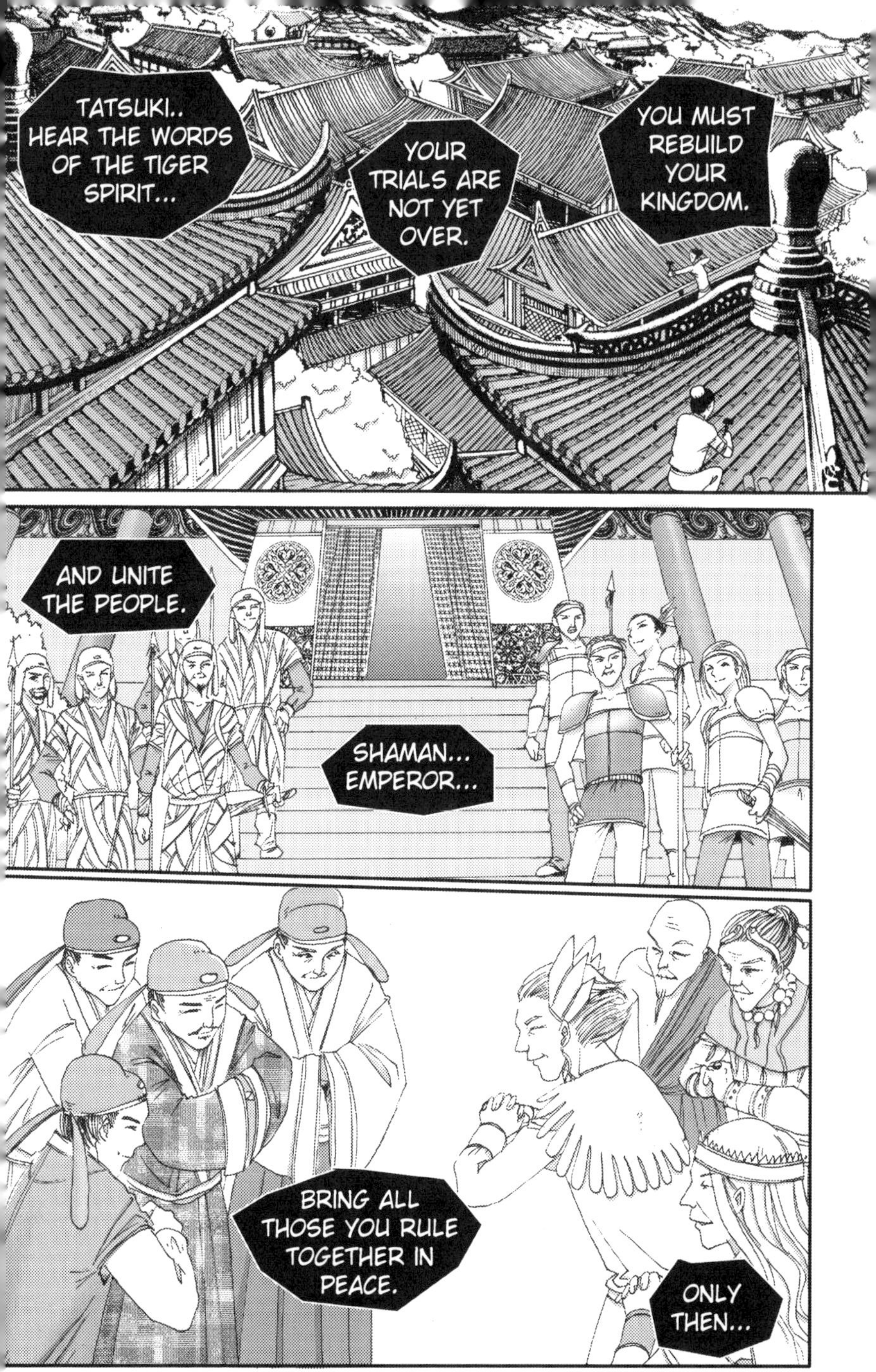
TATSUKI.. HEAR THE WORDS OF THE TIGER SPIRIT...
YOUR TRIALS ARE NOT YET OVER.
YOU MUST REBUILD YOUR KINGDOM.
AND UNITE THE PEOPLE.
SHAMAN... EMPEROR...
BRING ALL THOSE YOU RULE TOGETHER IN PEACE.
ONLY THEN...

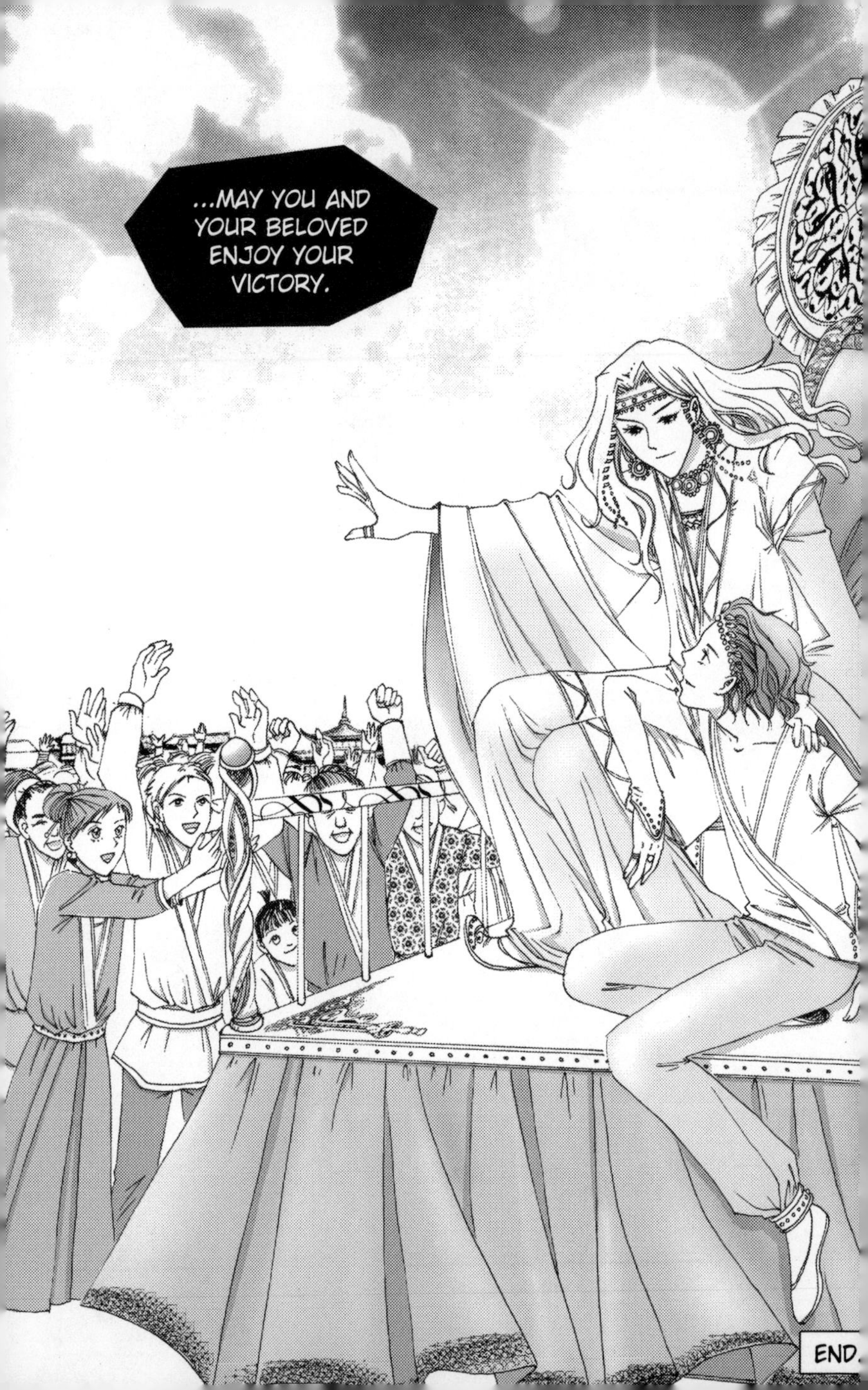
...MAY YOU AND YOUR BELOVED ENJOY YOUR VICTORY.
END.

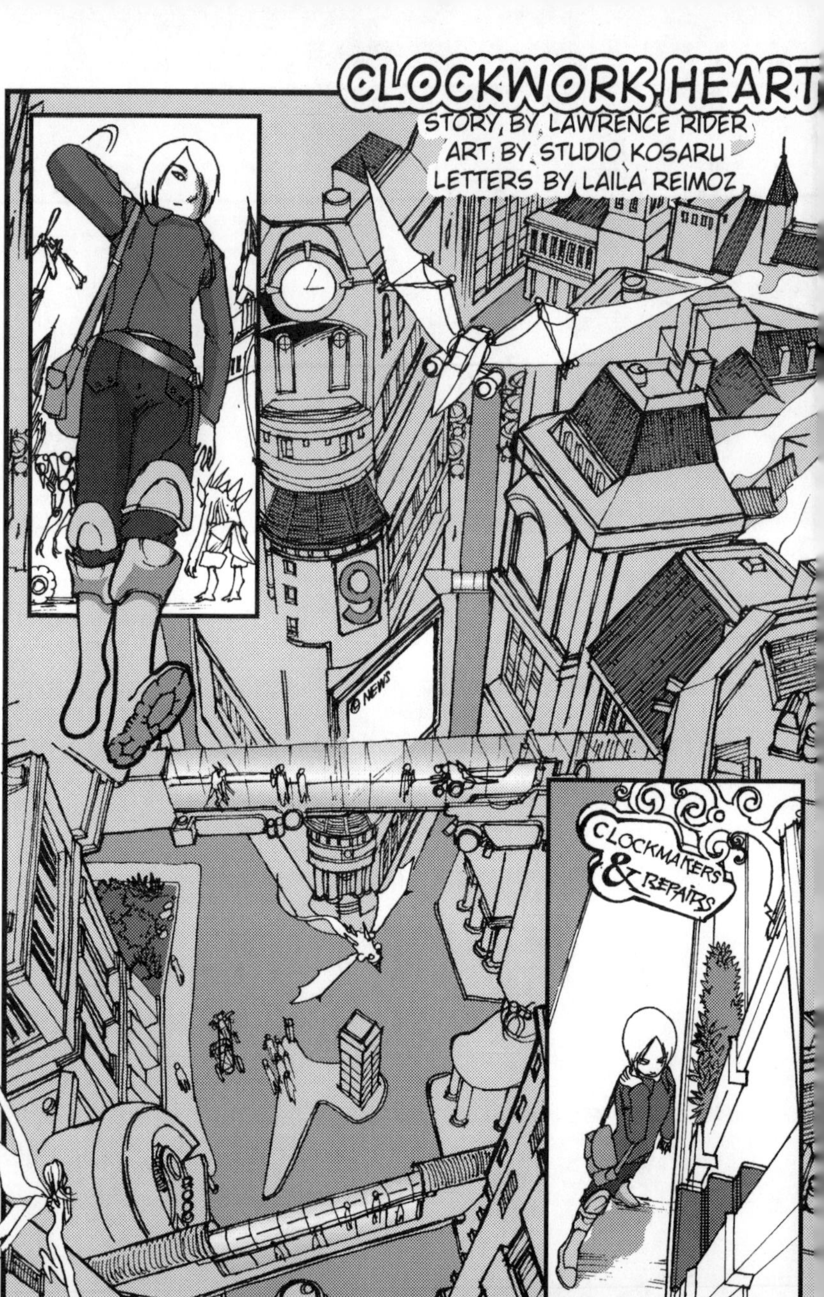
CLOCKWORK HEART
STORY BY LAWRENCE RIDER
ART BY STUDIO KOSARU
LETTERS BY LAILA REIMOZ
NEWS
CLOCKMAKERS & REPAIRS

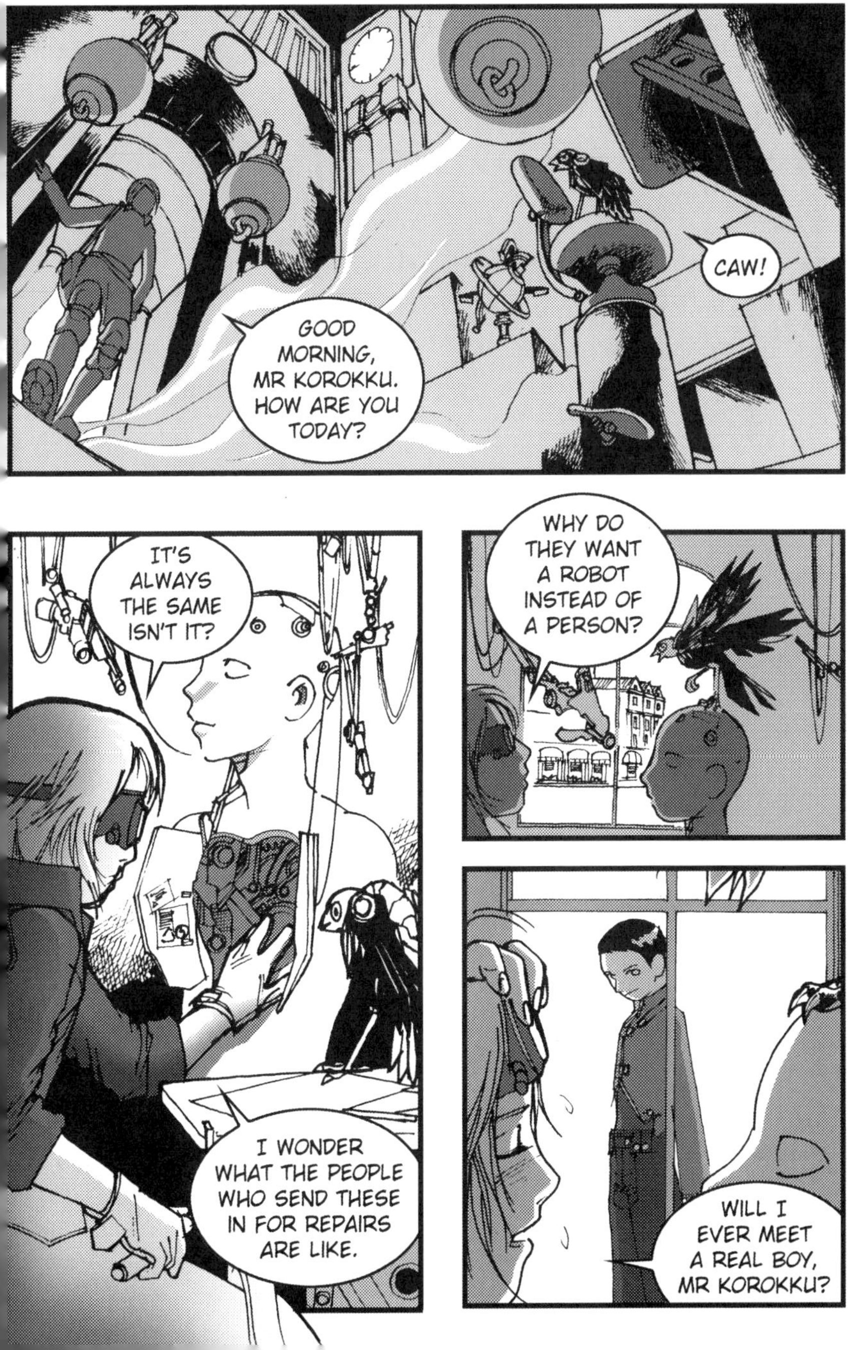
GOOD MORNING, MR KOROKKU. HOW ARE YOU TODAY?
CAW!
IT'S ALWAYS THE SAME ISN'T IT?
I WONDER WHAT THE PEOPLE WHO SEND THESE IN FOR REPAIRS ARE LIKE.
WHY DO THEY WANT A ROBOT INSTEAD OF A PERSON?
WILL I EVER MEET A REAL BOY, MR KOROKKU?

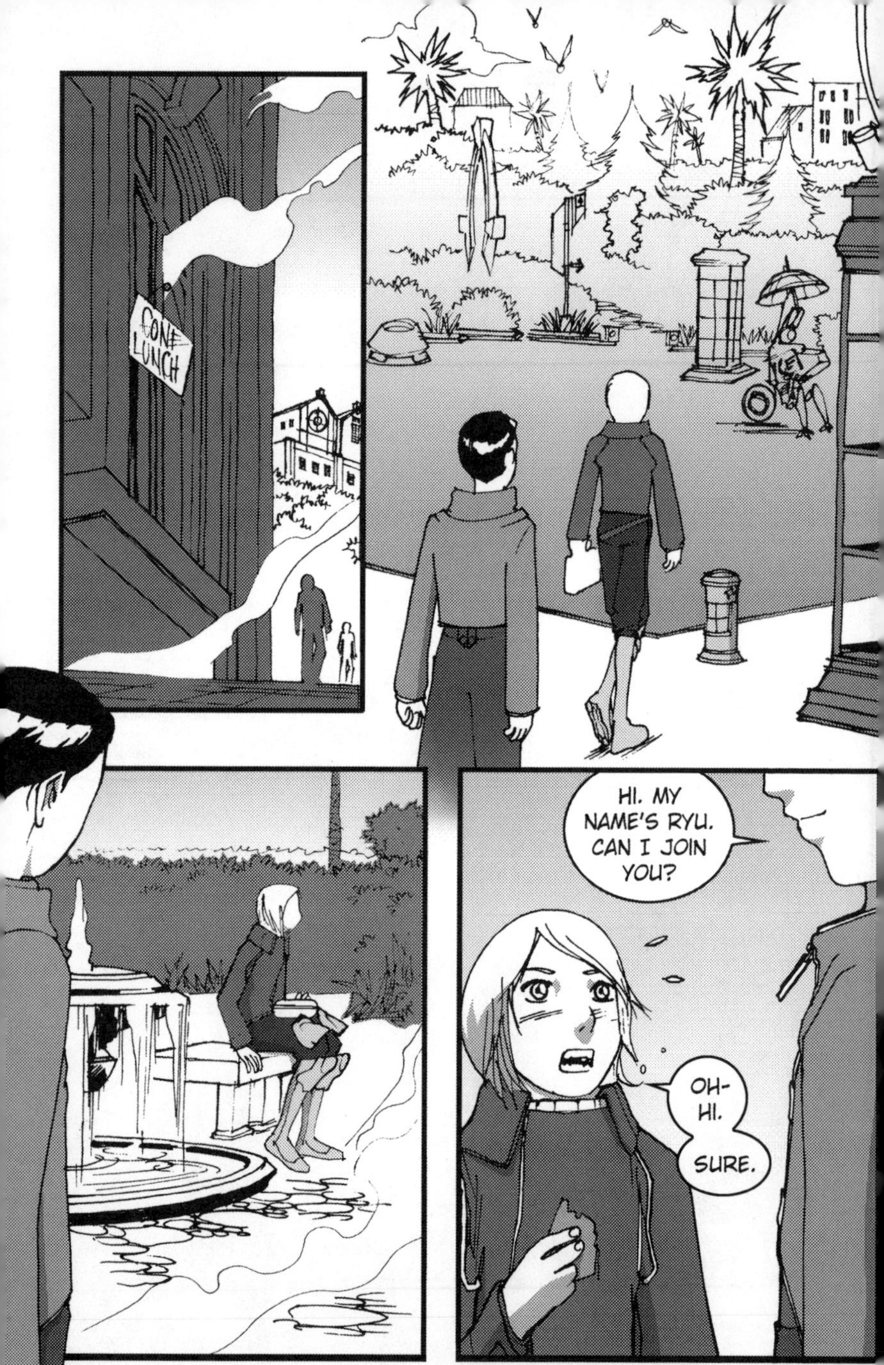
GONE
LUNCH
HI. MY NAME'S RYU. CAN I JOIN YOU?
OH- HI.
SURE.

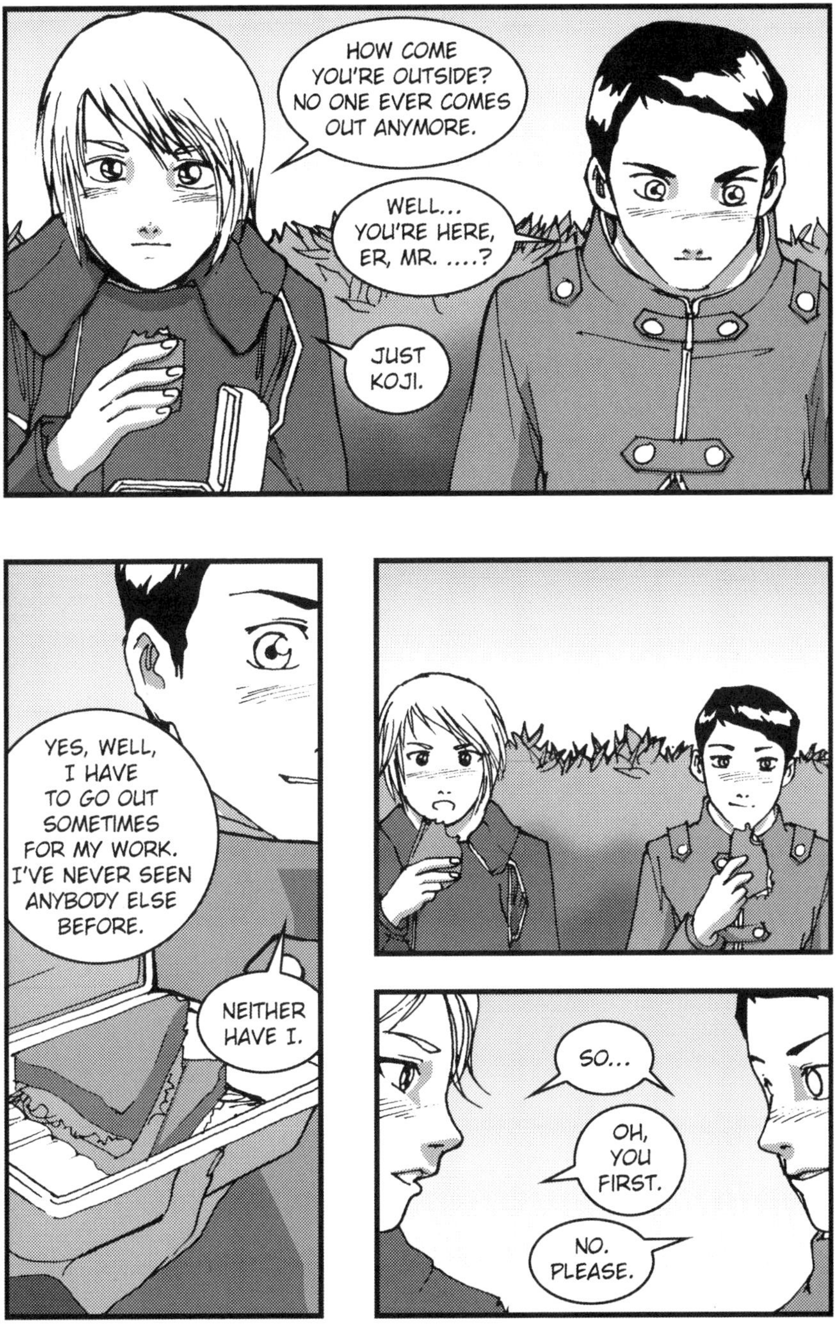
HOW COME YOU'RE OUTSIDE? NO ONE EVER COMES OUT ANYMORE.
WELL... YOU'RE HERE, ER, MR. ....?
JUST KOJI.
YES, WELL, I HAVE TO GO OUT SOMETIMES FOR MY WORK. I'VE NEVER SEEN ANYBODY ELSE BEFORE.
NEITHER HAVE I.
SO...
OH, YOU FIRST.
NO. PLEASE.

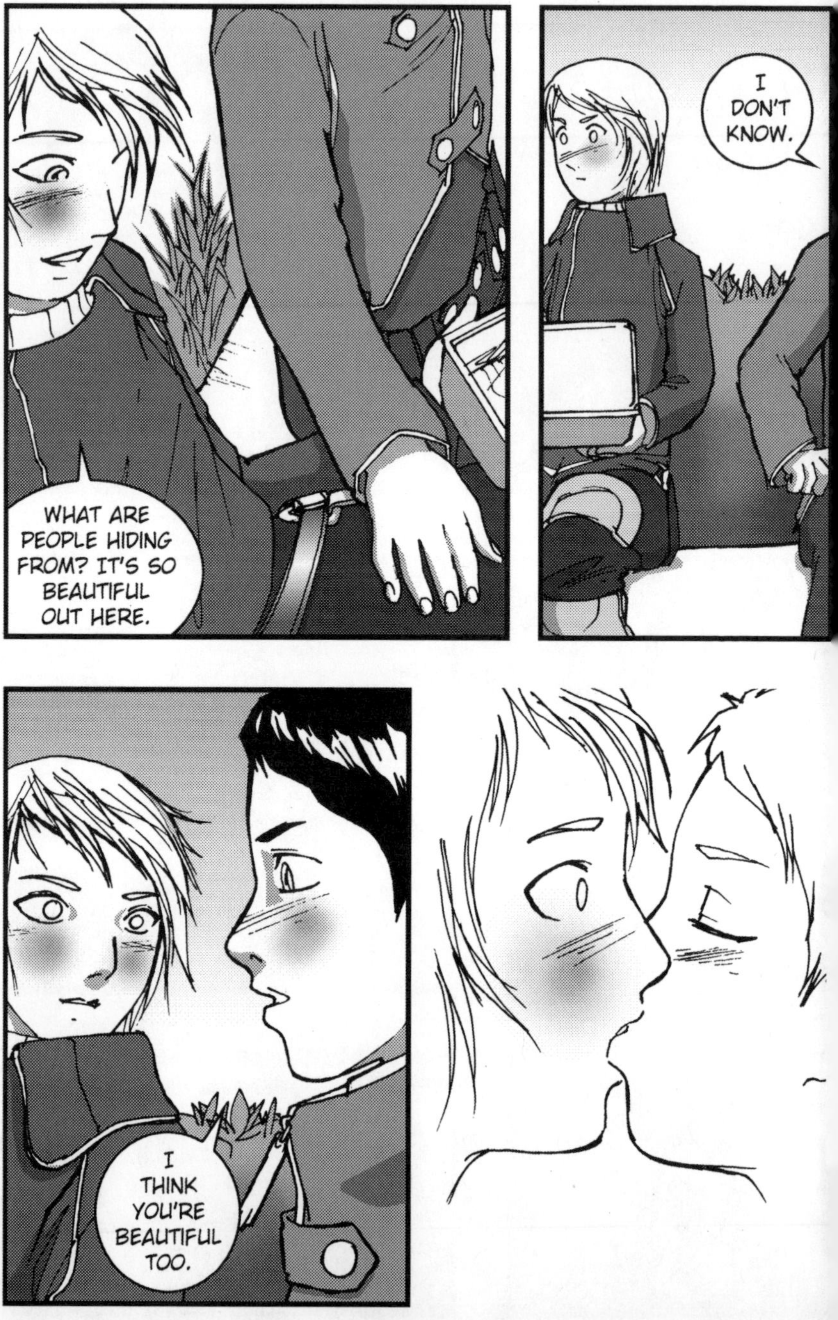
WHAT ARE PEOPLE HIDING FROM? IT'S SO BEAUTIFUL OUT HERE.
I DON'T KNOW.
I THINK YOU'RE BEAUTIFUL TOO.

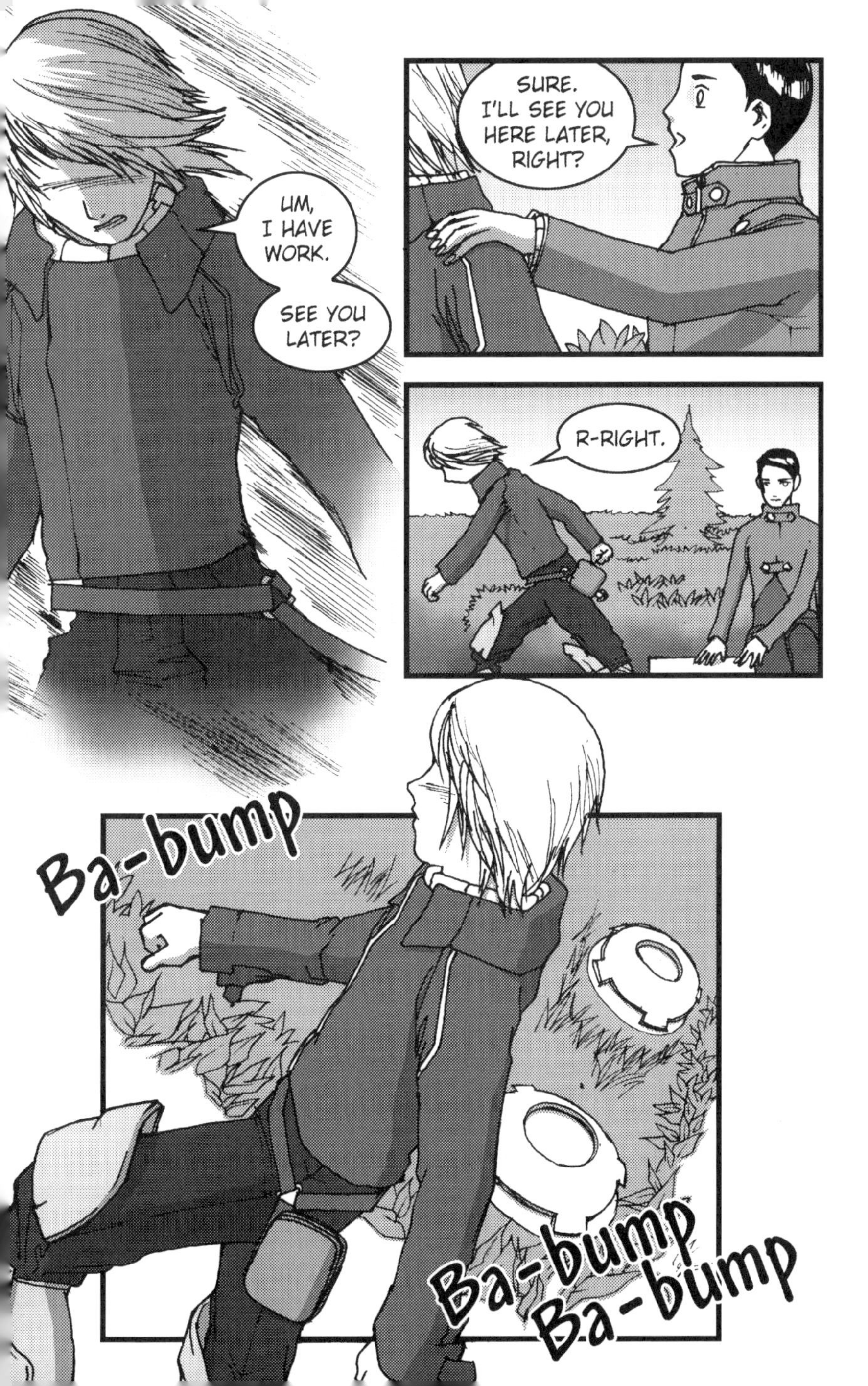
UM, I HAVE WORK.
SEE YOU LATER?
SURE. I'LL SEE YOU HERE LATER, RIGHT?
R-RIGHT.
Ba-bump
Ba-bump
Ba-bump

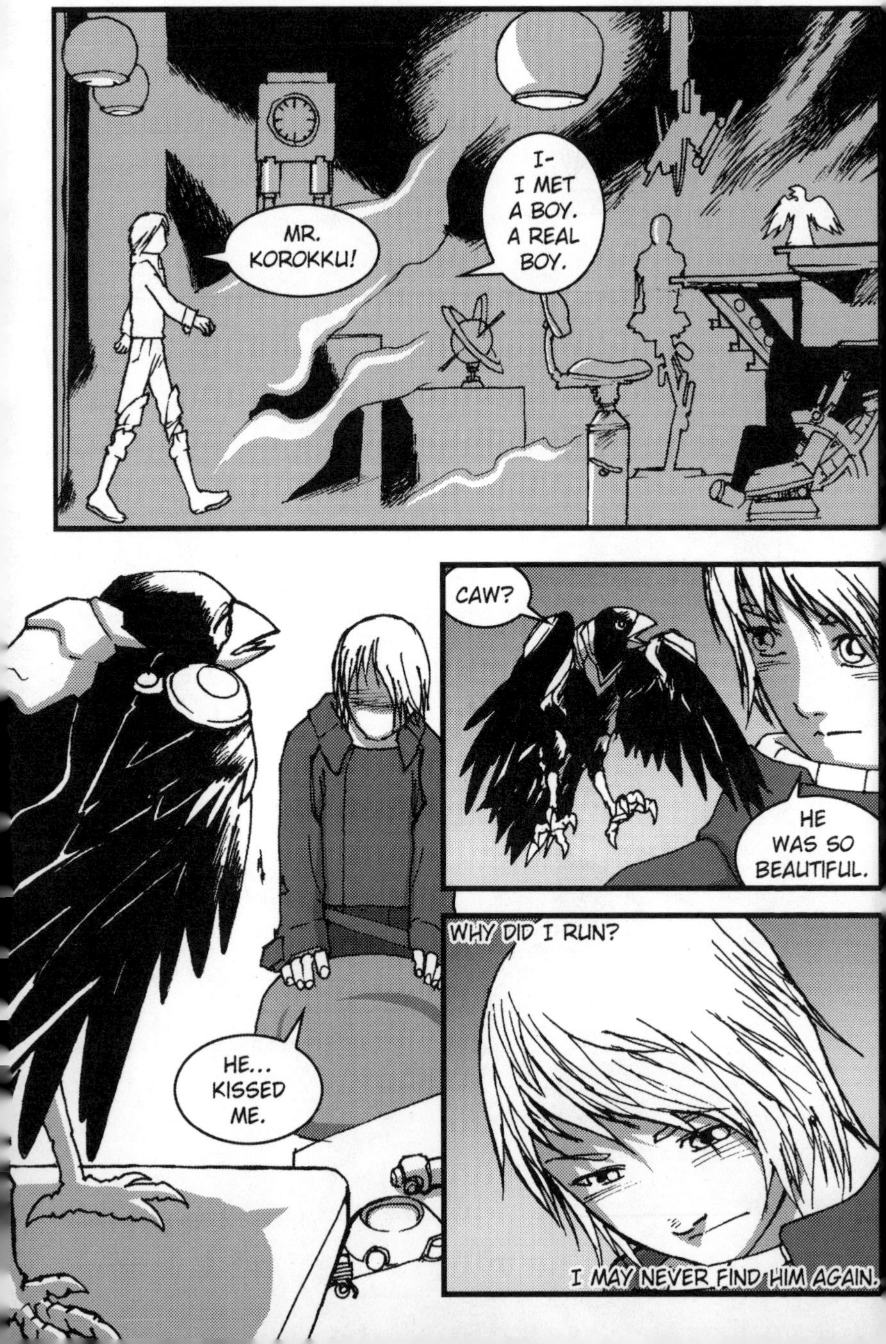
MR. KOROKKU!
I- I MET A BOY. A REAL BOY.
CAW?
HE WAS SO BEAUTIFUL.
HE... KISSED ME.
WHY DID I RUN?
I MAY NEVER FIND HIM AGAIN.

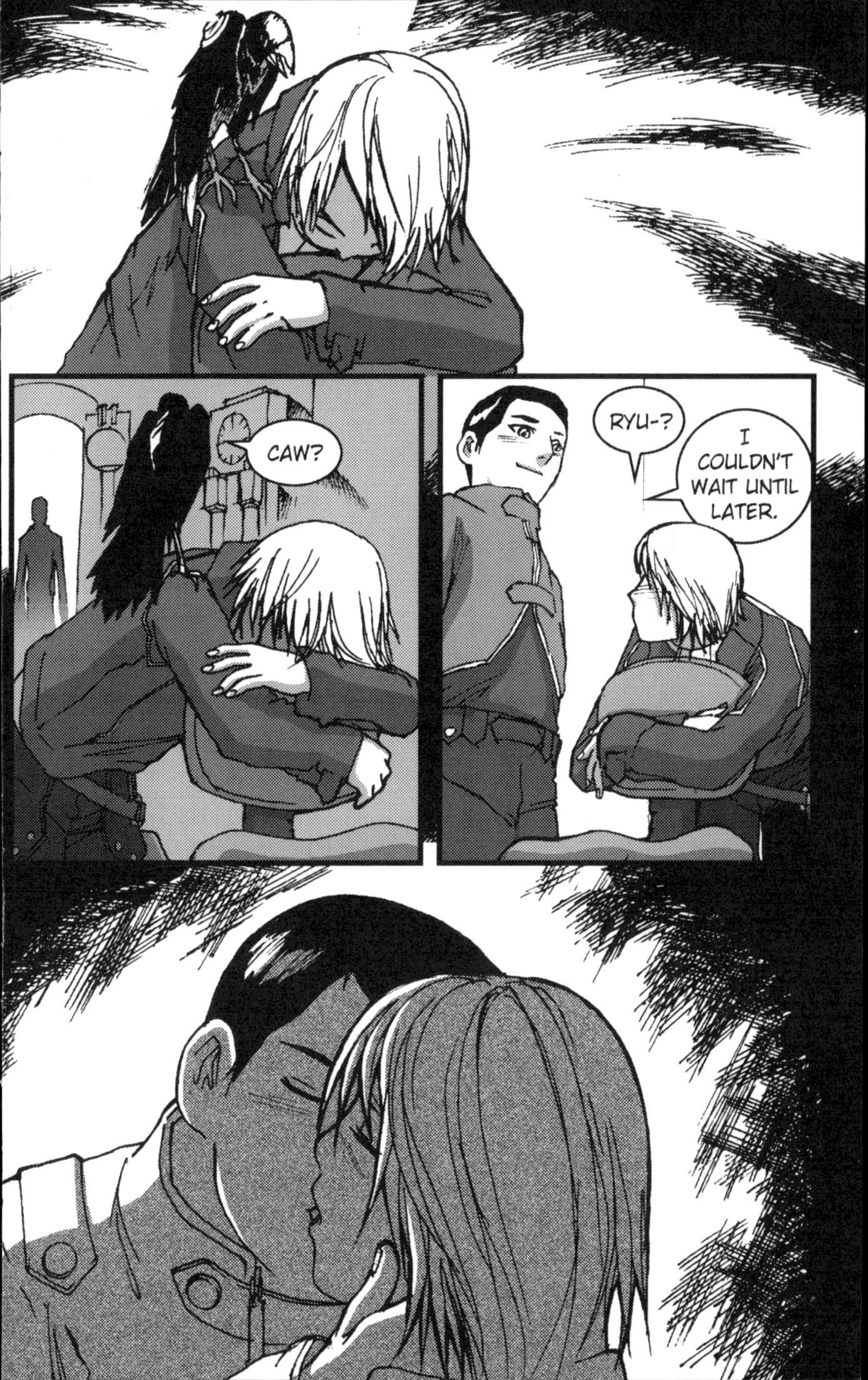
CAW?
RYU-?
I COULDN'T WAIT UNTIL LATER.

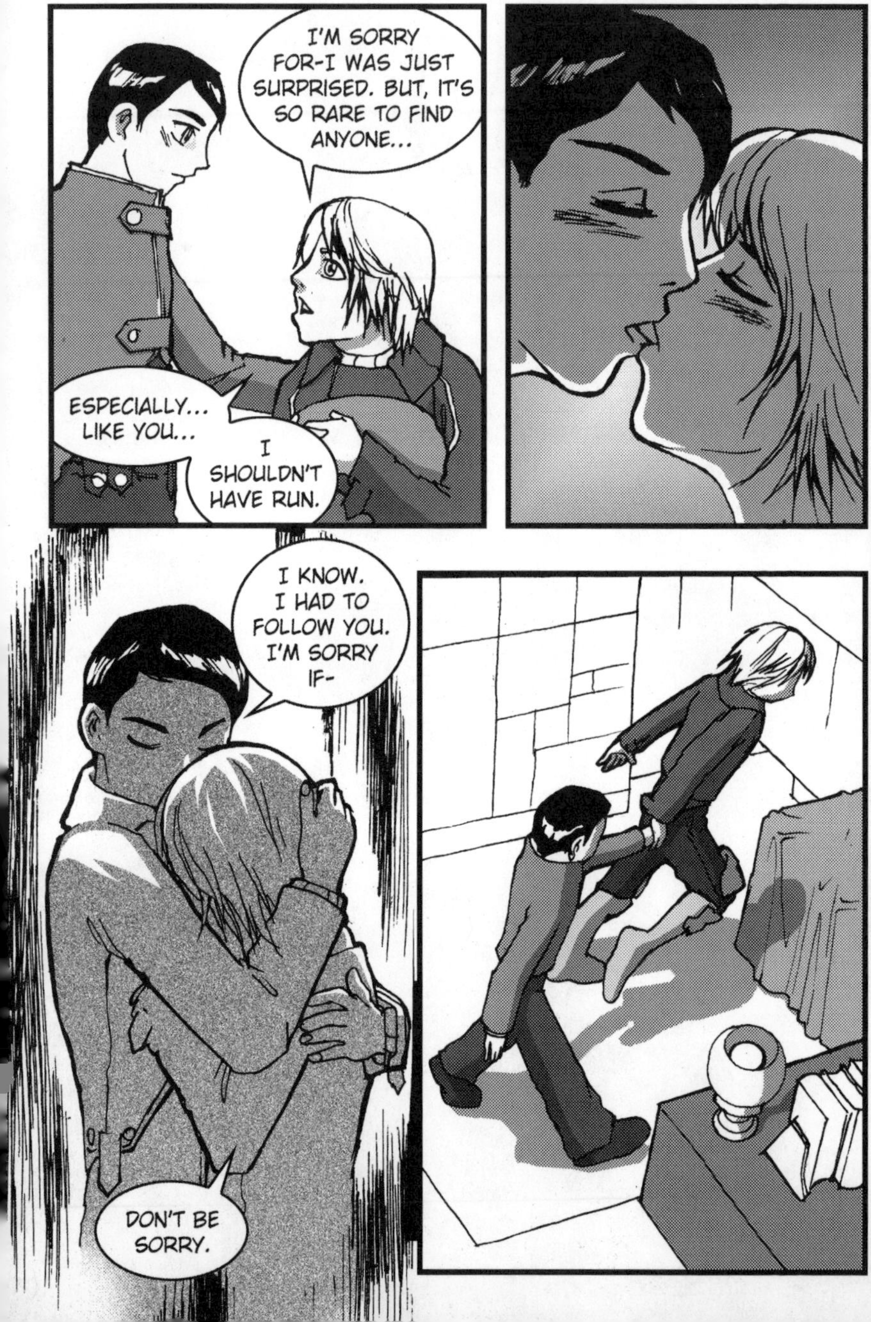
I'M SORRY FOR-I WAS JUST SURPRISED. BUT, IT'S SO RARE TO FIND ANYONE...
ESPECIALLY... LIKE YOU...
I SHOULDN'T HAVE RUN.
I KNOW. I HAD TO FOLLOW YOU. I'M SORRY IF-
DON'T BE SORRY.

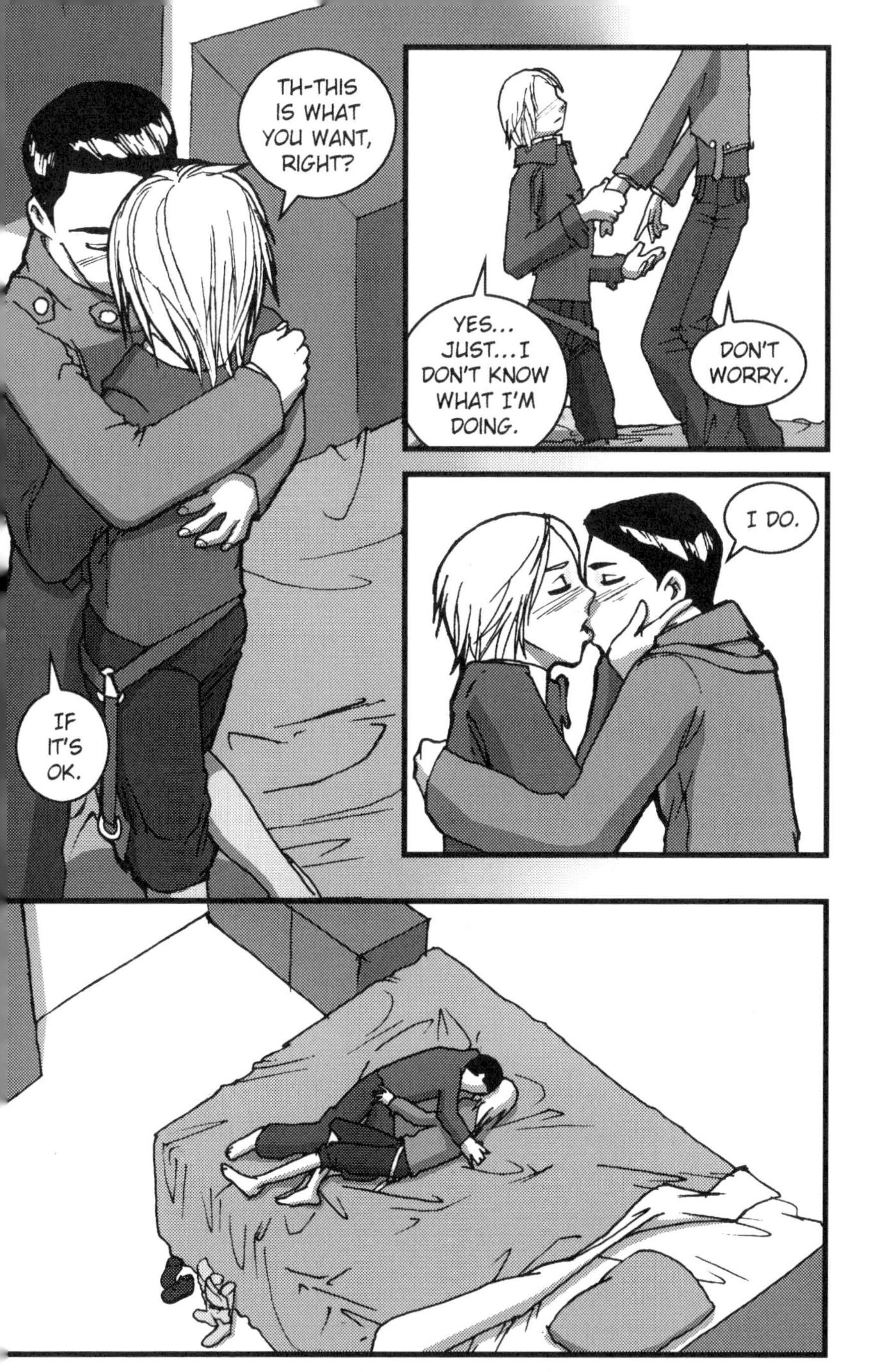
TH-THIS IS WHAT YOU WANT, RIGHT?
IF IT'S OK.
YES... JUST...I DON'T KNOW WHAT I'M DOING.
DON'T WORRY.
I DO.

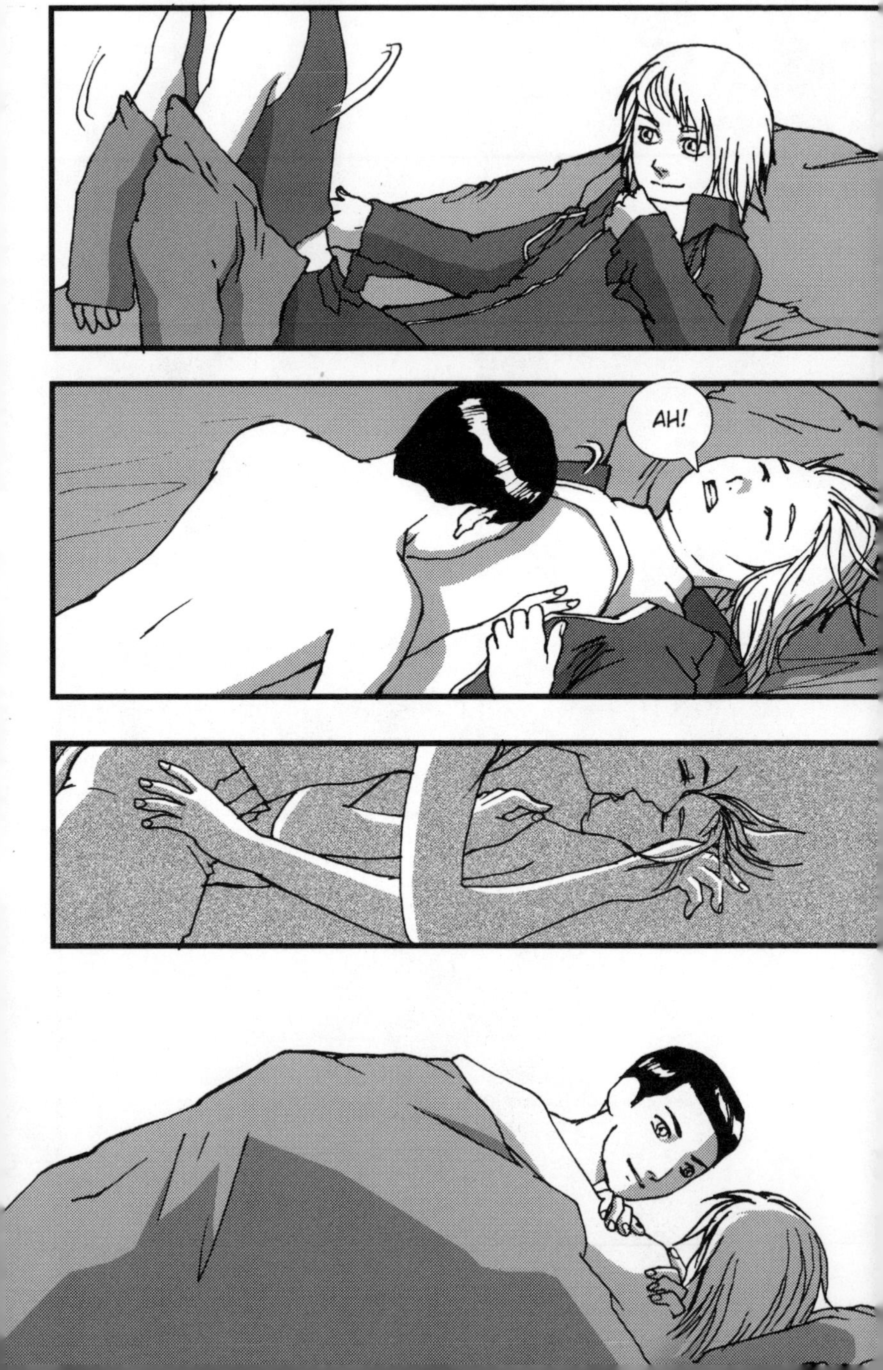
AH!

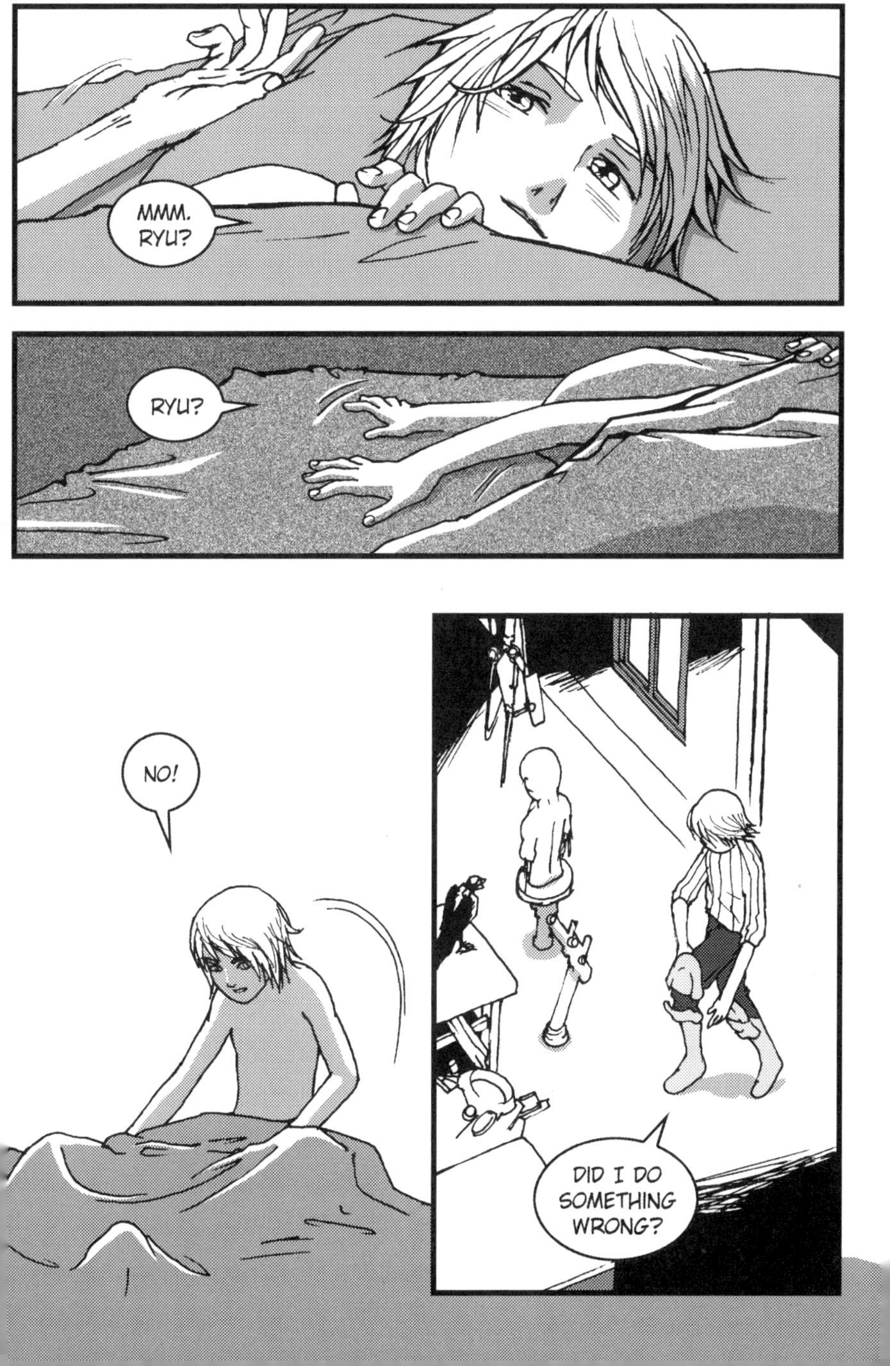
MMM.
RYU?
RYU?
NO!
DID I DO SOMETHING WRONG?

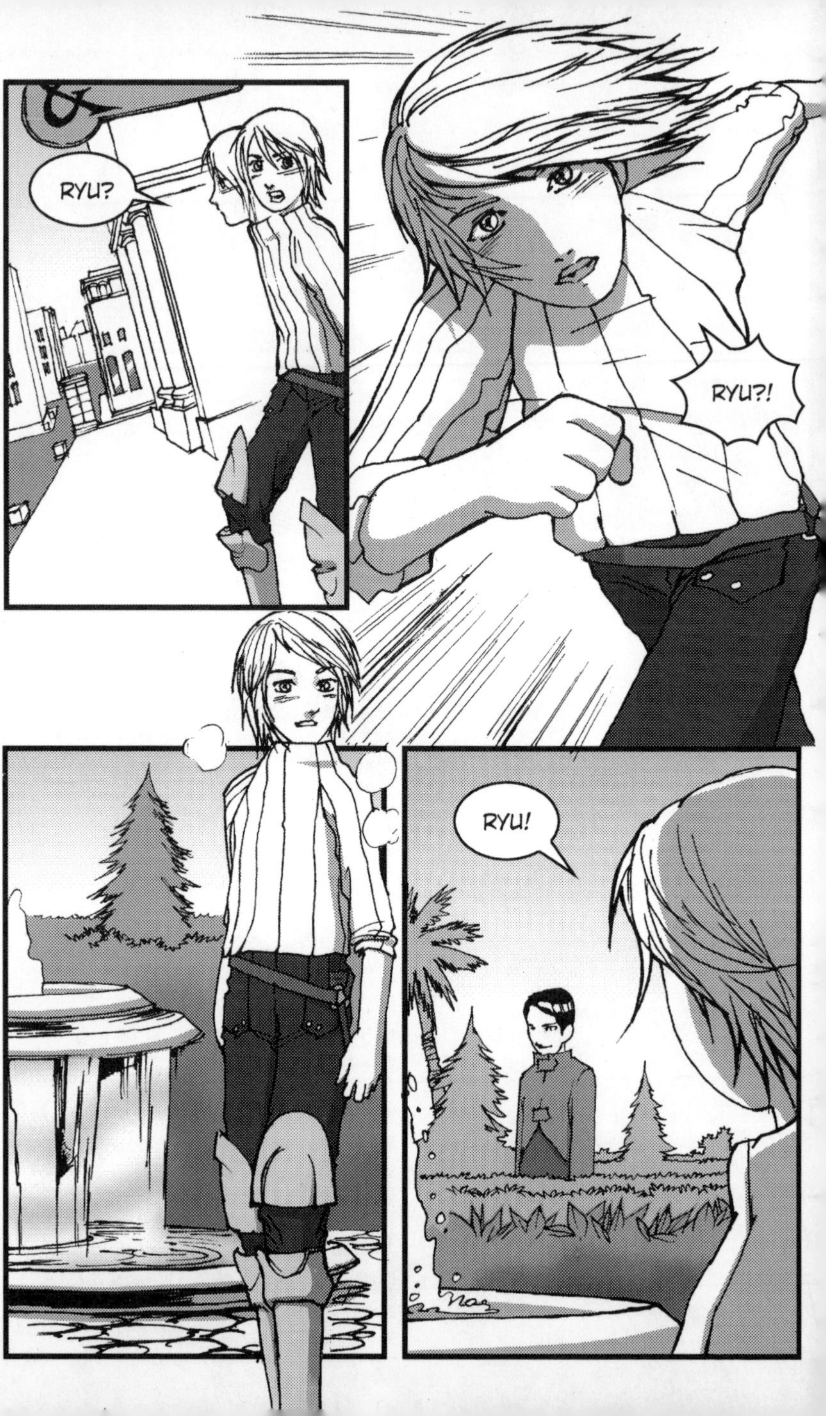
RYU?
RYU?!
RYU!

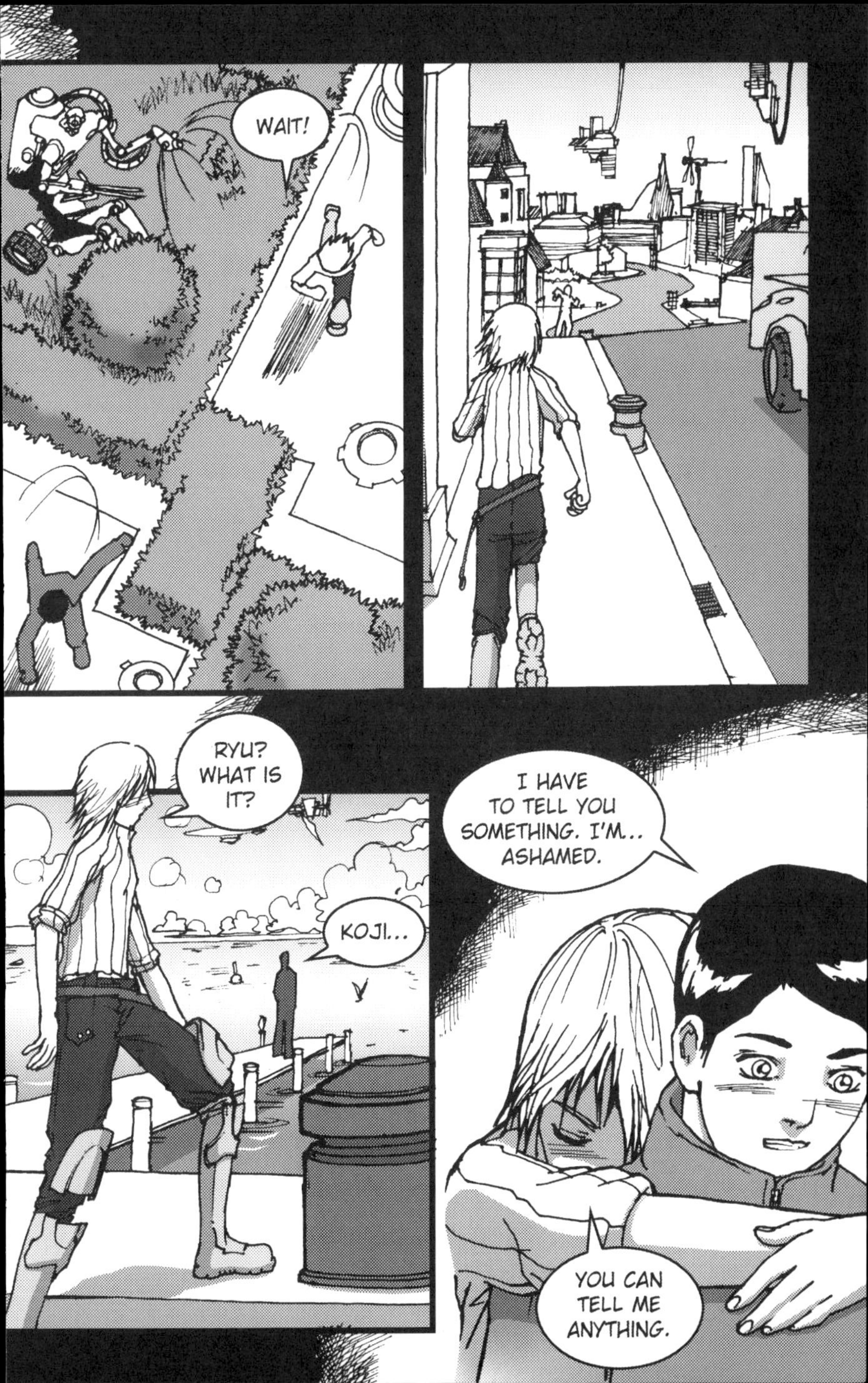
WAIT!
RYU? WHAT IS IT?
KOJI...
I HAVE TO TELL YOU SOMETHING. I'M... ASHAMED.
YOU CAN TELL ME ANYTHING.

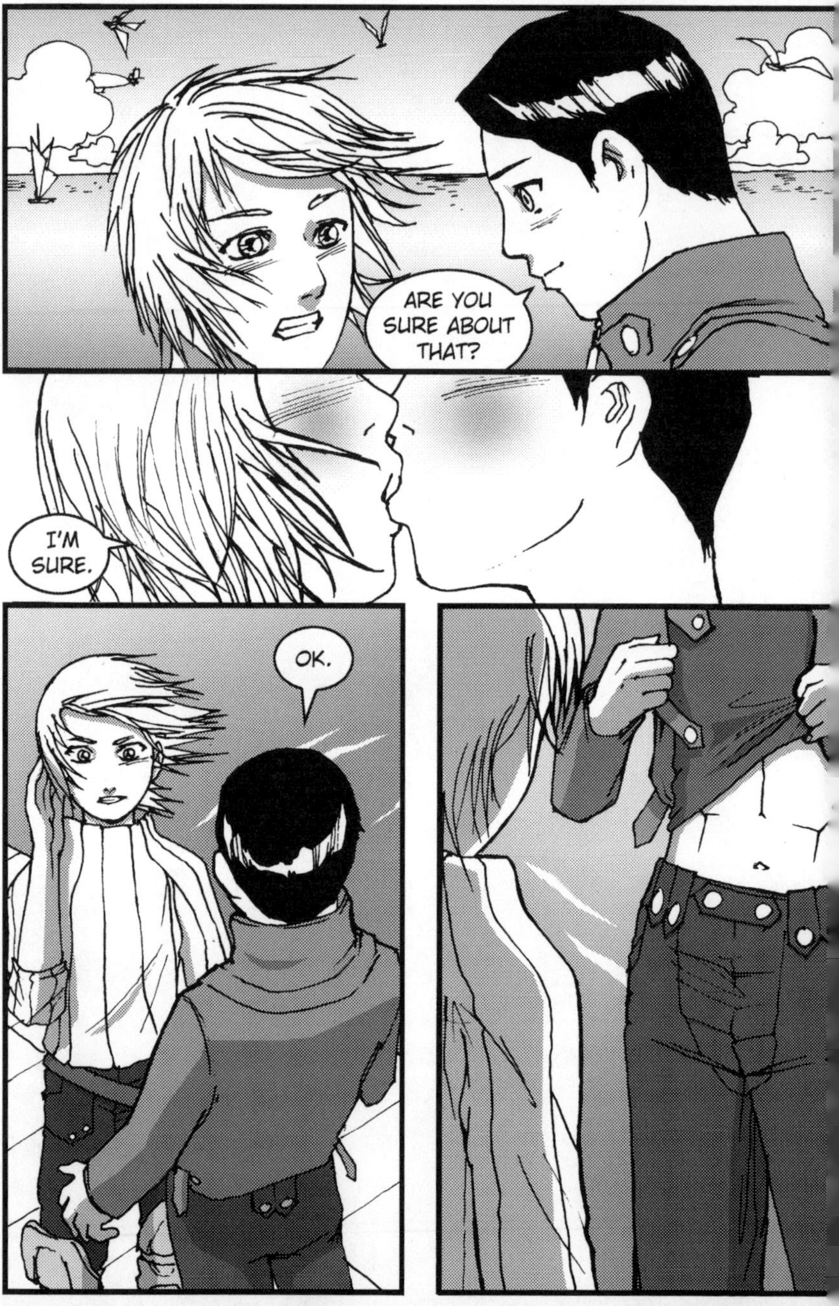
ARE YOU SURE ABOUT THAT?
I'M SURE.
OK.

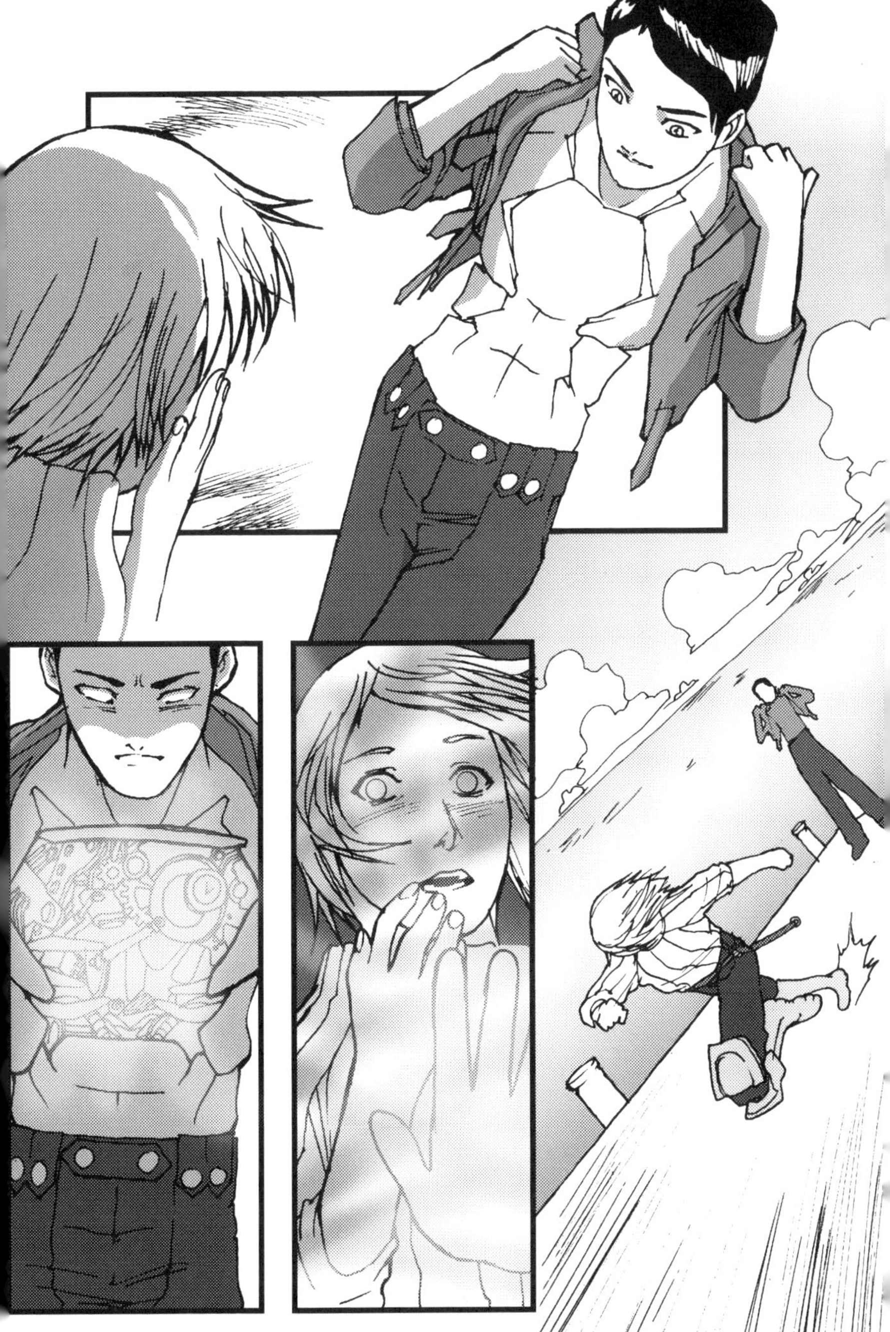

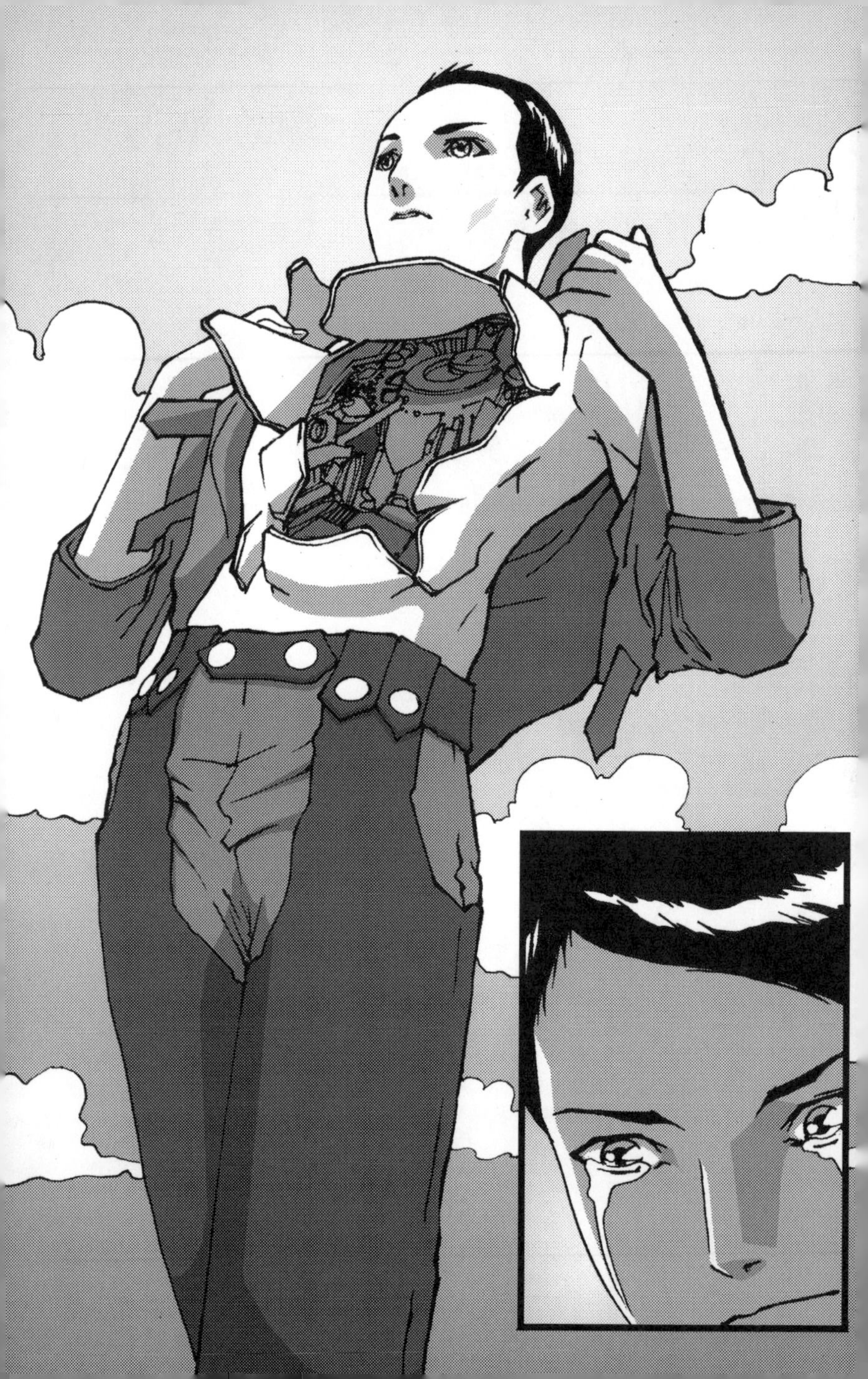

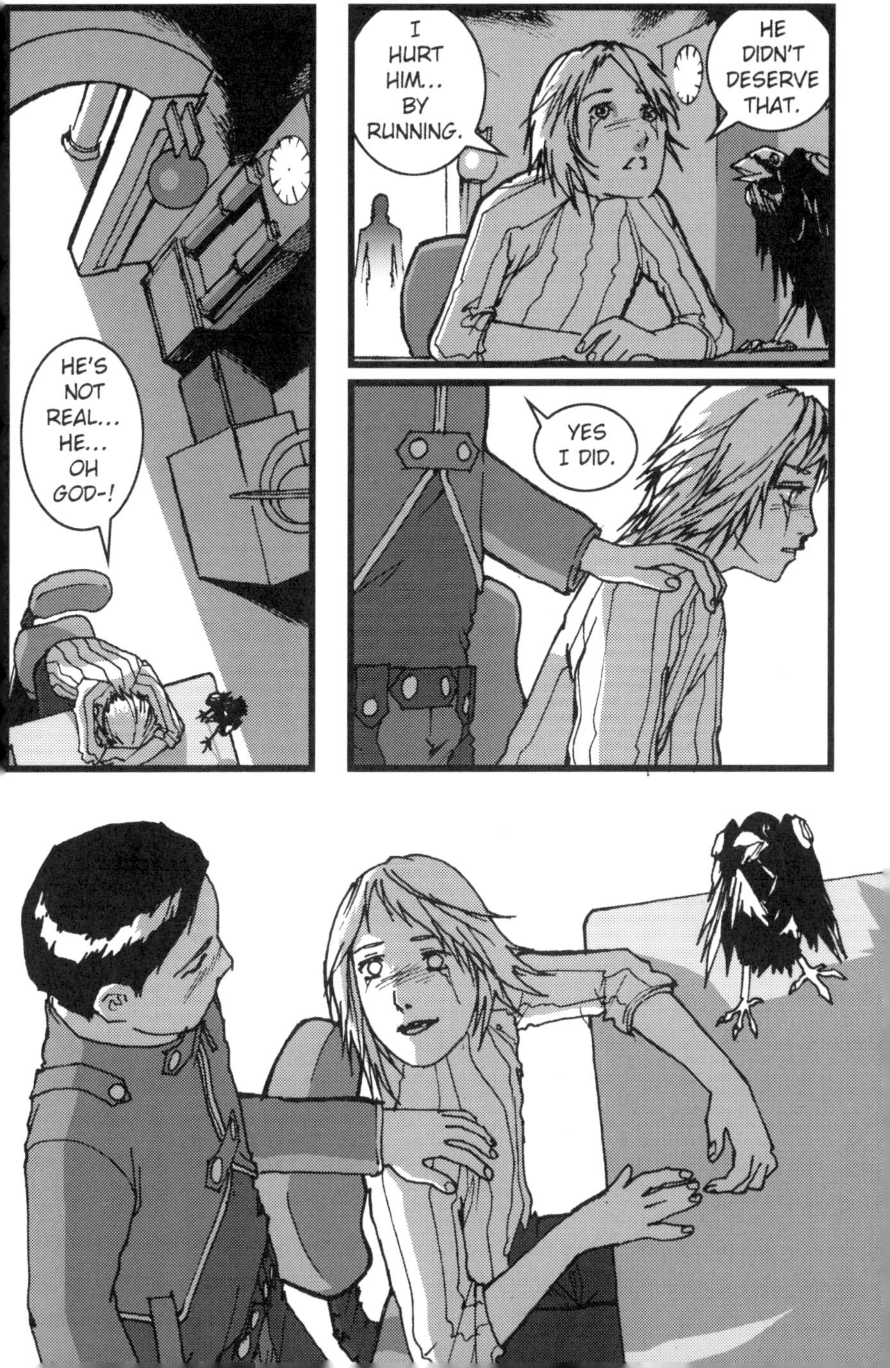
HE'S NOT REAL... HE... OH GOD-!
I HURT HIM... BY RUNNING.
HE DIDN'T DESERVE THAT.
YES I DID.

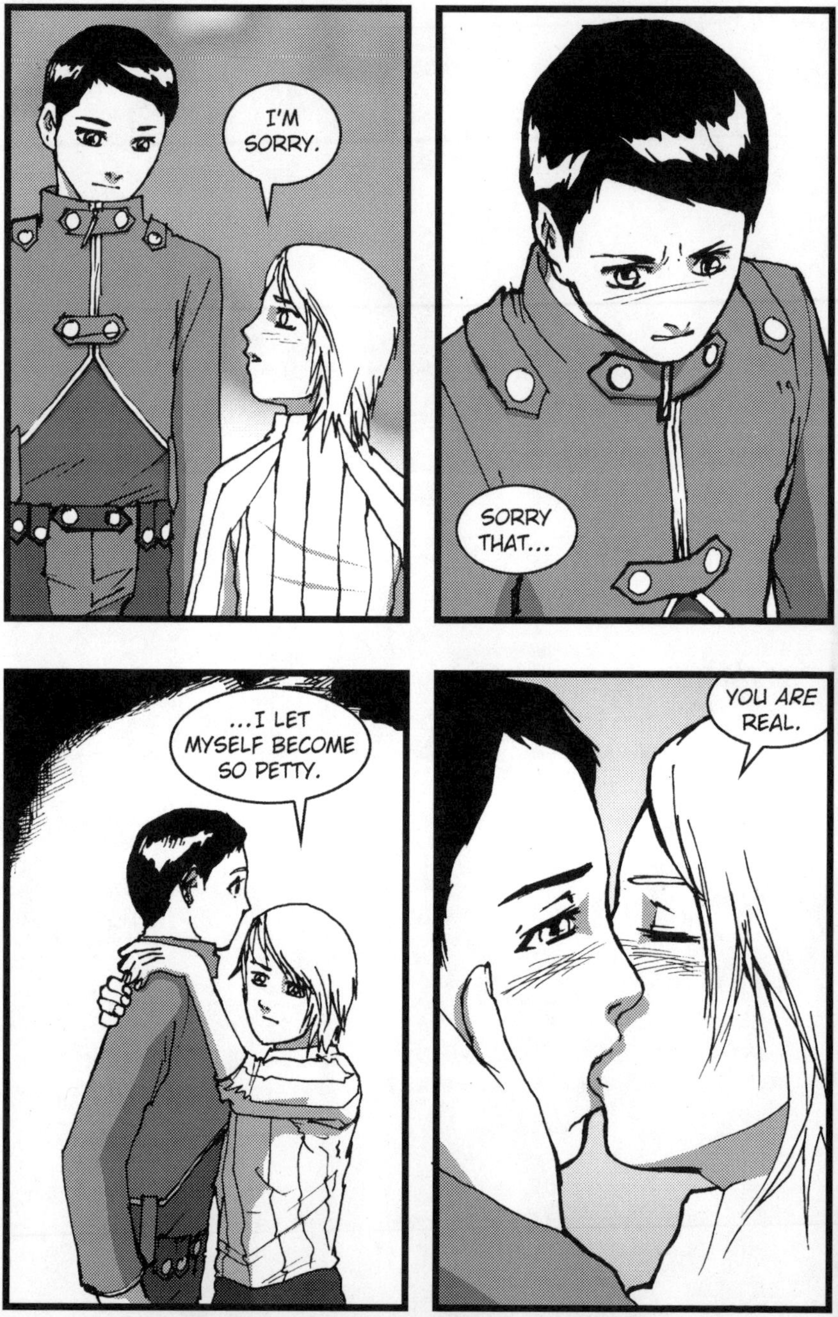
I'M SORRY.
SORRY THAT...
...I LET MYSELF BECOME SO PETTY.
YOU ARE REAL.

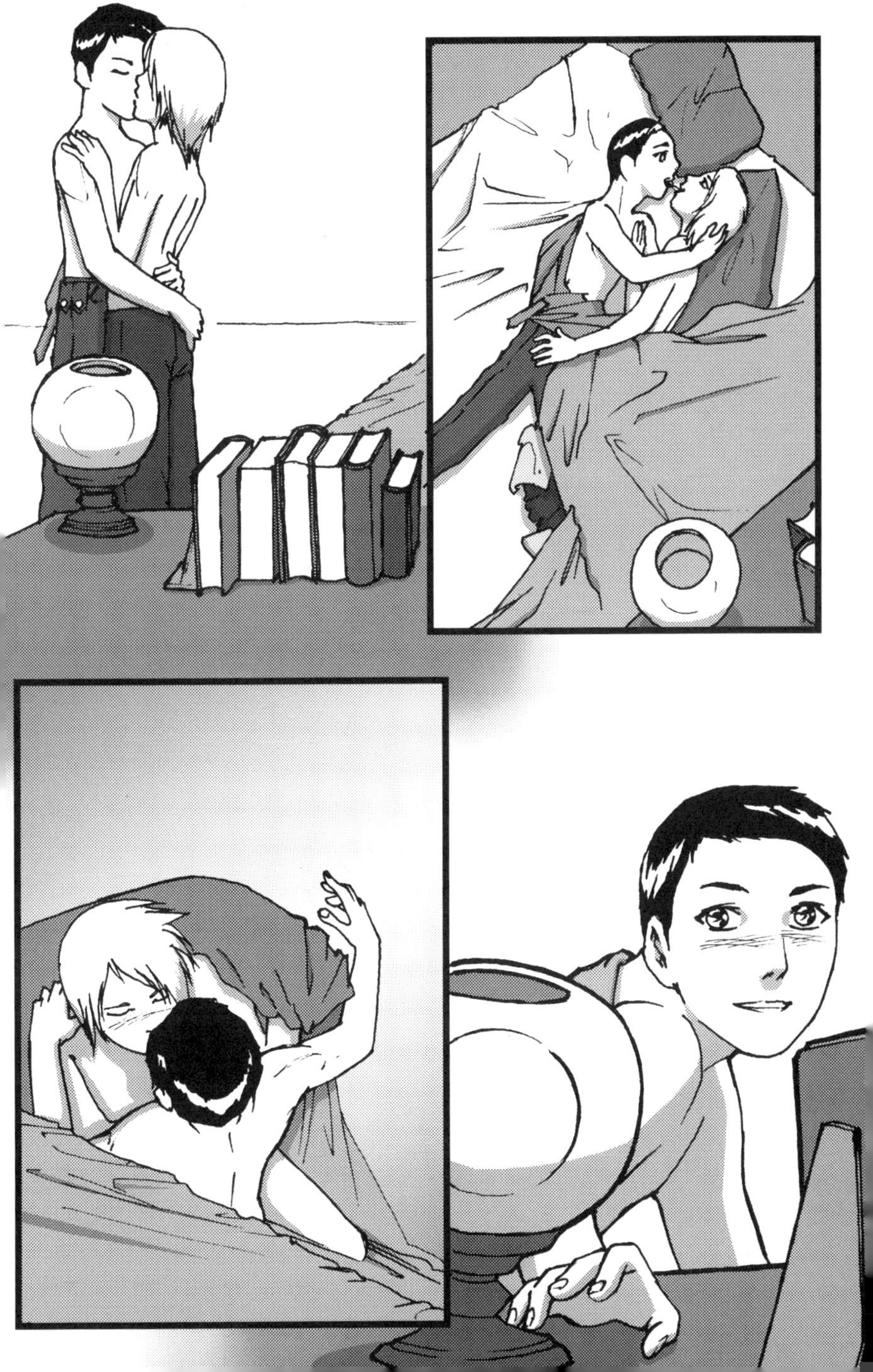

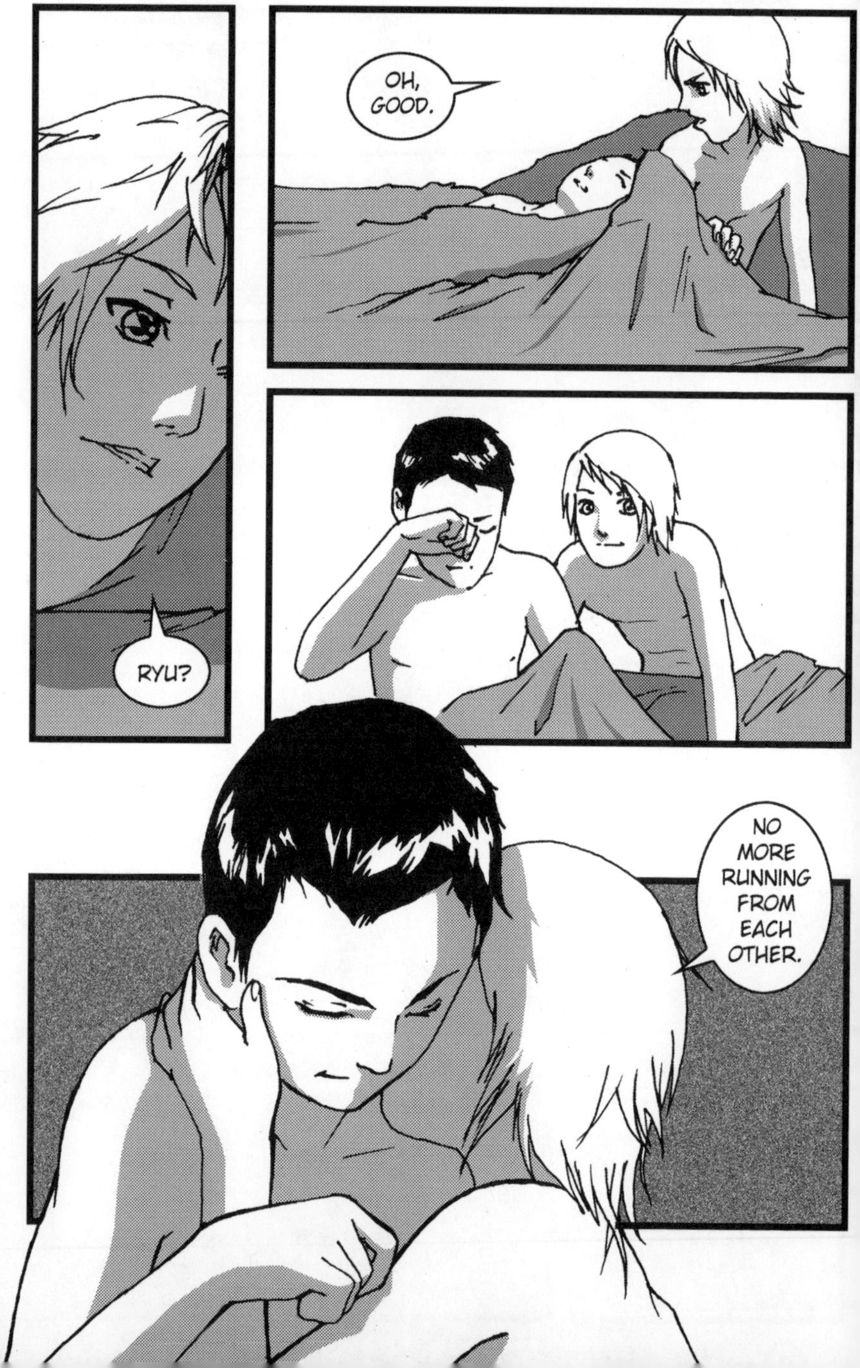
RYU?
OH, GOOD.
NO MORE RUNNING FROM EACH OTHER.

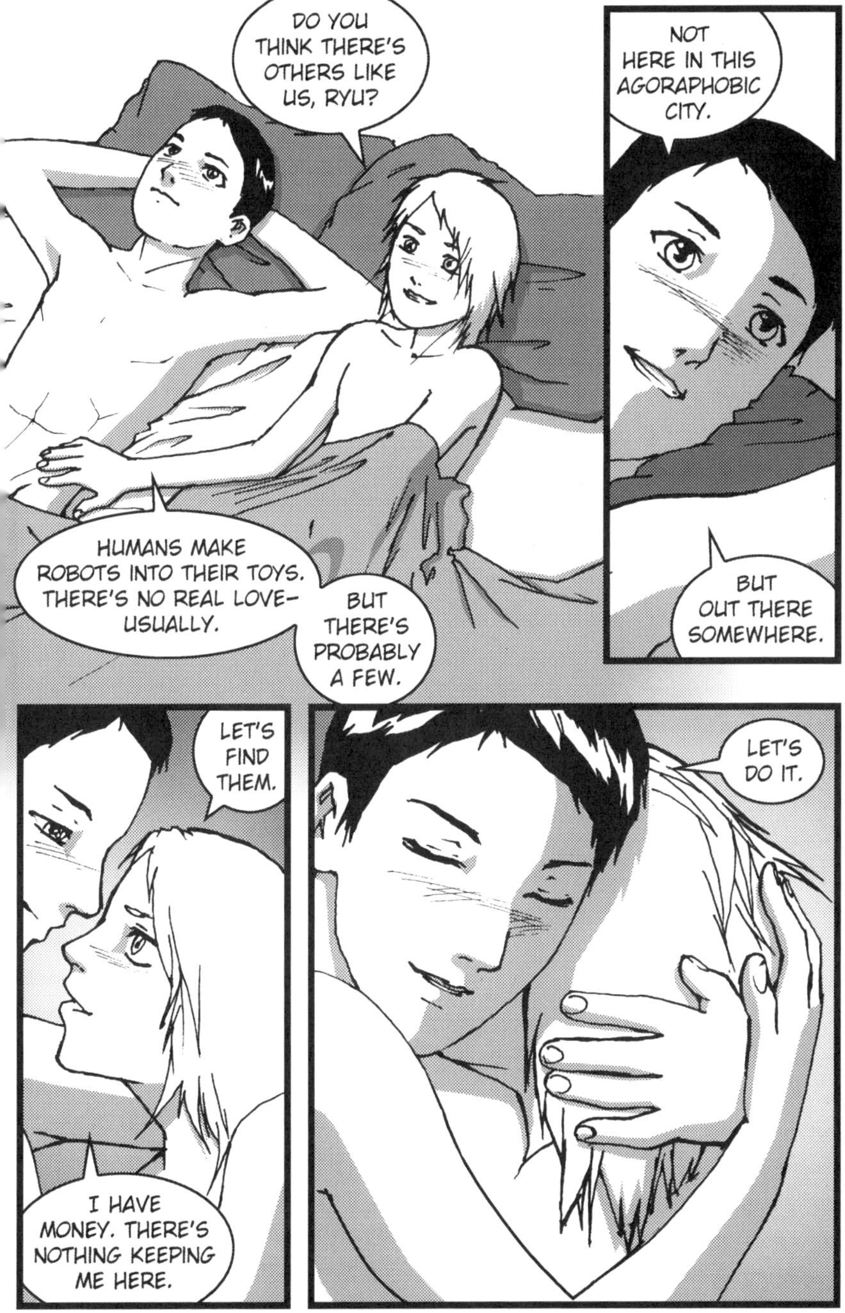
DO YOU THINK THERE'S OTHERS LIKE US, RYU?
NOT HERE IN THIS AGORAPHOBIC CITY.
HUMANS MAKE ROBOTS INTO THEIR TOYS. THERE'S NO REAL LOVE-USUALLY.
BUT THERE'S PROBABLY A FEW.
BUT OUT THERE SOMEWHERE.
LET'S FIND THEM.
I HAVE MONEY. THERE'S NOTHING KEEPING ME HERE.
LET'S DO IT.

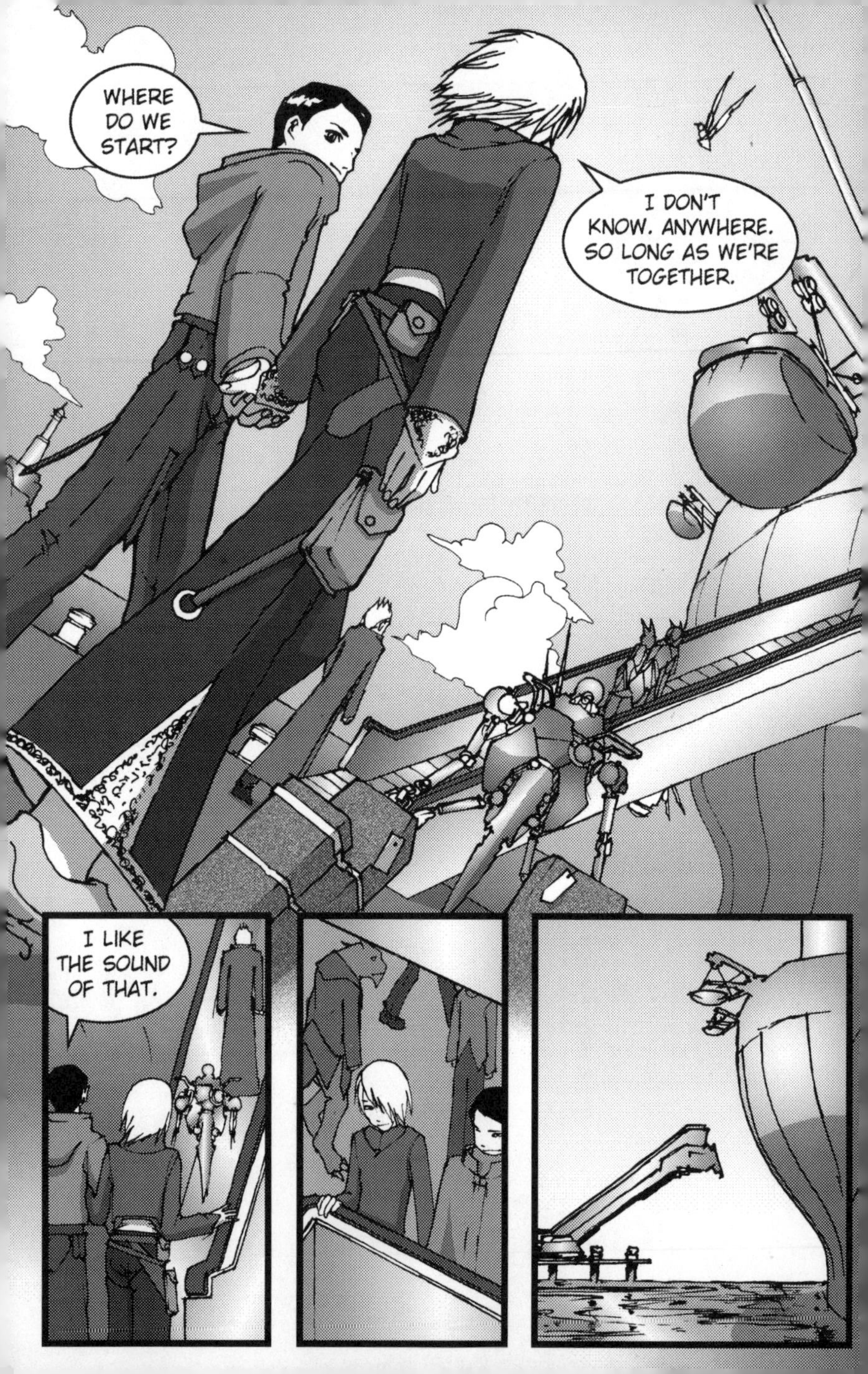
WHERE DO WE START?
I DON'T KNOW. ANYWHERE. SO LONG AS WE'RE TOGETHER.
I LIKE THE SOUND OF THAT.

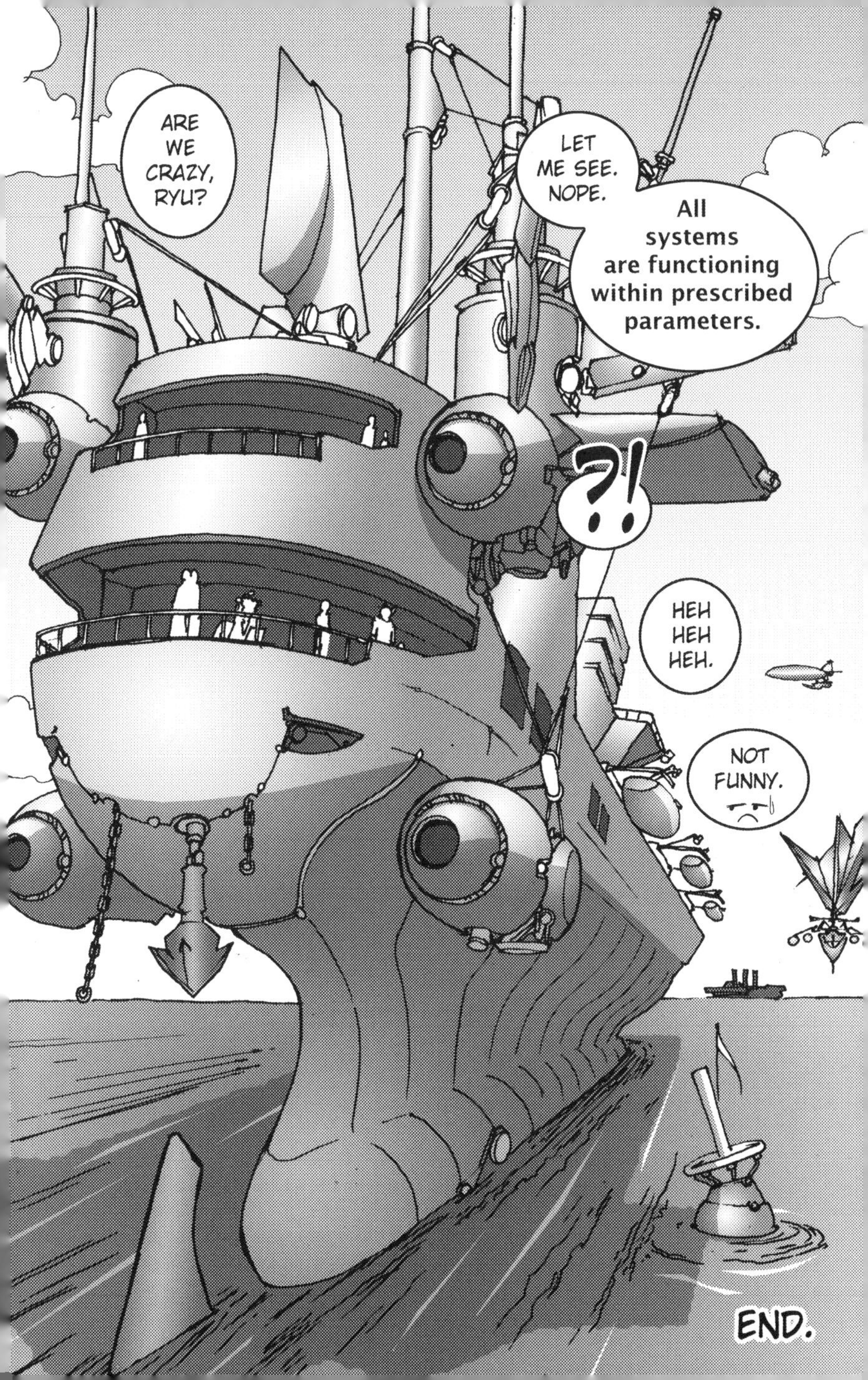
ARE WE CRAZY, RYU?
LET ME SEE. NOPE.
All systems are functioning within prescribed parameters.
?!
HEH HEH HEH.
NOT FUNNY.
END.

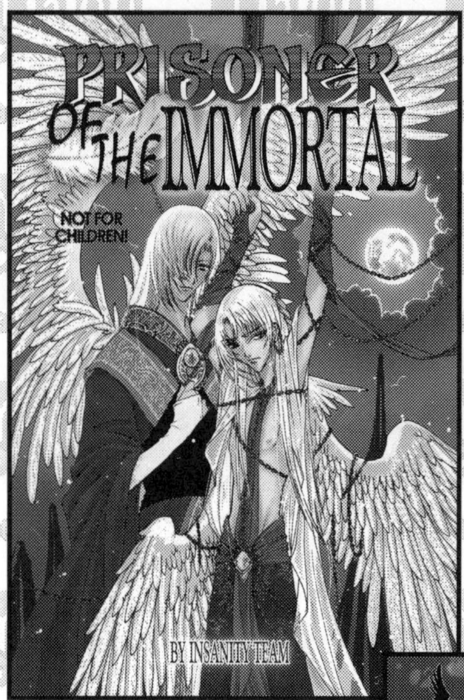
PRISONER OF THE IMMORTAL
NOT FOR CHILDREN!
BY INSANITY TEAM

Available Now!

Prisoner of the Immortal
by Insanity Team

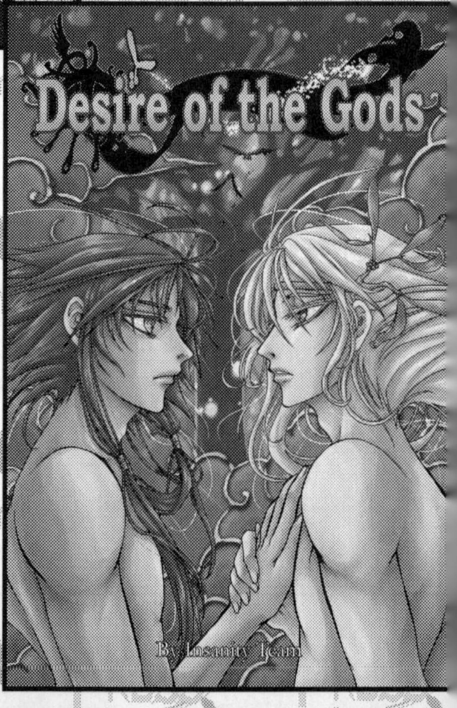
Desire of the Gods
By Insanity Team

Coming JAN-2006!

Desire of the Gods
by Insanity Team

Available Now!

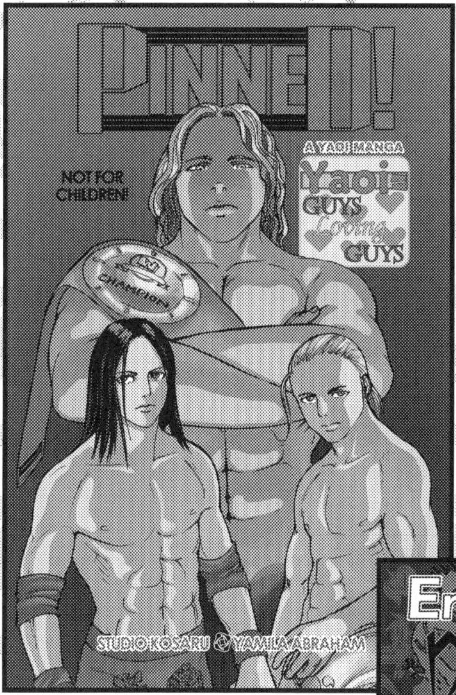

PINNED!
A YAOI MANGA
Yaoi
GUYS Loving GUYS
NOT FOR CHILDREN!
CHAMPION
STUDIO KOSARU
YAMILA ABRAHAM

Pinned
by Studio Kosaru
& Yamila Abraham

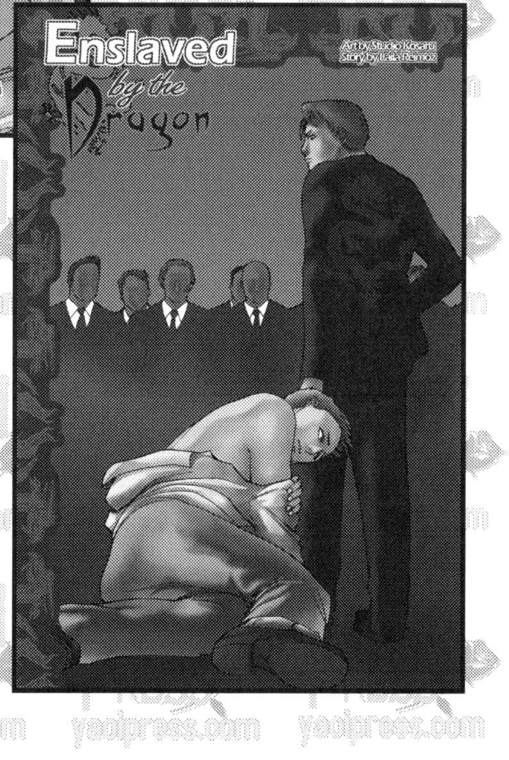

Enslaved by the Dragon
Art by Studio Kosaru
Story by Laila Reimoz

Enslaved by the Dragon
by Studio Kosaru
& Laila Reimoz

Coming 2006!

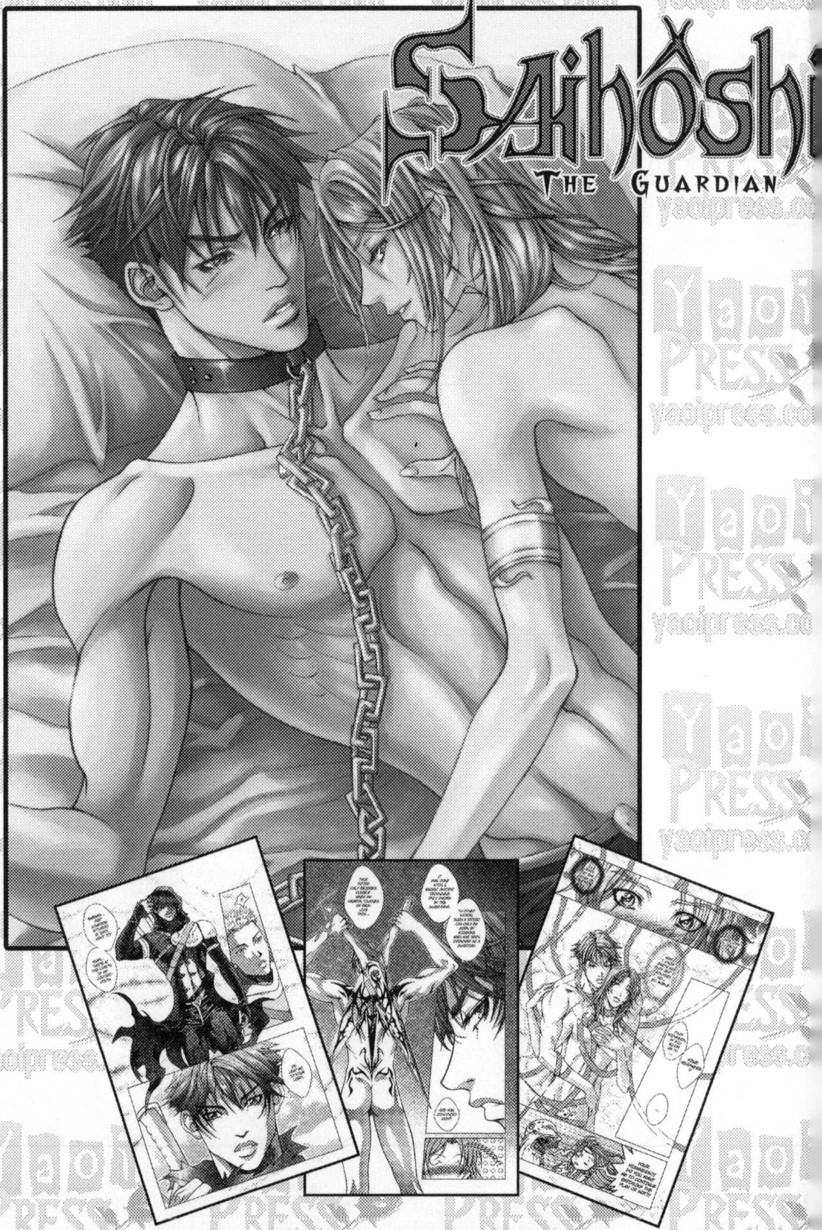
Saihôshi
THE GUARDIAN